SURVIVING
WOCS

A GUIDE TO APPLYING FOR
WARRANT OFFICER CANDIDATE SCHOOL

D1302149

CW4(R) JIM BOROCH

Copyright© 2013–2016 CW4(R) Jim Boroch

All rights reserved. No parts of this publication may be reproduced or transmitted in any form or by any means, electronic or mechanical, including, photocopy, recording, or any information storage and retrieval system, without the expressed permission, in writing, from the author.

The views expressed in this book are those of Jim Boroch and do not reflect the official policy or position of the Army, Defense Department or the United States Government.

©2016 All Rights Reserved

ISBN-13   978-0-9839714-7-4

ISBN-10   0-9839714-7-1

3ᴿᴰ EDITION, 1ˢᵀ PRINTING, 2016

2ᴺᴰ EDITION, 1ˢᵀ PRINTING, 2014

1ˢᵀ EDITION, 1ˢᵀ PRINTING, 2013

Published by:

MENTOR®
ENTERPRISES, INC.

121 Castle Drive STE F
Madison, AL 35758
info@mentorinc.us

Please send us your feedback, thoughts, or recommendations at:
info@mentorinc.us

Cover Design, Layout, and Typesetting by Matthew Dail

Acknowledgements

This book is dedicated to my sons Jerry and Peter, who inspired me to write down all the random thoughts I had about being a Warrant Officer. Hopefully this book will inspire them just as they inspire me.

A special thanks to my wonderful publisher Mark Gerecht, who honcho's Mentor Enterprise, Inc. Mark publishes and distributes many excellent military oriented books and called one day to ask me to take over this project. Mark's faith in my abilities, plus a few encouraging phone calls, was sufficient to get me typing away at the keyboard. Mark, thanks for seeing the writer lurking behind the cartoonist!

I also thank my beautiful wife Diane, who always supports the untold number of projects I undertake, and whose love always inspired me to do better and to succeed. I am a much better person for having her in my life.

Special Announcements

****Attention 350F, 350G and 352S Applicants****The MI Proponent has opened these critical WO MOSs to the following USMC Feeder MOSs (MOS 350F - USMC MOS 0231; MOS 350G - USMC MOS 0241; MOS 352S - USMC MOS 2631). Army or Sister Service applicants who meet the requirements for these critical MOS's have a HIGH potential for selection. Contact the MI Proponent POC DSN: 821-1181, COMM: (520) 533-1181 with questions about your eligibility. Do not wait to begin your packet process!

****Did you know you could also apply to be a Warrant Officer in the Army Reserve? ****

Explore your options as a Reserve Warrant Officer under the Warrant Officer Transition Program "09W" and find out if you qualify for a $20,000 BONUS (for specific MOS's)!

Contact your local Reserve Component Career Center (RCCC)/Transition Center for all the details. Web Directory ~ 23 February 2016

****Attention 255A (Information Services Technician) and 255N (Network Management Technician) Applicants***** For MOS 255A and 255N the minimum prerequisites have changed you must have a current TS/SCI clearance or eligible to obtain a TS/SCI clearance. Applicants who do not have a TS/SCI clearance will initiate procedures to obtain the proper level of clearance immediately upon selection to MOS 255A or 255N. Failure to obtain an adjudicated TS/SCI clearance by 1 OCT 2017 precludes you from holding the MOS. Applicants requiring periodic reinvestigation (PR) must submit their PR paperwork prior to submitting a WO Accession Application.

**** Attention all Ordnance Branch 890A, 913A, 914A, 915A, 919A, 948B, and 948D applicants**** All applicants that will compete with their first selection board in MARCH 2016 (or later) must comply with the newly published English College Credit and/or TABE prerequisites. National Guard applicants who submit their applications on/after 1 MAR 2016 must met this requirement. English Credit and TABE Requirements (if applicable) are listed on your desired MOS page under "Prerequisites ". Please direct all questions concerning English/TABE prerequisites to the OD Proponent POCs.

****Updated HQDA G-1 Tattoo Guidance (For ALL Applicants to include Sister Services) **** AR 670-1, dated 10 April 2015, no longer provides a provision for grandfathering tattoos. The grandfathering provision was provided in the March 2014 iteration of AR 670-1, and provided ample time for Soldiers and CDRs to documented eligible tattoos in the Soldier's iPERMS. HQDA G-1 will NO LONGER accept tattoo ETPs (from Army Applicants) for WO appointment unless the procedures outlined in AR 670-1 par3-3f are followed. Soldier MUST provide separation board proceedings indicating the CDR retained the Soldier along with a Tattoo Waiver Request (found under the "Downloads" tab). Additionally, as part of the WO application checklist (under downloads tab), the applicant's servicing Battalion S-1/S-1 NCO or PSD/MPD Supervisor must verify that the CDR has completed a tattoo verification, been found in compliance with AR 670-1 (dated 10 APR 15) and that all tattoos are properly documented in iPERMS. If a Soldier is in compliance with the tattoo guidance in AR 670-1 Para 3-3 (dated 10 April 2015) and has verified with their BN S-1 (indicated on the application checklist) that their "non-compliance" tattoos below the wrists (on the hands) and/or above the neck line (on head/face/inside mouth) were properly uploaded into iPERMS (ICW the March 2014 version of AR 670-1, i.e. grandfathered) they DO NOT require a tattoo waiver/ETP.

ALL Sister Service applicants still MUST submit a signed Tattoo Validation and Waiver Request Memo (regardless if applicant has tattoos) but are NOT required to separation board proceedings if tattoos are not ICW AR 670-1 Para. 3-3b and 3-3c, dated 10 April 2015*.

DA PAM 670-1, Para 3-3 provides guidance on the photos to be included with a Tattoo Waiver Request. Based on photos previously received, the DA G1 has additional guidance:

 1. Applicant should be in the IPFU (authorized PT uniform for applicants from other Services) when having their tattoo(s) photographed.

2. Color photos are required using a white or neutral color background.

3. Photos will depict tattoo location and size by showing the entire area below the elbow, below the knee, and/or above the t-shirt neck line using a ruler.

4. In order to show perspective, a full-length photo of the applicant showing their tattoo(s) is also required.

5. There are no specific camera settings required; however, all photos must be clear and visible.

ATTENTION ALL SISTER SERVICE APPLICANTS: Any sister service applicant who has not successfully completed an Army Basic Training, Warrior Transition Course, Marine Basic Training, Air Force or Navy Special Operations Forces, Air Force Tactical Air Control Training or Air Force Security Police Training will be required to attend Army Basic Training prior to attendance to WOCS. A Statement of Understanding (SoU), which is required for all packets, will serve as acknowledgement (from applicant) of the requirement for sister-service applicants to attend Army BCT. Any questions, concerns, or requests for withdrawal of current packet submissions can be addressed to the Special Programs and Boards Branch Chief at (502) 626-1893 or the Warrant Officer Recruiting Team at (910) 432-2175.

FOR DEPLOYED SERVICE MEMBERS: IAW AR 135-100 and DA PAM 601-6: All Warrant Officer applicants must pass their appointment physical prior to submitting an application. Flight physicals are good for 18 months and Technicians for 24 months. This requirement will not be waived. If you are scheduled to deploy you will need to be proactive and get your physical complete prior to your departure as Afghanistan no longer has the capability to complete physicals.

APFT WAIVER GUIDANCE: Per AR 350-1, paragraph 3-14a, Soldiers with medical profiles due to operational deployment will be permitted by their immediate commanders to attend appropriate courses (to include PME) within the guidelines of their profile. Soldiers must arrive at the aforementioned courses of instruction with a copy of their current profile and a memorandum signed by their commander stating the profile is a result of injuries sustained due to operational deployment. Per AR 350-1, paragraph 3-13j(3), Candidates applying to WOCS or OCS must pass the standard three-event APFT as a enrollment requirement. An exception to policy may be granted by HQDA DCS, G3/5/7 for a permanent profile to the running event only. The exception only allows the Soldier to apply to compete for entry into WOC or OCS school. The permanent profile must be a result of extraordinary circumstances.

LETTERS OF RECOMMENDATION FOR ARMY APPLICANTS: Due to several fraudulent LOR submissions by applicants, all Active Duty Army applicants will now be required to use USAREC Form 3.3 and the recommender will be required to digitally sign the form. If a recommender cannot sign the form due to extenuating circumstance, these will be entertained on a case-by-case basis. Furthermore, the recommender MUST include their unit info, e-mail, and phone number in the bottom of the narrative.

12-MONTH TIS REMAINING REQUIREMENT: Given the constant changing of retention and the drawdown EXCEPTIONS will be granted on a case by case basis. Applicants will have to include a memorandum requesting to waive the 12 month requirement. At a minimum, an applicant must have six months remaining on their service contract by the time their packet will be board to even be considered for a waiver. Furthermore, approval consideration will be based on the strength of the MOS and number of applicants applying for the program!

USAF APPLICANTS: Per the USAF AFPC, conditional release paperwork should be routed through VMPF (Virtual Military Personnel Flight) by selecting "voluntary separations" and then "early release". The last page of that application allows individuals to upload the LOI and the DD Form 368.

Please check the WO selection board schedule for new packet submission cutoff dates:

http://www.usarec.army.mil/hq/warrant/WOgeninfo_boardschedule.shtml

Contents

Updates and corrections can be found online at:
http://asktop.net/wocs-3ed

Access Code:
WOCBOR3D

Chapter 1

What is a Warrant Officer?

The Warrant Officer is a total package. Today's Warrant Officer is educated, has a technical and tactical foundation coupled with leadership skills to efficiently lead Soldiers, while maintaining and employing all associated equipment.

The Warrant Officer is as comfortable in the motor pool as they are conducting a briefing at a staff meeting. They fill leadership roles when Real Live Officers (RLO)s are in short supply, and CW2s –CW5s are commissioned, giving them the same authority as their RLO counterparts.

The Army will always need good NCOs to supervise Soldiers turning wrenches, but the Army also needs dedicated, knowledgeable managers (Warrant Officers) to make the best use of essential resources (people, time, money, and equipment).

Why should you go Warrant Officer?

You picked this book up because you want more out of your Army career. You want more of a challenge, more responsibility, the ability to have a bigger influence, and because you believe you can make a difference. This isn't an unsolicited piece of spam email in your inbox or an unwanted envelope full of junk mail in your mail box. You deliberately chose this book because you want to be a Warrant Officer. You want to take on the challenge of becoming a professional Warrant Officer, you want to make more money, and become a respected technical expert in your field.

First things first, this book will not make you a Warrant Officer. You, and only you, can transform yourself into a Warrant Officer. Becoming a Warrant Officer is not easy but I can assure you it is well worth the effort in terms of the rewards, self satisfaction, and the challenges you will face. Receiving your first salute from a young enlisted Soldier is a moment you will remember for the rest of your life. You will also become a leader who is overall responsible for the technical competence of your subordinates and have a significant role in shaping and growing the future leaders of this great nation.

As a Warrant you will provide wisdom and experience from a technical aspect and provide input into promoting, training, and the leader development of your subordinates. Gone are the days when a Warrant was just a technical expert. Now Warrants are the technical expert and leaders.

If you are unsure about becoming a Warrant consider this: on average you will have to wait five to seven years for the 13% possibility that you'll get selected for your next stripe, while Warrant promotions rates for WO1-CW4 are above 80%.

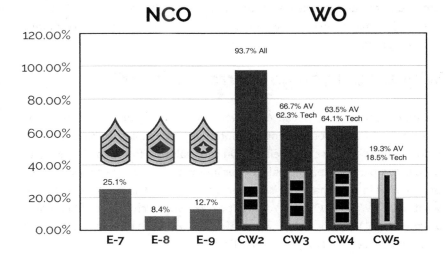

Army Promotion Comparison

Air Force Promotion Comparison

NCO   WO

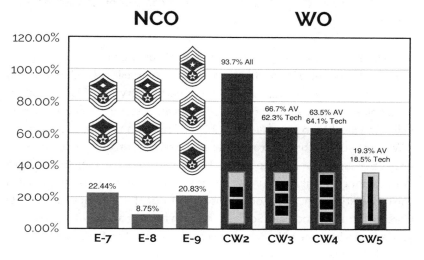

Navy Promotion Comparison

NCO   WO

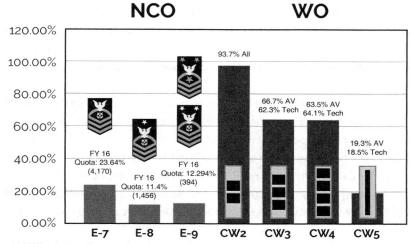

NOTE: Marine Promotion Comparison not available at time of publishing.

And earning Warrant Officer means there is a 94% chance of promotion to CW2 only two years after the successful completion of your Warrant Officer training.

So chances are you're still holding the book? You are not abandoning the Corps by becoming a Warrant; you're using that excellent NCO foundation to spring forward and start a new career path. Everything I learned as an NCO helped me to be a better Warrant Officer. Your experience as an NCO will be a valuable to you, the Soldiers you lead, and to your superiors. As a Warrant you will be able to give your superiors a unique perspective on issues because you have experience being an enlisted Soldier. Becoming a Warrant is not forsaking your NCO heritage. Becoming a Warrant gives you the capability to influence conditions in the future for the good of the NCO Corps, your unit, and your Soldiers. Keep in mind that one of the reasons you want to become a Warrant is because you want to make a difference. Your NCO experience helps you make that difference!

What's Your Motivation?

Most people don't become Warrant Officers for God, Country, or the American way. Don't get me wrong, I'm all for the above, but let's face it, all three fall short when the rent is due, when the kids need school supplies and you want the newest phone, or the car gives up the ghost. The reality is most Warrant Officers do it to satisfy their basic human needs.

There is nothing wrong with wanting to make changes in your life that will result in a better lifestyle and a financially secure future. Most of us joined the military because we have a high level of patriotism. If we could not take care of our family and pay our bills odds are we would not make the military a career. Others may be motivated leaders with a strong desire to be the head honcho and call the shots. Becoming a Warrant Officer will definitely require you to take on more responsibility and led your Soldiers.

So let's examine needs and motivation. Below are Maslow's Hierarchy of Needs. Take a moment to review them and think about them in terms of your desire to become a Warrant.

Maslow's Hierarchy of Needs, ranked first to last:

1. Physiological Needs (Air, Water, Food)

2. Safety Needs (Personal and Financial Security, Health and Well-being, Protection from Accidents and Illness)

3. Love and Belonging (Friendship, Intimacy, Family)

4. Esteem (Self-Respect and Respect from Others)

5. Self-Actualization (To be all you can be)

6. Self-Transcendence (To go beyond one's self) added by Viktor Frank

So where did your need or motivation to become Warrant fall within the hierarchy? Now let's do a pay comparison. As the chart on the next page indicates there is a significant difference between an E-8 with 20 years of service and a CW3 with 16 years of service; $481.00 a month to be exact. In my professional opinion you stand a better chance of being promoted to CW4 than you do making E-9. Now several factors will influence promotion potential including the number of slots in your MOS, your evaluation reports, etc. The bottom line is your span of influence and your compensation levels as a Warrant will far outweigh those in the NCO ranks. You must decide if you want to remain an NCO or become a Warrant.

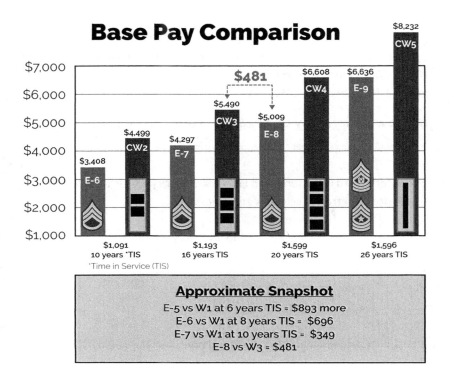

Base Pay Comparison

Approximate Snapshot

E-5 vs W1 at 6 years TIS = $893 more
E-6 vs W1 at 8 years TIS = $696
E-7 vs W1 at 10 years TIS = $349
E-8 vs W3 = $481

To become a Warrant Officers, applicants must, at minimum:

1. Be a U.S. citizen or naturalized citizen.

2. Have a general technical (GT) score of 110 or higher.

3. Pass the standard three-event Army Physical Fitness Test (APFT) and meet the height and weight standards required of your age and gender category.

4. Technicians and aviators must pass a physical.

5. Have a secret clearance.

6. The maximum age for applying for almost all Warrant Officer MOSs is 46. Aviator Warrant applicants cannot have passed their 33rd birthday at the time of selection. Age Waivers will be considered if required.

APFT Requirements
(within 6 Mo's of Board Date)

Specifics on the APFT test can be found in AR 350-1 and FM 7-22 Appendix A.

For those of you who are unfamiliar with the APFT standards here are two sample standards:

A male, age 22-26, will need to do a minimum of forty correct push-ups, fifty correct sit-ups, and complete the two-mile run in 16:36, or faster.

A female, age 22-26, will need to do a minimum of seventeen correct push-ups; thirty-four correct sit-ups, and complete the two-mile run in 23:06, or faster.

Acronyms for Warrants

WOCS—Warrant Officer Candidate School

WOES—Warrant Officer Education System

WOCC—Warrant Officer Career College

WOILE—Warrant Officer Intermediate Level Education

WOSSE—Warrant Officer Senior Service Education

RLO—Real Live Officer (Lieutenant - General)

And most importantly, WOPA—Warrant Officer Protection Association (AKA "Da' Mafia")

Summary

In this chapter we have covered the basics of becoming a Warrant Officer: What is a Warrant Officer, why should you consider becoming a Warrant Officer, promotion potential, pay comparison, qualification requirements, and acronyms to assist you in your WOC journey. Now you have the basics and you made your decision to become a Warrant Officer Candidate (WOC). So let's learn a bit of the Warrant Officer history, cover a few tips on applying for WOCS, and learn the basics of preparing for WOC school and how to not only survive but thrive while attending the course.

Chapter 2

History of the Warrant Officer Corps

Warrant Officer Corps Birthday: 9 July 1918,

Warrant Officer Corps Color: Brown (original), Since 2004 Warrant Officers wear their branch colors

Introduction

As an Enlisted Soldier or as an NCO you learned basic Army history and more than likely were required to learn unit specific history as you studied for various boards. As a WOC it is important that you have a basic understanding of Warrant Officer history. This chapter will give you a basic understanding of the Warrant Officer Corps and general expectations that are inherent with the rank.

Inception
1916-1940

The predecessor of the Warrant Officer was the Army Field Clerk, formerly the Headquarters Clerk, and the Field Clerk, Quartermaster Corps, formerly the Pay Clerk.

The use of Warrant Officers was expanded by the Congressional Act of 1920, which authorized appointment of Warrant Officers in clerical, administrative, and band leading activities. The rank of Warrant Officer has a long history; for example, evidence suggests that Napoleon used Warrant Officers as communications links between his commissioned Officers and the Soldiers.

The military grade of "Warrant Officer" dates back two centuries before Columbus, during the fledgling years of the British Navy. At that time, nobles assumed command of the new Navy, adopting the Army ranks of Lieutenant and Captain. These royal blood Officers often had no knowledge of life on board a ship, let alone how to navigate such a vessel or operate the guns. They often relied on the technical expertise and cooperation of a senior sailor, who tended to the technical aspects of running the ship and operating the cannons. These sailors, sometimes referred to as "Boat Mates" or "Boswans Mates," became indispensable to less experienced Officers, and were subsequently rewarded with a Royal Warrant. This Royal Warrant was a special designation, designed to set them apart from other sailors, without violating the strict class system that was so prevalent during the time.

In the U.S. Navy, Warrant Officers have traditionally been technical specialists whose skills and knowledge were an essential part of the proper operation of the ship. The Navy has had Warrant Officers among its ranks, in some form or another, since its conception.

For the U.S. Army, we can trace the lineage of the Warrant Officer back to the Headquarters and Field Clerks.

Eight of the original forty-three mine planter Warrant Officers from 1922
Image source: http://www.usawoa.org/woheritage/Hist_of_Army_WO.htm

Eight Of The Original 48 Army Mine Planter Service
Warrant Officers Appointed In 1922,
Photo Taken At Fort McPherson, Georgia

In World War I, the Coast Artillery Corps was responsible for mine defenses in major ports. Vessels, ranging in size from small motorboats to 1,000-ton ocean-going ships, laid and maintained minefields. Conflict between Soldiers and civilian employees who manned these vessels revealed the need to ensure that military personnel manned the vessels. Officially, the birth date of the Army Warrant Officer Corps is 9 July 1918, the day that Congress established the Army Mine Planter Service as part of the Coast Artillery. This action ensured these vessels were exclusively manned by Army personnel.

The Army opened a school to train its mariners at Fort Monroe, Virginia, commanded by an Officer who had graduated from the Naval Academy. The official color of the Warrant Officer Corps was brown, as Warrant

Officers in the Mine Planter Service wore simple bands of brown cloth on their uniform sleeves as their insignia of rank.

Warrant Officers served in four positions aboard the vessels: masters, mates, chief engineers and assistant engineers. Masters wore four bands. Deck Officers also wore an embroidered brown, fouled anchor above the braid, while engineer Officers wore an embroidered brown three-bladed propeller in a similar position.

In 1921, Warrant Officers were excluded from performing as a summary court Officer, defense counsel, Officer of the day, and assistant adjutant because enlisted personnel were prohibited from performing those same duties. During this time, only one pay grade existed, except in the Army Mine Planter Service.

Warrant Officers of the Tank Corps first wore the distinctive insignia approved on 12 May 1921; which consisted of an eagle rising with wings displayed, standing on two arrows and enclosed in a wreath. It was adapted from the great seal of the United States, with the arrows symbolizing the military arts and science, "The Eagle Rising."

In 1922, the Warrant Officer authorized strength dropped from 1,120 to 600, not including the Army Mine Planter Service Warrant Officers and Army Bandmasters. Consequently, there were no Warrant Officer appointments other than Bandmasters and Army Mine Planter Service personnel between 1922 and 1935.

After 1922 laws were passed that authorized the appointment of additional classes of personnel with certain qualifications, In 1936, the Army held competitive examinations to replenish lists of eligible's candidates that could serve in Regular Army appointments. The Army began appointing Warrant Officers from this list to fill authorized vacancies. This list was used from 1936 until the beginning of World War II.

In 1939, Warrant Officers who were qualified as pilots were declared eligible for appointments as air corps lieutenants in the Regular Army. In 1940, Warrant Officers began serving as "disbursing agents." At this time, Warrant Officer appointments began to occur in significant numbers for the first time since 1922; however, a large number of Warrant Officers transferred to active duty as commissioned Officers, causing a continuing decrease in Warrant Officer strength until 1942.

Warrant Officer Definition
1957 – The First Definition of the Warrant Appears

The first published definition for Army Warrant Officers was established in AR 611-112, and defined the Warrant Officer as follows:

"The Warrant Officer is a highly skilled technician who is provided to fill those positions above the enlisted level which are too specialized in scope to permit effective development and continued utilization of broadly trained, branch qualified commissioned Officers."

1985 Definition of Warrant Officer Modified

In 1985 the Army developed a clear and concise definition of the Warrant Officer that encompassed all Warrant Officer specialties:

"An Officer appointed by warrant by the Secretary of the Army, based upon a sound level of technical and tactical competence. The Warrant Officer is the highly specialized expert and trainer, who, by gaining progressive levels of expertise and leadership, operates, maintains, administers, and manages the Army's equipment, support activities, or technical systems for an entire career."

1999 Definition of the Warrant Officer with regard to Army Leadership

Army Field Manual 22-100, Army Leadership, 31 August 1999, defined the role of Army Warrant Officers as:

"Warrant Officers are highly specialized, single-track specialty Officers who receive their authority from the Secretary of the Army upon their initial appointment. However, Title 10 U.S.C. authorizes the commissioning of Warrant Officers (WO1) upon promotion to Chief Warrant Officer (CW2). These commissioned Warrant Officers are direct representatives of the President of the United States. They derive their authority from the same source as commissioned Officers but remain specialists, in contrast to commissioned Officers, who are generalists. Warrant Officers can and do command detachments, units, activities, and vessels as well as lead, coach, train, and counsel subordinates. As leaders and technical experts, they provide valuable skills, guidance, and expertise to commanders and organizations in their particular field."

(Source Paragraph A-3, Army Field Manual 22-100).

Army Pamphlet 600-3 outlines the current definitions of the Warrant Officer

The Army WO is a self—aware and adaptive technical expert, combat leader, trainer, and advisor. Through progressive levels of expertise in assignments, training, and education, the WO administers, manages, maintains, operates, and integrates Army systems and equipment across the full spectrum of Army operations. Warrant Officers are innovative integrators of emerging technologies, dynamic teachers, confident War fighters, and developers of specialized teams of Soldiers. They support a wide range of Army missions throughout their career. Warrant Officers in the Army are accessed with specific levels of technical ability. They refine their technical expertise and develop their leadership and management skills through tiered progressive assignment and education.

Characteristics and Responsibilities by Grade
Warrant Officer 1

This is an Officer, appointed by warrant, with the requisite authority pursuant to assignment level and position, given by the Secretary of the Army. WO1s are basic-level, technically and tactically-focused Officers who perform the primary duties of technical leader, trainer, operator, manager, maintainer, sustainer, and advisor. They also perform any other branch-related duties assigned to them. They also provide direction, guidance, resources, assistance, and supervision necessary for subordinates to perform their duties. WO1s have specific responsibility for accomplishing the missions and tasks assigned to them and, if assigned as a commander, the collective or organizational responsibility for how well their command performs its mission. WO1s primarily support levels of operations from team or detachment through battalion, requiring interaction with all Soldier cohorts and primary staff. They provide leader development, mentorship, and counsel to enlisted Soldiers and NCOs.

Chief Warrant Officer 2

CW2s are commissioned Officers with the requisite authority pursuant to assignment level and position as given by the President of the United States. CW2s are intermediate-level technical and tactical experts who perform the primary duties of technical leader, trainer, operator, manager, maintainer, sustainer, and advisor. They also perform any other branch-related duties assigned to them. They provide direction, guidance, resources, assistance, and supervision necessary for subordinates to perform their duties. They have specific responsibility for accomplishing the missions and tasks assigned to them and, if assigned as a commander, the collective or organizational responsibility for how well their command performs its mission. CW2s primarily support levels of operations from team or detachment through battalion, requiring interaction with all Soldier cohorts and primary staff. They provide leader development, mentorship, advice, and counsel to NCOs, other WOs, and company-grade branch Officers.

Chief Warrant Officer 3

CW3s are commissioned Officers with the requisite authority pursuant to assignment level and position, as given by the President of the United States. CW3s are advanced-level technical and tactical experts who perform the primary duties of technical leader, trainer, operator, manager, maintainer, sustainer, integrator, and advisor. They also perform any other branch-related duties assigned to them. They provide direction, guidance, resources, assistance, and supervision necessary for subordinates to perform their duties. CW3s have specific responsibility for accomplishing the missions and tasks assigned to them and, if assigned as a commander, the collective or organizational responsibility for how well their command performs its mission. CW3s primarily support levels of operations from team or detachment through brigade, requiring interaction with all Soldier cohorts and primary staff. They provide leader development, mentorship, advice, and counsel to NCOs, other WOs, and branch Officers. CW3s advise commanders on WO issues.

Chief Warrant Officer 4

CW4s are commissioned Officers with the requisite authority pursuant to assignment level and position, as given by the President of the U.S. CW4s are Senior-level technical and tactical experts who perform the primary duties of technical leader, manager, maintainer, sustainer, integrator and advisor. They also perform any other branch-related duties assigned to them. They provide direction, guidance, resources, assistance, and supervision necessary for subordinates to perform their duties. CW4s have specific responsibility for accomplishing the missions and tasks assigned to them and, if assigned as a commander, the collective or organizational responsibility for how well their command performs its mission. They primarily support battalion, brigade, division, corps, and echelons above corps operations. They must interact with NCOs, other Officers, primary staff, and special staff. CW4s primarily provide leader development, mentorship, advice, and counsel to NCOs, other WOs and branch Officers. They have special mentorship responsibilities for other WOs and provide essential advice to commanders on WO issues.

Chief Warrant Officer 5

CW5s are commissioned Officers with the requisite authority pursuant to assignment level and position as given by the President of the United States. CW5s are master-level technical and tactical experts who perform the primary duties of technical leader, manager, integrator, advisor, or any other particular duty prescribed by branch. They provide direction, guidance, resources, assistance, and supervision necessary for subordinates to perform their duties. CW5s have specific responsibility for accomplishing the missions and tasks assigned to them. CW5s primarily support brigade, division, corps, echelons above corps, and major command operations. They must interact with NCOs, other Officers, primary staff and special staff. They provide leader development, mentorship, advice, and counsel to WOs, and branch Officers. CW5s have special WO leadership and representation responsibilities within their respective commands. They provide essential advice to commanders on WO issues.

Warrant Officer compared to Branch Officer (RLO)s:

	Warrant Officer	Branch Officer
Available Ranks	Warrant Officer (WO1)– Chief Warrant Officer 5 (CW5)	Second Lieutenant (O1)– General (O10)
Leadership	Warrant Officers (WOs) are leaders in their field, often the unit commander's go-to source for information.	Branch Officers are unit commanders, ultimately responsible for the success or failure of their troops.
Career Track	A WO is a technical and tactical expert in one career field; WOs generally stay in a single field for their entire career.	Branch Officers are generalists; their primary job is leading troops. They may be reassigned to other branches as they progress in rank.
Pay & Benefits	WO pay is more than enlisted personnel, but less than branch officers. Some WOs are eligible for additional pay based on their field(e.g., flight pay).	Branch Officers have the highest earning potential in the military.
Assignments	A Warrant Officer's job is to be the best at their position (example: A WO aviator might be assigned as an Instructor Pilot or Maintenance Test Pilot).	A branch officer's assignment is to lead troops (example: An aviation officer might start out as a Platoon Leader, then progress to Company Commander, etc.)

Chapter 3

Applying for WOCS

In the first two chapters we established your desire to become a Warrant and took a journey back in time to acquaint you with the history of the Warrant Corps. Now we are taking the first step in preparing for your new career as a Warrant Officer.

As we discussed in Chapter One, most NCOs are tactically and technically proficient but where you have the advantage is you have the dedication, desire, and ambition to become a Warrant Officer.

Are You or Can You?

1. Are you the best candidate available?
   ☐ Yes   ☐ No

2. Are you technically and tactically proficient?
   ☐ Yes   ☐ No

3. Can you gather all the items on the Warrant Officer Application Checklist and put them in the right order like some madcap scavenger hunt?
   ☐ Yes   ☐ No

If you at least checked off Number 3 you've passed go and collected the figurative $200 dollars. Did you check yes to all three? Great, you hit a grand slam homerun, or for the horse racing fans out there, you got the trifecta.

You think I'm kidding? Number 1 and 2 don't mean anything if you miss ONE item on the Warrant Officer Application Checklist or fail to meet the submission date. Your application will never make it to the selection board if it's not 100% complete. It will be weeded out. You will be waiting by the phone for a call that will never come. Warrant Officers are expected to be detail oriented, and here we have an applicant who can't even follow a simple checklist? Imagine the shame and agony of never hearing from the selection board because your packet never made it past the Branch Chief's In-Box. Attention to Detail!

Common Application Mistakes (Summary)

The following items summarize the common mistakes that will delay or stop processing of your Warrant Officer application:

Application Checklist:

• Not reviewed and signed by a Warrant Officer.

• Not endorsed by S-1/PSB verifying completeness and not pending UCMJ action.

USE THE CHECKLIST AS A GUIDE FOR THE PROPER ORDER OF APPLICATION WHEN SCANNING.

DA Form 61 (Application for Appointment):

• Block 1- ALL Applicants must select WARRANT OFFICER-ARMY RESERVE.

• Block 3- Must state WO1.

- Block 5a and b- Must have MOS code and the complete title of the MOS applying for.

- Block 27f and g – Must be filled in ETS date and date of last promotion.

- Bock 41- Unit Commander must sign verifying APFT information is accurate.

- Block 42 Applicant must sign.

USAREC Form 1935 (Warrant Officer Resume):

- Section II-Must include Civilian Education (should match ERB or included transcripts)

- Section VII- Summary- The idea is to be able to articulate to the board why you deserve to be a warrant officer and how you plan to serve as a WO. (THERE IS NO EXAMPLE)

- Section VIII- Signature- Must be signed and dated.

USAREC Form 1936 (Letter of Recommendation):

- Section I - Blocks 1-5 – APPLICANT (your) Information

- Section I - Blocks 8 – Relation to applicant should be either Interviewer, Supervisor, Company Commander or Battalion Commander.

- Section IV - Blocks 1-5 - RECOMMENDER Information and signature/date.

- If the Letter of Recommendation is from a Chief Warrant Officer, they must hold the MOS you are applying for.

- The recommender MUST include their unit info, e-mail, and phone number in the bottom of the narrative.

- This is the preferred form, but a memorandum style LOR is acceptable for sister services.

USAREC Form 1932 (Physical Cover Sheet):

- Take this form with you to the physical

- Must have current PULHES

- Must be marked either "Qualified" or "NOT Qualified"

- Must be signed by a Medical Doctor, Physician Assistant, or Nurse Practitioner.

- If applying for 150A or 153A you must also submit page 1 of your DD Form 2808 with qualified stamp from Ft. Rucker in your packet.

DA Form 160-R (Application for Active Duty):

- Block 1 - Date!

- Block 2 - Must State: U. S. ARMY RECRUITING COMMAND, FORT KNOX, KY 40121

- Block 7 – Duration must be month and year assigned to current unit.

- Block 9 - Must check a. and State for a period of 6 years.

- Block 10 - You should choose 3 DIFFERENT locations.

How to Submit your Packet:

- Send NEW packets to: usarmy.knox.usarec.mbx.9sbn-new-warrant-packets@mail.mil

- Emails must be less than 5MB each.

- All forms should be in PDF Format.

- DA Photo can be in JPEG format and a color copy.

- ALL PACKETS MUST BE COMPLETE BEFORE SUBMITTING.

How to Submit Corrections:

- Send CORRECTIONS to usarmy.knox.usarec.mbx.9sbn-new-warrant-corrections@mail.mil

- Follow the instructions in the email you receive from the Recruiting Team.

- Include all corrections required.

How to Submit Updates:

- Your Application must be in "B" status to submit updates

- If you need to update your packet, submit updates to: usarmy.knox.usarec.mbx.9sbn-new-warrant-updates@mail.mil

NOTES:

- It is imperative that you become very familiar with the Warrant Officer Website www.usarec.army.mil/hq/warrant

- NO ONE should care more about your packet than YOU!!

- Keep in mind that you are applying for a Professional Position, your packet should reflect as such. Your packet is how you represent yourself to the board

- If you are scanning in documents, open the document and verify that it is legible. Rule of thumb- If you can't read it, then the board cannot read it.

- Do not submit your packet directly from a digital sender. Send it to yourself then submit it to the WO recruiting team.

- Do not have someone else submit your packet. Have them email it to you, you review it, and then YOU submit it from your email address. Your Government Email account is preferred.

NOTE: The selection board is reviewing hundreds of applications and will only take a few minutes to review your file. Make sure EVERYTHING is present and legible.

Avoid these items for a successful application process:

1. Incomplete packets. INCOMPLETE packets will be REJECTED without action.

2. Poorly Written Letters of Recommendation

3. Sloppy Paperwork

4. Typos

5. Misspelled Words

6. Bad Evaluations

7. Bad Photo

8. Overweight

9. APFT failure

10. Illegible Transcripts

11. Missing the submission dates for the selection board

12. Disapproved Waivers

Think about it this way. The board members know what they are looking for and they know what right looks like. Any reason you give them to view something as a bad indicator can and most likely will reduce your chances receiving the highest possible recommendation.

Your Packet represents you so ensure it provides the very best image of you, your career, and your potential to the Army.

Feeder MOS - Enlisted MOS Conversion List (Army)

Not sure what Warrant MOS you should apply for?

Use the chart on the **next 2 pages** to choose the correct Warrant Officer MOS you will apply for or that you are qualified to apply for. You can apply for up to 3 WO-MOS. Selecting a Warrant Officer MOS you have prior enlisted experience in will dramatically improve your chances of selection.

Feeder MOS - Enlisted MOS Conversion List (Army)

WOMOS	Warrant Officer Title	Enlisted Feeder MOS
120A	Construction Engineering Technician	12H, K, N, P, Q, R, T, W
125D	Geospatial Engineering Technician	12Y, 35F, 35G
131A	Field Artillery Targeting Technician	11C, 13B, D, F, M, P, R, T
140A	Command and Control Systems Technician	14G, 14H & 14S
140E	Air and Missile Defense (AMD) Tactician/Technician (Patriot Systems Technician)	14E, 14H, 14T, 94S
150A	Air Traffic Control Technician	15Q
150U	Tactical Unmanned Aerial Systems (TUAS) Operations Technician	15W, 15E - US Army Combat Arms MOSs (11B, C, H, M, B; ALL CMF 12, 13, and 19 series) with Certified SUAS IO (MOS Prerequisite Waiver Required), USMC MOS 7314/6214, USAF AFSC 1U0X1, USN NEC 8361-4, 6-8 (MOS Prerequisite Waiver Required for ALL sister service)
151A	Aviation Maintenance Technician	All CMF 15 MOS (Excluding 15P & 15Q)
153A	Rotary Wing Aviator	All MOSs
170A	Cyber Operations Technician	Preferred CMF 25 and 35 MOS (All other enlisted MOSs - including Sister Service - applicants may apply with strong related technical background and minimum Bachelor's of Science in Computer Science, Programming, or a similar degree.)
180A	Special Forces Warrant Officer	All CMF 18 MOS
255A	Information Services Technician	All MOSs (Must have 4 years IT experience IAW prerequisites)
255N	Network Management Technician	All MOSs (Must have 4 years IT experience IAW prerequisites)
270A	Legal Administrator	27D
290A	Electronic Warfare Technician	29E, 25E, or 13F with ASI 1J
311A	CID Special Agent	31D
350F	All Source Intelligence Technician	35F
350G	GEOINT Imagery Technician	35G

WOMOS	Warrant Officer Title	Enlisted Feeder MOS
351L	Counterintelligence Technician	35L
351M	Human Intelligence Collection Technician	35M
352N	SIGNET Analysis Technician	35N, 35P
352S	Signals CollectionTechnician	35S
353T	Military Intelligence Systems Maintenance/Integration Technician	35T
420A	Human Resources Technician	42A/42F
420C	Bandmaster	All CMF 02 MOS's (ALL CMF 42R and 42S)
640A	Veterinary Services Food Safety Officer	68R, 68S
670A	Health Services Maintenance Technician	68A
740A	Chemical, Biological, Nuclear and Radiological (CBRN) Technician	74D
880A	Marine Deck Officer	88K
881A	Marine Engineering Officer	88L ; 12P, w/ASI S2
882A	Mobility Officer	88N, 88M. 88H
890A	Ammunition Warrant Officer	89A, 89B, 89D
913A	Armament Systems Maintenance Warrant Officer	91A, M, 91F, 91G
914A	Allied Trades Warrant Officer	91E, X
915A	Automotive Maintenance Warrant Officer	91A, B, H, M, P, S, X
919A	Engineer Equipment Maintenance Warrant Officer	91B, C, D, L, H, X, 91J
920A	Property Accounting Technician	92Y, 68J
920B	Supply Systems Technician	92A
921A	Airdrop Systems Technician	92R
922A	Food Service Technician	92G, 68M
923A	Petroleum Systems Technician	92F, 92L, and 92W
948B	Electronic Systems Maintenance Warrant Officer	94D, E, F, H, M, R, W, Y & Z (25S/with waiver only)
948D	Electronic Missile Systems Maintenance Warrant Officer	94A, M, P, S, T, X, & Z

Feeder MOS - Enlisted MOS Conversion List (USAF)

USAF MOS	Job Title	Army MOS	Warrant MOS	Warrant Officer Title
1A6xx	Transportation MGMT Coordinator	88N	882A	Mobility Officer
1C0xx	Aviation Operations Specialist	15P	153A	Rotary Wing Aviator
1C1xx	Air Traffic Control Operator	15Q	150A	Air Traffic & Air Space Management Tech.
1N1xx	Imagery Analyst	35G	125D	Geospatial Engineering Technician
			350G	Imagery Intelligence Technician
1N2x1	Communication Signals Intelligence Production	35N	290A	Electronic Warfare Technician
			352N	SIGINT Analysis Technician
1N5xx	Electronic Signal Intelligence Ex.	35S	290A	Electronic Warfare Technician
	Elct Signal Intel Exploitation JM		352S	SIGNALS Collection Technician
	Elct Sig Intel Exploitation Supt			
1N6x1	Electronic System Security Assessment	35G	125D	Geospatial Engineering Technician
			290A	Electronic Warfare Technician
1U0X1	UAV	15W/15E	150U	Tactical Unmanned Aerial System
2A0x1	Avionics Test Station and Components	*	290A	Electronic Warfare Technician
2F0xx	Petroleum Supply Specialist	92F	153A	Rotary Wing Aviator
2G0xx	Automated Logistics Specialist	92A	920B	Supply Systems Technician
2M0xx	Missile & Space Systems Electronic Maintenance	*	948B, 948D	Electronic Systems Maintenance Warrant Officer, Electronic Systems Missile Warrant Officer
2S0x1	Unit Supply Specialist	92Y	920A	Property Accounting Technician
2S0x2	Automated Logistics Specialist	92A	920B	Supply Systems Technician

USAF MOS	Job Title	Army MOS	Warrant MOS	Warrant Officer Title
2T0xx	Transportation Management Coord	88N	882A	Mobility Officer
2T1xx	Motor Transport Operator	88M	153A	Rotary Wing Aviator
2T2xx	Transportation Management Coord	88N	882A	Mobility Officer
2T3xx	Metal Worker	44B	914A	Allied Trades Warrant Officer
2T370	Vehicle Maintenance Specialist	91B	915A	Automotive Maintenance Warrant Officer
2W0xx	Ammunition Specialist	89B	890A	Ammunition Technician
3A0xx	Administrative Specialist	42L	153A	Rotary Wing Aviator
3C0x1	Informations Systems Opns/ Analyst	25B		250N, 251A or 254A
3E0xx	Electrical Systems/ Production	12R/P	120A	Construction Engineering Technician
3E4x1	Utilities	12K	120A	Construction Engineering Technician
3E3x1	Structural	12W	120A	Construction Engineering Technician
3E5x1	Engineering	12T	120A	Construction Engineering Technician
3E7xx	Firefighter	12M	153A	Rotary Wing Aviator
3M0xx	Food Service Specialist	92G	922A	Food Service Technician
3N0xx	Journalist	46Q	153A	Rotary Wing Aviator
3P0xx	Military Police	31B	153A	Rotary Wing Aviator
4A1xx	Medical Logistics Specialist	68J	920A	Property Accounting Technician
4A2xx	Biomedical Equipment Specialist	68A	153A	Rotary Wing Aviator
4B0xx	Preventive Medicine Specialist	68S	153A	Rotary Wing Aviator
4D0xx	Hospital Food Service Specialist	68M	922A	Food Service Technician
4E0xx	Preventive Medicine Specialist	68S	153A	Rotary Wing Aviator

USAF MOS	Job Title	Army MOS	Warrant MOS	Warrant Officer Title
4N1x1	Operating Room Specialist	68D	153A	Rotary Wing Aviator
4P0x1	Pharmacy Specialist	68Q	153A	Rotary Wing Aviator
4T0xx	Medical Lab Specialist	68K	153A	Rotary Wing Aviator
4Y0xx	Dental Specialist	68E	153A	Rotary Wing Aviator
5J0xx	Paralegal Specialist	27D	270A	Legal Administrator
5R0xx	Chaplain Assistant	56M	153A	Rotary Wing Aviator
6C0xx	Automated Logistics Specialist	92A	920B	Supply Systems Technician
8J0xx	Corrections Specialist	31E	153A	Rotary Wing Aviator
9R0xx	Aviation Operations Specialist	15P	153A	Rotary Wing Aviator

Feeder MOS - Enlisted MOS Conversion List (Navy)

Navy MOS	Job Title	Army MOS	Warrant MOS	Warrant Officer Title
1733	Electronic Warfare Systems Technician (AN/SLQ-32(V)2)	29E	290A	Electronic Warfare Technician
1734	Electronic Warfare Systems Technician (AN/SLQ-32(V)3)	29E	290A	Electronic Warfare Technician
1736	Electronic Warfare Systems Maintenance Technician (AN/SLQ-32(V)4)	29E	290A	Electronic Warfare Technician
1737	Electronics Warfare Systems Technician (AN/SLQ-32A(V)5/ AN/SLQ-32(V)5)	29E	290A	Electronic Warfare Technician
8278 8279	Traffic Management Coordinator	88N	882A	Mobility Officer
8284	Imagery Ground Station Operator	35G	125D	Geospatial Engineering Technician
8361-4, 6-8	UAV	15W/15E	150U	Tactical Unmanned Aerial System
9525	Automated Logistics Specialist	92A	920B	Supply Systems Technician
9549	Automated Logistics Specialist	92A	920B	Supply Systems Technician
9550 9562 9563	Water Craft Operator	88K	880A	Marine Deck Officer
AK	Automated Logistics Specialist	92A	920B	Supply Systems Technician
BM	Water Craft Operator	88K	880A	Marine Deck Officer
BU	Builder	12W	120A	Construction Engineering Technician
CE	Construction Electrician	12R	120A	Construction Engineering Technician
CM	Construction Mechanic	*	919A	Engineer Equipment Maintenance Warrant Officer

Navy MOS	Job Title	Army MOS	Warrant MOS	Warrant Officer Title
CS	Culinary Specialist	92G	922A	Food Service Technician
CTM CTN CTO	Crypto Technician - Maintenance Crypto Technician - Networks Crypto Technician - Communications	*	255N	Network Management Technician
EA	Engineering Aid	12T	120A	Construction Engineering Technician
GS	Gas Turbine Systems Technician	88L	881A	Marine Engineering Officer
IS	Intelligence Specialist	35G	125D	Geospatial Engineering Technician
IT	Information System Technician	25B	255A	Information Services Technician
LN	Legalman	27D	270A	Legal Administrator
MM	Machinist Mate	88L	881A	Marine Engineering Officer
MR	Machinary Repairman	44E	914A	Allied Trades Warrant Officer
SK	Storekeeper	92A	920B	Supply Systems Technician
SK 2821	Storekeeper - Traffic Management	88N	882A	Mobility Officer
SK 2829	Storekeeper - Unit Supply	92Y	920A	Property Accounting Technician
GM	Gunner's Mate	*	890A	Ammunitions Technician
			948D	Electronic Missile Systems Maintenance
UT	Utilitiesman	12R	120A	Construction Engineering Technician

Feeder MOS - Enlisted MOS Conversion List (Marines)

Marine MOS	Job Title	Army MOS	Warrant MOS	Warrant Officer Title
231	Intelligence Specialist	*	350F	All Source Intelligence Technician
241	Imagery Analysis Specialist	35G	350G	GEOINT Imagery Technician
261	Geographic Speciallist	12Y	125D	Geospatial Information Technician
431	Logistics/Embarkation and Combat Service Support (CSS) Specialist	88N	882A	Mobility Officer
451	Air Delivery Specialist	92R	921A	Airdrop Systems Technician
511	MAGTF Planning Specialist	88N	882A	Mobility Officer
08xx	Field Artillery	*	131A	Field Artillery Targeting Technician
1141	Electrician	12R	120A	Construction Engineering Technician
1169	Utilities Chief	12H	120A	Construction Engineering Technician
1361	Engineering Assistant	12T	120A	Construction Engineering Technician
1316	Metal Worker	*	914A	Allied Trades Warrant Officer
1341	Engineer Equipment Mechanic	*	919A	Engineer Equipment Maintenance Warrant Officer
1391	Bulk Fuel Specialist	*	923A	Petroleum Systems Technician
2111	Small Arms Repairer / Technician	*	913A	Armament Systems Maintenance Warrant Officer
2161	Machinist	*	914A	Allied Trades Warrant Officer
2171	Electro-Optical Ordnance Repairer	*	890A	Ammunition Technician
2311	Ammunition Technician	*	890A	Ammunition Technician
2621	Special Communications Signals Collection Operator	29E	290A	Electronic Warfare Technician
2629	Signals Intelligence Analyst	29E	290A	Electronic Warfare Technician
			352N	SIGINT Analysis Technician

Marine MOS	Job Title	Army MOS	Warrant MOS	Warrant Officer Title
2631	Electronic Intelligence (ELINT) Intercept Operator/Analyst	29E	352S	SIGNALS Collection Technician
2691	Signals Intelligence/ Electronic Warfare Chief	29E	290A	Electronic Warfare Technician
28xx	Data / Communcations Maintenance	*	255N 255A	Most 28xx series MOSs will fit under one of the three Signal Warrant Officer MOSs.
3112	Traffic Management Specialist	88N	882A	Mobility Officer
3381	Food Service Specialist	92G	922A	Food Service Technician
3529	Motor Transport Maintenance Chief	*	915A	Automotive Maintenance Warrant Officer
40xx	Data System	*	255N 255A	Most 28xx series MOSs will fit under one of the three Signal Warrant Officer MOSs.
4421	Legal Services Specialist	*	270A	Legal Administrator
5819	Military Police Investigator	*	311A	CID Special Agent
59xx	Electronics Maintenance	*	948B	Electronic Systems Maintenance Technician
59xx	Electronics Maintenance	*	948D	Electronic Missile Systems Maintenance Technician
6214	UAV Repairman	15E	150U	Tactical Unmanned Aerial System
6531	Aircraft Ordnance Technician	*	890A	Ammunition Technician
6541	Aviation Ordnance Systems Technician	*	890A	Ammunition Technician
6591	Aviation Ordnance Chief	*	890A	Ammunition Technician
7314	UAV Operator	15W	150U	Tactical Unmanned Aerial System

34

So What Items Do I Need For A Warrant Packet?

- Most all branches require that the applicant have experience in the enlisted feeder MOS.

- **Rank:** It varies based on the Warrant Officer MOS you are applying for.

- **NCOERS:** Must submit copies of ALL NCOERs. The preponderance of your NCOERs must reflect outstanding and exceptional duty performance ratings noted with "among the best" ratings by the Rater and "successful" and/or "superior" ratings by the Senior Rater.

- **College:** Must possess six semester hours of composition-based English (Grade of C or better) from an accredited institution of higher learning. Successful completion of the College Level Examination Program (CLEP) in English Composition or Freshman College Composition is acceptable. You must provide a memorandum signed by an Army Education Center official which certifies that the college or university is an Army accredited institution of higher learning.

- **Letters of Recommendation:** Must possess a Letter of recommendation from a Senior Warrant Officer (CW3-CW5), in the desired MOS, assigned to the applicant's organization that attests to your technical and tactical competence in the desired MOS. In organizations where no Senior Warrant Officer in the desired MOS is assigned, a letter of recommendation from a Senior Warrant Officer in the desired MOS assigned to the applicant's installation will also meet this requirement.

- **Experience:** Most must possess a minimum of five most recent years documented experience in the desired MOS. Civilian experience related to the desired MOS will also be taken into consideration.

MOS's Available to All Applicants Regardless of Experience

The following MOS's are open to all candidates and do not require a feeder MOS:

- 153A - Rotary Wing Aviator

- 255N - Network Management Technician (Must have 4 years IT experience IAW prerequisites)

- 255A - Information Services Technician (Must have 4 years IT experience IAW prerequisites)

Administrative Requirements

A Soldier must meet these nine Administrative Requirements before applying for the Warrant Officer Program

1. US Citizenship (No Waivers).

2. General Technical (GT) score of 110 or higher (No Waivers).

3. High school graduate or have a GED (No Waivers).

4. Final Secret or Top Secret Security Clearance - **Interim clearances will not satisfy the requirement!**

5. Pass the standard 3-event Army Physical Fitness Test (APFT) and meet height/weight standards. **APFT must be current and not older than six months by the time the applicant's packet will be boarded.**

6. Pass the commissioning physical for technical specialties or the Class 1 (Warrant Officer candidate) flight physical for Aviators.

7. All applicants must have 12 months remaining on their enlistment contract.

8. Active Federal Service (AFS): All applicants must have 12 years of AFS or less prior to their packet being boarded. Applicants must submit an **AFS waiver request with the application** if they have 12 or more years of AFS.

9. Age Requirements: For 153A, 33rd birthday or less prior to their packet being boarded. For all other WO MOS', 46th birthday or less prior to their packet being boarded. Applicants must submit an **Age waiver request with the application** if they exceed the age requirements specified.

Deployment Information Page

If you are currently deployed in support of OIF or OEF, USAREC is keenly aware of the challenges you face trying to put your Warrant Officer application together.

Email works best from theater. usarmy.knox.usarec.mbx.9sbn-wo-team-questions@mail.mil

Policy Changes:

1. Letters of Recommendation are good for 12 months.

2. S-1 Letter can be substituted for the MILPO letter. (Our checklist will be better)

3. Photos taken during contingency operations must be of good quality and have a clear background. (It is preferred that photos are taken against a wall with a clear backdrop if possible. No unit flags, vehicles, outside scenery etc.,) Remove headgear, tactical gear and weapons. Duty uniform only. (Traditional or Multi-Cam patterns)

4. Resume.

5. Security Memorandum Change.

6. Rotating through SWA, Contact our multi-functional recruiter located in Kuwait at Camp Virginia (PSB Tent#3) DSN: 318-430-12149

7. Army Personnel Testing sites in SWA for personnel desiring to take the Selection Instrument for Flight Training (SIFT)

Warrant Officer Application Checklist

The following items are required as part of the WOC checklist. All documents should be single-sided and in the following order:

Name: _____

Board Packet

The following items make up your board packet and will be reviewed by board members. It is important these documents are clean and neat in appearance:

_____DA Form 61 (with valid HT/WT and APFT Statement, and Signed by CO CDR in Block 41)

_____Company Commander LOR (or applicable Company Grade UCMJ authority) USAREC Form 3.3

_____Battalion Commander LOR (or applicable Field Grade UCMJ authority) USAREC Form 3.3

_____Group Commander LOR - 180A ONLY

_____Group CCWO LOR - 180A ONLY

_____Senior Warrant Officer Letter of Recommendation (CW3-CW5 for most MOS' – check MOS prerequisites) USAREC Form 3.3

_____Resume USAREC Form 3.2 (ensure summary page is filled in)

_____ERB or equivalent document (used to verify DOB, GT, AFS, and ETS)

_____Evaluations [All NCOERS (up to ten years) and all Army Evaluation Reports (AERs) (1059s) in order oldest to newest]

_____College Transcript(s): Official or Unofficial

_____COPIES of Professional Certificates (i.e. Licenses/Certificates issued to Engineers, Mechanics, Pilots, etc.)

_____SIFT Results (153A applicants only)

_____DA Photo (all applicants must include a color quality photo -.jpeg prefered)

Supporting Documents

These documents are required to qualify your packet, but will not be reviewed by the board)

_____Security Clearance verification memorandum (Prepared by the S-2 or facility security manager)

_____Physical Coversheet USAREC Form 3.1 (Technicians only—expires after 24 months). Include whole physical if medical waiver required.

_____DD 2808 with Stamp from USAAMC, Ft. Rucker (153A and 150A applicants only) Include whole physical if medical waiver is required.

_____DA Form 160-R (ensure that you sign it and block 9a is checked)

_____DA Form 7434-Application for US Army Marine Certification (880A, 881A)

_____Re-enlistment/extension documents-if required (if ERB does not show 12 months remaining on current contract)

_____Statement of Understanding (a copy of this memo is in this book)

_____Conditional Release—if required (if you are not an active Duty Army Applicant) DD Form 368

_____Conditional Resignation Memorandum (Army Commissioned Officer only)

_____Conditional Release Memorandum from current Branch (Army Commissioned Officer only)

_____English credit document—if required (255A, 255N, 420A, 890A, 913A, 914A, 915A, 919A, 948B, 948D)

_____TABE score document—if required (255A, 255N, 880A, 881A, 890A, 913A, 914A, 915A, 919A, 920A, 920B, 921A, 922A, 923A, 948B, 948D)

_____Achilles Dagger Certificate or Level III qualified-180A ONLY

_____DA 330 with at least a 1/1 language proficiency-180A ONLY

_____REDD Report/GT Conversion (Air Force, Marine, Navy and Coast Guard applicants)

_____Body Fat Content Worksheet—if required (if you do not meet the height/weight standards set forth in AR 600-9)

_____Tattoo Validation Waiver -if required (If you are not in compliance with AR 670-1 dated 10 April 2015)

_____Tattoo (related) Separation Board Proceedings - if required (indicating CDR retained Service Member)

_____Moral waiver request—if required (as identified in blocks 26 on DA Form 61)

_____Age waiver request—if required (required if older than 33 AVN, 46 TECH by start date of your 1st board)

_____Prerequisite waiver request—if required (verify with MOS on web site)

_____AFS (Active Federal Service) waiver request—if required (if you have more than 12 years AFS by date DA 61 is signed)

_____APFT (Army Physical Fitness Test) waiver request—if required (must include current Profile, complete Physical, APFT score card)

_____Remaining Hard Copy documents from OMPF not included on your ERB (awards, certificates)

This section to be completed and authenticated by PSD/MPD personnel or the Battalion S-1/S-1 NCO

I certify that service member is not flagged or barred and have verified that the service member's tattoos (if applicable) are in compliance with AR 670-1 (dated 10 April 2015) and are properly documented in IPERMS/AMHRR: Service member is eligible for this program.

CERTIFYING OFFICIAL (printed name and title): _____

SIGNATURE: _____
DATE: _____
DSN PHONE #: _____COMM PHONE #: _____
EMAIL: _____

_____Entire Packet administratively reviewed by unit CSM.

REVIEWER (printed name and title):_____

SIGNATURE_____

_____ Entire Packet administratively reviewed by recommending Senior Warrant Officer.

REVIEWER (printed name and title):_____

SIGNATURE_____

Applicants must send their packets as a PDF attachment via email or by use of a Digital Sender, (file size restricted to 5mbs or less per transaction) to to: usarmy.knox.usarec.mbx.9sbn-new-warrant-packets@mail.mil

Check your application status on-line at www.usarerc.army.mil/hq/warrant after allowing 7–10 business days for processing.

Good luck!

Check here for the most updated version:
http://usacac.army.mil/cac2/WOCC/

Joint Service Agreement for Non-Army Personnel

A joint service agreement allows service members who are selected for this program to be discharged from their service and enlist in the Army. Applicants must apply for this program while on active duty and must have 12 months or more remaining on their enlistment contract. Civilians must contact their local Army recruiter. Applications are forwarded from the individual to the United States Army Recruiting Command (USAREC). After screening, the application is forwarded to the appropriate proponent who evaluates the applicants' technical experience and determines if the applicant is qualified to compete against other qualified applicants for the limited Warrant Officer positions. Applications from those who are not technically qualified will be returned to the applicant without further processing. Further requirements for Non-Army personnel are listed below under "Additional Requirements for Non-Army Personnel".

A selection board will consider fully qualified applications. Selection is highly competitive and board members select applicants based upon the whole person concept. Leadership and technical abilities will be evaluated and only the best qualified will be selected.

Note: Commissioned Officers from the Air Force, Navy, Marines, and Coast Guard cannot apply through the Warrant Officer Selection Board (WOSB). They have to resign their commission and apply through the WOFT Program or apply for an Inter-Service Transfer through the Army Human Resources Command (AHRC).

Additional Requirements for Non-Army Personnel

1. Armed Services Vocational Aptitude Battery (ASVAB)

Air Force, Navy, and Coast Guard service members who want to get their scores converted first must ensure they qualify with a minimum Army General Technical (GT) score of 110.

If the Armed Services Vocational Aptitude Battery (ASVAB) or Armed Forces Classification Test (AFCT) or in-service ASVAB was administered prior to 1 July, 2004 the following applies:

1. Air Force members need a minimum General (G) score of 64.

2. Navy and Coast Guard Service members must combine their Arithmetic Reasoning (AR) and Verbal (VE) and have a minimum combined score of 109.

   If the ASVAB or AFCT was administered after 1 July 2004 the following applies:

   1. Air Force members need a minimum General (G) score of 70.

   2. Navy and Coast Guard Service members must combine their Arithmetic Reasoning (AR) and Verbal (VE) and have a minimum combined score of 111.

ASVAB scores can be converted by mailing (Cannot be faxed) a True Certified Copy of the service member's ASVAB record. A "True Certified Copy" is a photocopy of the service member's ASVAB or AFCT scores that has the statement "Certified True Copy" or "True Copy" either stamped or hand-written on the page and is accompanied by a blue or black ink signature of a military personnel clerk, test control officer, or Commander. In addition, include rank, position, and phone number of the individual certifying the scores. Photocopied signatures will not be accepted. Please do not send originals. Documentation provided for conversion will not be returned.

A memorandum containing the following information must be submitted along with the True Certified Copy of scores:

1. Full Name, Rank/Grade, Social Security Number.

2. Complete Current Command Address (NO ABBREVIATIONS OR ACRONYMS ACCEPTED).

3. Complete mailing address (can be individual's home).

4. What program individual is applying for? i.e. Warrant Officer Flight/ Engineer Programs.

5. Request to take the Selection Instrument for Flight Training (SIFT), if necessary.

6. POC information, email addresses and phone numbers. Please include commercial and DSN phone numbers.

Both documents must be mailed to the following address:

Education Division (AHRC-PDE/APT)
U.S. Army Human Resources Command
1600 Spearhead Div Ave
Ft Knox, KY 40122

POC: You can contact The Army Personnel Testing (APT) Program Office at (502) 613-8594 / DSN 983-8594 or by email at: usarmy.knox.hrc.tagd-army-personnel-testing@mail

Retesting procedures (Improve ASVAB score or take initial SIFT) for individuals who do not meet the aptitude requirement (110 GT) for entry into the Warrant Officer Program. They will need to take the Armed Forces Classification Test (AFCT). The AFCT is the in-service version of the ASVAB. Individuals will need to take the test within their service, have the scores posted to their official military file, and have their personnel component certify a true copy of the record.

Individuals should ensure that they study for this test, as failure to achieve the required score will result in a retest of the AFCT in its entirety. Baron's and ARCO have good study guides that are available at most local libraries and bookstores. Procedures to covert scores to Army standards as outlined above apply.

Those individuals who request to take the SIFT must take a copy of the letter certifying their ASVAB scores to the nearest Army Education Center or testing facility in order to schedule the exam with them. The original letter must accompany the application packet for the Warrant Officer Program. If you are unsure where the closest Army Test facility is, go to the web site:

https://www.armyeducation.army.mil

Click on Testing at the top of the screen, then scroll down to see local test accounts.

Marines:
Marines needing ASVAB scores converted must contact:

HQMC M&RA MPP-50 Testing
3280 Russell Road
Quantico, VA 22134

A letter request from the individual's commanding officer to HQMC is required to convert ASVAB scores to Army Standards. HQMC will submit a letter certifying GT scores. This letter will be an enclosure for the package that will be submitted for the Army Warrant Officer Program.

Marines who request to take the AFAST will need to submit a letter request from the parent unit Commanding Officer to HQMC. The request should include last ASVAB test date (if the test date is not the original test, and was a retest prior to 2003 the Marine must test with the ASVAB before scores can be converted) and where the exam is to be taken with a point of contact and phone number.

The SIFT must be administered at an Army facility. An authorization letter from HQMC will be forwarded to the Army Personnel Testing Coordinator who will give the Army Test Control Officer (TCO) authorization to test the Marine. The entire process takes a minimum of two weeks. If you are unsure where the nearest Army test facility is located, go to the web site:

https://www.armyeducation.army.mil

Click on "Testing" at the top of the screen, then scroll down to select "Local Test Accounts".

The Contact Numbers for HQMC MPP-50 is:

COM: (703) 784-9615
DSN: 278-9615
FAX: (703) 784-9574
DSN 278-9574.

E-Mail: SMBManpowerMPP50Testing@usmc.mil

2. Approved Conditional Release:

This is a memorandum granting approval of separation contingent upon selection into the Warrant Officer program. Approval authority for each service is listed below:

Navy

For information on how to apply for conditional release, refer to:

MILPERSMAN 1910-102, para 6.
http://buperscd.technology.navy.mil/bup_updt/508/milpers/1910-102.htm

COMNAVPERSCOM
5720 Integrity Drive Millington, TN 38055

Enlisted Favorable Separation Section:
Ph: (901) 874-4431
Fax: (901) 874-2754
DSN prefix: 882-XXXX

This is a memorandum granting approval of separation contingent upon selection into the Warrant Officer program. Approval authority for each service is listed below:

Air Force

Per the USAF AFPC, conditional release paperwork should be routed through VMPF (Virtual Military Personnel Flight) by selecting "voluntary separations" and then "early release". The last page of the application allows individuals to upload the LOI and the DD Form 368.

U.S. Air Force Conditional Release
HQ AFPC DPPRSOA
550 C Street West Suite 11
Randolph AFB, TX 78150-4713
DSN prefix: 665-3769

Note: AFPC requires a Letter of Interest (LOI) before granting your conditional release. You can email your request to the WO website. Please provide your Full Name, Rank, SSN,

Note: A Warrant Officer recruiter will reply with your LOI.

Marines
Hqs, USMC, Manpower & Reserve Affairs (MMSR 3)
3280 Russell Rd.
Quantico, VA 22134-5103

Coast Guard
US Dept of Trans
2100 Second Street S.W.
Washington DC 20593

3. Army 3-Event Physical Fitness Test (APFT):

Push-ups, sit-ups, and 2 mile run administered by an Army E7 or above. Check with a nearby Army installation or the local Army recruiting office for someone to administer the test. The APFT score is valid for 6 months but should not be close to expiration when forwarding the packet. Results must be recorded on DA Form 705, signed by an Army E7 or above, and included in the packet. Be sure to read the Test Procedures in Training Manual 21-20 that address the instructions and additional points for each event before testing. You should make every effort to exceed the APFT minimum standards. The Warrant Officer Candidate School will administer the APFT to very strict standards.

4. Personnel data record equivalent of the Army Enlisted Record Brief (ERB). Equivalent forms are listed below:

Navy: Personnel data record pages 1, 4, and 5
Air Force: Data Verification Brief (DVB) or RIP pages 1 - 11
Marines: Master Brief Sheet (MBS) (Usually only 1 page)
Coast Guard: Personnel data record pages 1, 3, 4, and 5

5. Tattoo Validation/Waiver Memo.

ALL Sister Service applicants are required to provide a Tattoo Validation/ Waiver Memo signed by the first O-5 (or above) in their chain of command. The Commander will verify/document any extremist, indecent, sexist or racist tattoos anywhere on applicant's body (IAW AR 670-1. Para 3-3b) and any tattoos below the wrist/above the collar (in Summer Pt Shirt) (IAW AR 670-1. Para 3-3c) and provide recommendation on waiver approval. If applicant does not have any tattoos on their body; any extremist, indecent, sexist or racist tattoos; or any tattoos below the wrist/above the collar (in Summer Pt Shirt), the Commander will indicate "None" on lines 1.a. and 2.a though 2.d (respectively). Sample memo can be found in this book and at Warrant Officer Recruiting website.

6. Official Military Personnel File.

As a minimum, this file contains your enlistment and reenlistment documents, awards, evaluations, training certificates, and promotion orders. If your personnel records are not on microfiche, then a hard copy of these documents are sufficient. Documents missing from your record should be provided in hard copy. It is your responsibility to ensure your records are accurate and current.

7. 12 Months Enlistment Remaining.

An applicant can now apply with 12 months remaining on his or her current active duty enlistment. The reference to a two-year requirement will remain on our web site until AR 611-85 is published eliminating the two-year requirement. Reenlistment or extension documents are needed if your personnel records do not reflect at least 15 months or more remaining on your active duty contract. This must be completed before submitting application.

Note: The above requirements must be met, in addition to, or in place of the other requirements in the sample application and governing regulations. Include the supporting document that proves you have completed each requirement as a part of your application.

8. Sister Service 153A (Rotor Wing Aviator) Flight Physical

Option 1: (Preferred): Applicant completes their flight physical (on the DD 2808) the through their closest Army Flight surgeon. (Army flight surgeon submits to Ft Rucker Aero-med)

Option 2: Applicant completes their flight physical (on the DD 2808) through their servicing physician and the physician submits to Ft Rucker Aero-med electronically through the medical system "AERO".

Option 3: Applicant completes their flight physical (on the DD 2808) through their servicing physician and submits to Ft Rucker Aero-med through their closest Army flight surgeon.

Option 4: Applicant completes their flight physical (on the DD 2808) through their servicing physician and the physician mails the completed flight physical to the address below (with delivery receipt signature). Preferred method of mail is 1. FEDEX (for expedited delivery) or 2. US Postal Service (takes 2-3 weeks in most cases).

Mail completed Flight Physicals to:
ATTN: Mr. Stephen Gaarcia
453 Novosel St (RM 160)
Fort Rucker, AL 36362

Sister Service Physicians can direct Flight Physical questions to:
Mr. Stephen Garcia (Ft Rucker Flight Physical Section)
(334) 355-3233.

Additionally, you can phone Ft Rucker Aero-med at:
(334) 255-0750.

SIFT Study Guide Link:
http://www.usarec.army.mil/hq/warrant/download/militaryflight.pdf

Chapter 4

Your Resume & Letters of Reference

Your Resume- Use USAREC Form 3.2

Section 1 – Administrative Data

Use the example below to get started. Read Sections I thru VIII thoroughly and start by typing your last name **IN ALL CAPs** as shown. Do not deviate from the example. Use your legal name; not your nickname. When in doubt, use what's printed on your birth certificate or social security card.

Warning: This is the only resume the board will accept!

Section II – Civilian Education

Only list your education here, and be sure to add your GPA and any academic honors you earned while attending. If you are currently enrolled indicate your intended graduation date.

Section III - Objective

WARRANT OFFICER RESUME
(This form will be used in place of the resume.)

PRIVACY ACT STATEMENT
AUTHORITY: Collection of this information is authorized by Title 10, USC, Sections 503, 505, 508, 3013, and 12102 and Executive Order 9397.   **PRINCIPAL PURPOSE:** Information collected will be used by selection board members to determine qualifications of warrant officer candidates.   **ROUTINE USES:** Blanket routine use disclosures as described in AR 340-21, The Army Privacy Program, paragraph 3-2.   **DISCLOSURE:** Voluntary; however, failure to provide the information may delay or terminate the warrant officer candidate's application process.

SECTION I - ADMINISTRATIVE DATA		
1. NAME *(Last, first, middle initial)* : SAMPLE, Joe E.	2. RANK/GRADE: SSG / E6	3. PMOS: 42A20P
4. UNIT, ORGANIZATION, STATION, ZIP CODE OR APO, MAJOR COMMAND: C DET 1-4 INF BATTALION, FT ATTERBURY, KY 40121 (CENTCOM)	5. E-MAIL ADDRESS: Joe.e.sample@mail.mil	

SECTION II - CIVILIAN EDUCATION
(Include the highest degree level obtained. Include your GPA, Dean's List, and any other special recognition.)
BA Degree - Libery University (intended graduation May 2018), 108 credits completed, 3.2 GPA   AA Degree - University of Pheonix, 2015 GPA 3.5, Dean's List

SECTION III - OBJECTIVE
(List all of the warrant officer MOSs to include 4-digit code and official title you are applying for in order of preference.)
1. 153 A - Rotary Wing Aviator
2. 420A - Human Resources Technician
3.

Use the MOS to Enlisted Feeder MOS List in Chapter 3 to complete SECTION III - OBJECTIVE

Some Candidates qualify for several MOS's. List your top 3 choices.

Section IV — Military Experience

Accomplishments should appear in chronological order, by date, starting with the most current assignment. List ALL military assignments; especially those in an NCO position. Focus on quantifiable measurements of success that set you apart by the unique characteristics of each assigned position. Write in a clear, concise, yet complete sentences - not in fragments or bullets.

SECTION IV - MILITARY EXPERIENCE	
(List in order from most recent to earliest duty assignment or position. Be sure to mention any accomplishments, special recognition, or achievements that will illustrate to the board your potential for leadership as a warrant officer.)	
1. DATES *(YY/MM)*: 07/07 to Present	ORGANIZATION: 95th Special Troops Battalion, Ft Carson, CO
POSITION TITLE: TITLE should match ERB or evaluation reports	
DUTIES *(list below to include significant contributions)*:	

Examples:

04/2016 to Present Organization: 108th Air Defense Artillery, Fort Bragg, NC. As the Readiness NCO and technical expert provided support for 24 Patriot systems and associated equipment. I advised 4 senior leaders on logistical issues and solutions for dead-lined equipment. Monitored requisitions and resolved long lead times using computer based programs and coordination with Defense Logistics Agency. Prepared readiness data blasts and transmitted to Standard Army Maintenance System 2 terminal. Trained 17 Soldiers to apply preventative maintenance checks and services to missile systems, test equipment, tools, and training equipment to improve efficiency. Responsible for a $1.2 million hand receipt with no losses over a 2 year period.

6/2014 - 4/2016 As the Maintenance Section Chief I authored a logistic plan for support to 2 theaters of operations. I developed logistics policies for Material Management Center operations interrelated to 3 subordinate Air Defense Brigades. I was assigned to Lead 3 Mission Rehearsal Exercises and fully coordinated all execution details. My squad arranged multi-service high priority resupply operations and transfer of critical Class V, float Patriot equipment and parts to restore Air Defense coverage of vital Defended Asset List (DAL) locations culminating in a successfully deployment to a Combat Zone and 2 Multi-National exercises. As Squad leader I supervised 6 Soldiers and managed $120K annual budget as the Government Credit Card Holder.

2.	DATES (YY/MM): 05/06 to 05/05	ORGANIZATION: HHC, IIId ACA, Ft Hood, TX
	POSITION TITLE: PROMOTION SECTION NCOIC	
	DUTIES (list below to include significant contributions):	

List outstanding achievements and additional duties performed in that position. Spell out terms that apply to your assignment especially buzzwords in your MOS, e.g. Prescribed Load List (PLL). Avoid the use of jargon, slang, and other types of informal terms. Look over your NOCER for good bullets to use to build narrative sentences based on noteworthy achievements. See NCO bullet examples below.

- Successfully performed duties during one Combat deployment and 3 NTC deployments

- Maintained 146 Bradley's and related support equipment above 95% readiness rate for 2 consecutive years.

- Supervised 6 Soldiers and 2 contact teams.

- Accountable for hand receipts valued at over $2M with zero losses.

- Submitted creative solution to TOW Visual Module component saving $320K annually.

- Completed 100% of counseling and awards for 8 Soldier's on-time.

- Corrected all site violations as Brigade HAZMAT NCO with zero post and state violations.

SECTION IV - MILITARY EXPERIENCE *(continued)*
(List in order from most recent to earliest duty assignment or position. Be sure to mention any accomplishments, special recognition, or achievements that will illustrate to the board your potential for leadership as a warrant officer.)

3.	DATES *(YY/MM):* 03/09 to 05/05	ORGANIZATION: A Det, 82d PSB, Ft Bragg NC
	POSITION TITLE: ENLISTED RECORDS NCO	
	DUTIES *(list below to include significant contributions):*	

Focus on measurements of success, NOT just a job description, but how well you performed the job. Use NCOER/evaluation bullets as a "reference only", not as the actual written entry for the resume. Mention if you exceeded standards on a significant inspection, evaluation, or leadership school. List deployments or make a separate assignment entry if deployed for several months.

Example: Received Fort Benning Basic NCO Leadership class award.

4.	DATES *(YY/MM)* 02/09 to 03/08	ORGANIZATION: C Det 516th PSC, Korea
	POSITION TITLE: REASSIGNMENTS CLERK	
	DUTIES *(list below to include significant contributions):*	

List service, impact, or achievement awards received during each tour or assignment. List significant contributions in major deployments and field training exercises e.g. OIF/OEF. ULCHI FOCUS LENS, JROTC, NTC. List career enhancement recognition awarded such as Soldier/NCO of the month as well as Audie Murphy and similar association inductions.

56

SECTION IV - MILITARY EXPERIENCE *(continued)*	
(List in order from most recent to earliest duty assignment or position. Be sure to mention any accomplishments, special recognition, or achievements that will illustrate to the board your potential for leadership as a warrant officer.)	
6. DATES *(YY/MM)* _____ to _____	ORGANIZATION:
POSITION TITLE:	
DUTIES *(list below to include significant contributions):*	

Use this side as a continuation page from the previous page. Be sure to summarize assignments but don't exceed the last 11 duty positions or ten years on record. Again, focus on measurements of success NOT just a job description. Look at the examples on the previous page

Section V – Civilian Experience

Here is where you list related civilian job experience that correlates to the Warrant Officer MOS you are applying for. Examples: HVAC Repair, Electrician, Mechanic, Pilot, Computer Repair, Engineer. Duties should focus on skills that would benefit a Warrant Officer.

SECTION V - CIVILIAN EXPERIENCE	
(List in order any civilian experience that specifically relates to the warrant officer position for which you are applying. Be sure to mention any accomplishments, special recognition, or achievements that will illustrate to the board your potential for leadership as a warrant officer.)	
1. DATES *(YY/MM)* 98/01 to 00/05	ORGANIZATION: Kelly Temporary Services, Grand Rapids MI
POSITION TITLE: Administrative Assistant	
DUTIES *(list below to include significant contributions):*	

Do not list civilian employment/experience if it is not related to the Warrant Officer MOS you entered in Section III. Avoid Listing: Taco Bell, Car Salesman, Pizza Delivery, Hotel Clerk, Exterminator.

Section VI – Military Education

SECTION VI - MILITARY EDUCATION	
(List up to 21 military courses and give a brief description focusing on the main learning objective.)	
1. DATES *(YY/MM)* 00/08 to 00/07	COURSE: Unit Movement Officer Course (UMO), Ft Sill, OK
DESCRIPTION:	

Special skill courses such as airborne, air assault, pathfinder, etc. are NOT necessary to list as they should appear on your Enlisted Record Brief. Do list correspondence courses that PERTAIN to the Warrant Officer MOS you are applying for. Add a brief course overview for each.

2. DATES *(YY/MM)* 98/01 to 98/03	COURSE: Advance Individual Training (AIT) Ft Atterbury, IN
DESCRIPTION:	
Make all entries reader-friendly and avoid overuse of acronyms. There will be board members unfamiliar with your MOS so use	

Make sure all entries are reader-friendly and avoid overuse of acronyms. There will be board members unfamiliar with your MOS so use commonly understood terms. Keep all descriptions short, concise, and to the point while focusing on the main learning objective of the course.

Section VII - Summary

SECTION VII - SUMMARY

Write a paragraph or two explaining why you are fully qualified to perform the duties of a Warrant Officer in your skill. This is a very important part of the resume. Make this a call to action, but do so without turning off the reader. Summarize all of your significant accomplishments/achievements (below-the-zone promotions, awards, noteworthy distinctions, deployments, challenging assignments, unique skills in MOS, standards exceeded on a significant inspection/evaluation, etc). Explain how you are exceptionally qualified and have the leadership, management and technical skills needed to become a Warrant Officer. Time to brag!

Answer this question:

Why are you qualified to be an Army Warrant Officer?
Why are you qualified to be an Army Aviator, HR Technician, Logistician?
What will you contribute to the Army as a Warrant Officer?
Why do you want to be an Army Warrant Officer?

Other notes:

No other resume formats are acceptable beyond USAREC FORM 3.2. Therefore, don't go through the big expense of having someone professionally prepare your resume. Take your time and follow the examples above and prepare the form yourself. If you are non-Army, the resume takes on increased importance in conveying your qualifications to become an Army Warrant Officer. In this case you might want to find someone you respect in the Army to assist you in developing or reviewing your resume. They may be able to assist you in finding a Warrant in the MOS you are applying for. This could be of significant help. The Army uses a software package to complete Army Forms. The software is called PureEdge Viewer. Download the software at: http://www.e-publishing.af.mil/viewerdownload.asp

Download USAREC Form 3.2 at:
http://www.usarec.army.mil/hq/warrant/WOpdownload_forms.shtml

Resumes won't be processed without the applicant's signature/date!

SECTION VIII - SIGNATURE			
1. NAME *(Last, first, middle initial)*: SAMPLE, Joe E.	2. RANK: SGT/E5	3. SIGNATURE:	4. DATE *(YYYYMMDD)*:

HQ USAREC Form 1936, Rev 1 Dec 2008   Page 13 of 13

Ensure you sign SECTION VIII-SIGNATURE, Block 3. A digital signature is preferred. You may also print out the form and sign/date (YYYYMMDD) it manually, and then scan the entire packet.

Security Clearance Requirement

Your Security Clearance Verification Memorandum is prepared by the S2 or Facility Security Manager. The memo format form of secret clearance is the same as the memo used to verify a security clearance if the JPAS print it not available. The memo will indicate a secret clearance is granted. See Chapter 6 for an example copy. You are required to confirm your secret clearance in order to submit an application. You will not get orders to attend WOCS until you receive a final secret clearance—follow the directions you receive in your packet when you are selected for school.

Summary

Remember: Warrant Officer jobs are highly technically and require precision and attention to detail. This is one of the few documents prepared by you and will make a huge impression on board members. Whether that impression is positive or negative is determined by how much care you take in preparing this resume. Grammar, spelling, verb tense, whether you used

Caps or Lowercase, the reading level reflective in your summary, did you use the correct date format, YYYYMMDD, are all being evaluated while your resume is being considered.

Start early on the resume and continue to review and edit while you compile the rest of the application. Have the best English expert you know review the resume. Writing skills are very important to a Warrant Officer and the resume demonstrates your ability to communicate in written form. This is not a civilian resume limited to one page; you should state specifics but keep it brief and concise. Do follow the standard format example provided.

It provides an easy read for the board members.

Letters of Reference

Nearly all Warrant Officer applicants must provide 3 Letters of Reference (LOR).

The 1st LOR is from a Senior Warrant Officer in the MOS you're applying for, the 2nd LOR is from your Company Commander, and the 3rd LOR from your Battalion Commander. All LORs must be written up on the USAREC Form 3.3.

— Letters Must Not be Older than 12 Months
— If using former Commander - recommend having current your Commander review the packet! *(Only applicable if PCS occurred within 60 days)*
— Letters of Recommendation required:
  • Company Commander or First Level of UCMJ Authority *(Manadtory)*
  • Battalion Commander or Second Level of UCMJ Authority *(Manadtory)*
  • Senior Warrant Officer Letter of Recommendation *(CW3 to CW5 – Mandatory for most WOMOS;highly recommended for those that don't)*
— USAREC Form 3.3 must be Digitally Signed and recommender's Unit, Email and Phone Number is mandatory in the Bottom Narrative of the Form
- Unique Chains of Command provide explanation memo (Joint Activities/NCOAs)

– Note: If requesting an APFT Waiver, BN CDR LOR must state: <u>"You are physically capable of completing the training and worldwide deployment."</u>
– Note: Non-UCMJ LORs acceptable for Joint Service Organizations (JSOC, WHCA, etc) See memo example at WO website or in this book.
– Sister Service applicants can utilize respective command service letter-heads: hand-signatures are authorized. Contact information is mandatory.

DEPARTMENT OF THE ARMY
UNITED STATES ARMY SPECIAL OPERATIONS RECRUITING BATTALION
BUILDING D-2612 ARDENNES STREET
FORT BRAGG, NORTH CAROLINA 28310

RC-SORB   30 September 2015

MEMORANDUM FOR RECORD

SUBJECT: Exception to Policy for (UCMJ Authority) Letters of Recommendation (LORs) for Warrant Officer Applicants serving in Joint Service organizations.

1. Letters of Recommendation (LORs) are the cornerstone of Army Warrant Officer recruiting. Senior Warrant Officers (SWO) within the applicant's functional specialty and Officers overseeing the applicant's performance, potential and leadership abilities are required to endorse the application packet prior to submission to USAREC. For routine packet submissions, the Army requires first and second level Commanders with Uniform Code of Military Justice (UCMJ) authority over the applicant to endorse the applicant and provide LORs.

2. This memorandum serves as an exception to policy from the UCMJ requirement for Commanders/Directors writing LORs at Joint Service organizations (including but not limited to the Joint Special Operations Command (JSOC), White House Communications Agency (WHCA), Defense Information Systems Agency (DISA), Defense Intelligence Agency (DIA), National Ground Intelligence Center (NGIC), Intelligence and Security Command (INSCOM), etc.). Due to the unique organizational structure and leadership assignments, applicants in these types of organizations are commonly many echelons removed from company and field grade officers with UCMJ authority. Due to the low number of company grade officers at Joint Service organizations, (non-UCMJ authority) field grade level officers may provide either the company or field grade letter for the applicant. The U.S. Army Warrant Officer Recruiting Program will accept and process these packets.

3. Applicants must use separate field grade officers for each LOR. Letters from company grade officers without UCMJ authority will not be accepted.

4. This exception to policy will remain in effect until formally rescinded by the Chief of the U.S. Army Warrant Officer Recruiting Program.

5. The POC for this memorandum is CW4 Jeremy Addleman (Chief, U.S. Army Warrant Officer Recruiting Program), 910-432-2177, jeremy.b.addleman.mil@mail.mil .

ADDLEMAN.JEREMY.B   Digitally signed by ADDLEMAN.JEREMY.B.EAU.1259450140
EAU.1259450140   DN: c=US, o=U.S. Government, ou=DoD, ou=PKI, ou=USA, cn=ADDLEMAN.JEREMY.B.EAU.1259450140
                                    Date: 2015.09.30 13:36:30 -04'00'
JEREMY B ADDLEMAN
CW4, TC
Chief, Army Warrant Officer Recruiting Program

NOTE: The HQ USAREC Form 3.3 in fillable format are available for download at:

http://www.usarec.army.mil/hq/warrant/WOpdownload_forms.shtml

---

LETTER OF RECOMMENDATION
(Warrant Officer Procurement Program)

PRIVACY ACT STATEMENT

AUTHORITY: Collection of this information is authorized by Title 10, USC, Sections 503, 505, 508, 3013, and 12102 and Executive Order 9397.
PRINCIPAL PURPOSE: Information collected will be used by selection board members to determine qualifications of warrant officer candidates.
ROUTINE USES: Blanket routine use disclosures as described in AR 340-21, The Army Privacy Program, paragraph 3-2.
DISCLOSURE: Voluntary; however, failure to provide the information may delay or terminate the warrant officer candidate's application process.

SECTION I - ADMINISTRATIVE DATA

1. NAME (Last, first, middle initial):	2. SSN:	3. RANK:	4. DATE OF RANK:
SMITH, ROBERT A.	123-45-6789	SFC/E7	23 MARCH 2010

5. UNIT, ORGANIZATION, STATION, ZIP CODE OR APO, MAJOR COMMAND:	6. I am completing this form as the applicant's:
MNT TRP SPT SQDN 3ACR (RSSC) COMANCHE BASE, BOSNIA APO AE 09789	☐ Senior Warrant Officer ☐ Company Grade Officer ☒ Field Grade Officer ☐ Other _____ (Specify)

7. I have known this applicant from	2011/12 (Year/Month)	to	PRESENT (Year/Month)	8. RELATIONSHIP TO APPLICANT (i.e., supervisor, interviewer): COMMANDER

SECTION II - NARRATIVE
(Write a narrative explaining the applicant's leadership qualities, character, experience, and special expertise that uniquely qualify him or her to serve as a future warrant officer.)

NARRATIVE:

1. Letters should be three to five paragraphs with specific, quantifiable comments about the service member's character and tactical and technical competence.

2. You may use information from the service member's entire record, including comments about schools, completed assignments, deployments, impact awards, achievements and accomplishments.

3. Generic, flowery, comments are not effective in communicating the service member's attributes to the board members. If you can change the name of the person being recommended to someone else and the comments are not false, then the letter is probably too generic to communicate effectively to the board members.

EXAMPLE WRITE UP:

1. I strongly recommend you select SFC Smith as a Warrant Officer in either MOS 250N, Network Management Technician or 254A, Signal Systems Support Technician. I have observed SFC Smith over the past 2 years and during that time he has consistently impressed me with both his technical and leadership skills.

2. SFC Smith is currently working as the Ground Mobile Forces (GMF) Control Supervisor in the Regional SATCOM Support Center (RSSC) - Bosnia, where he plans, engineers, and coordinates satellite communications network accesses for four unified combatant commanders. In this function he interacts expertly with people from all services, government civilians, and even other country representatives. He has represented the Space and Missile Defense Command and the Army well in many missions and consistently displayed competence and abilities expected of a Warrant Officer.

3. SFC Smith will surely benefit the Army by serving as a Network Management Technician Warrant Officer. He has all the correct skills and proven experience in tough, high tempo organizations. What really makes him the correct choice to be a 250N is his determination to succeed. During Operation ENDURING FREEDOM, SFC Smith led his eight-man team into a hostile area and installed a communication network in two hours versus the eight hour average. Additionally, he earned the distinction of Honor Graduate during his ANCOC attendance and also secured a place on the Commandant's list. I am fully confident that he will represent the US Army as a Warrant Officer superbly.

4. POC for this recommendation is the undersigned at (123) 456-7890 or DSN 987-7890, email at william.a.galvin@us.army.mil.

SECTION III - DISCLAIMER

Notice: I understand by submitting this recommendation I am endorsing this applicant to be boarded for warrant officer selection.

SECTION IV - SIGNATURE

1. NAME (Last, first, middle initial):	2. RANK:	3. BRANCH:	4. SIGNATURE: *William A. Galvin* 1202-5326-93922 20130402	5. DATE (YYYYMMDD):
GALVIN, WILLIAM A.	MAJ	MI		20130402

HQ USAREC Form 1936. Rev   PREVIOUS EDITIONS ARE OBSOLETE   V4.00

REPLY TO
ATTENTION OF

1
2 OFFICE SYMBOL
1
2

1
2 Date

3 MEMORANDUM FOR Deputy Commandant, US Army Command and General Staff
College (ATZL-SWD), 1 Reynolds Avenue, Ft Leavenworth, KS 66027-1352

1
2 SUBJECT: Using and Preparing a Memorandum
1
2
3 1. Paragraph 2-2 defines the use of a memorandum.

2. Single-space the text of the memorandum; double-space between paragraphs.

3. When a memorandum has more than one paragraph, number the paragraphs consecutively.
When paragraphs are subdivided, designate first subdivisions by the letters of the alphabet and
indent them as shown below.

   a. When a paragraph is subdivided, there must be at least two subparagraphs.

   b. If there is a subparagraph "a," there must be a "b."

      (1) Designate second subdivisions by numbers in parentheses; for example, (1),
(2), and (3).

      (2) Do not subdivide beyond the third subdivision.

         (a) However, do not indent any further than the second subdivision.

         (b) This is an example of the proper indentation procedure for a third subdivision.

1
2 AUTHORITY LINE:
1
2
3
4
5 Encl   JOHN W. SMITH
                                          Colonel, GS
                                          Deputy Chief of Staff for Operations

1
2 CF:
   Director, Tactics Division (w/encl)

Sample Security Clearnce Verification Memo

FOR OFFICIAL USE ONLY

DEPARTMENT OF THE ARMY
(UNIT ORGANIZATION ADDRESS)

REPLY TO
ATTENTION OF:

(Office Symbol)   **(Date)**

MEMORANDUM FOR Commander, U.S. Army Recruiting Command, ATTN: RCRO-SPA, Fort Knox, KY 40121-2725

SUBJECT: Security Clearance Verification for **(Last Name, First Name, Middle Initial)**

1. References:

    a. AR 380-67, Personnel Security Program, 9 Sep 88.

2. **(Rank, Last Name, First Name, Middle Name, Social Security Number)** was granted **(Type of security clearance for example TS/SCI)** eligibility on **(date clearance was granted)** by the Army Central Clearance Facility (CCF). **(Rank Last Name)** had a PPR closed on **(date investigation was closed)**

3. The point of contact for this memorandum is **(Your S2/ Security Manager's Name, Phone Number, and E-mail address)**.

S2/Security Manager's Signature block with Signature

FOR OFFICIAL USE ONLY
This document and personal information contained herein is protected by the Privacy Act of 1974,
Section 5 U.S. C sub 552a as amended

64

Suggestions For Obtaining Letters of Recommendation

Some individuals may find its difficult to approach Senior Officers for a letter of recommendation. This section will explore suggestions and possible courses of action for obtaining letters of recommendation.

Typically you will have a relationship with your Company Commander. Usually this relationship will allow you to have a honest discussion with the commander regarding their evaluation of your professionalism and potential as a Warrant Officer. The Company Commander can also assist you in developing a draft letter for the Battalion Commander and Senior Warrant officer. So how should you approach your Company Commander?

There are two schools of thought on this activity. First you can simply depend on the Commander to write a letter of recommendation from scratch or you can prepare a draft for the commander to work from. The choice is yours and should be based on your relationship with the Commander and your chain of command. If you are well known and respected within the unit chances are the Commander will knock out a letter for you with no problem. If you are new or not well known then you may to need to provide the Commander with a starting point. Consider some of the following suggestions.

First, Read AR 25-50 Preparing and Managing Correspondence. This regulation will assist you in finding the proper format for the letter of recommendation. Next sit down and review your evaluation reports, awards, and other achievements that your commander may or may not be familiar with. Then, following the examples provided on the previous page, prepare a draft letter of recommendation. Be careful of overselling yourself or using language that the commander may be uncomfortable with or see as bragging or egotistical. You want to provide a good letter that the Commander can turn into an awesome letter. The goal is to develop a letter that is a strong recommendation and is supported by factual achievements you can document. In the review phase take your draft letter to someone that knows and understands the proper format of Army correspondence, for example, your S-1 NCOIC. Once the format is correct take the letter to senior individuals you trust and respect. They will review it and tweak the letter so that it is ready for review by the Commander. These individuals might consist of: your platoon sergeant, platoon leader, a Senior NCO or officer in another unit. Once your letter is ready you need to have an electronic copy available to present to the Commander. This will save him/her time since they can edit your draft. Now you are ready to see the Commander. When you are talking with the Commander you should always state something like: "Sir, I would greatly appreciate it if you could make this a strong letter in support of my desire to become a Warrant Officer". This lets the Commander know you are looking for their personal touch in the letter and you don't expect the Commander to sign it then and now.

You should make an appointment to see the Commander. Ensure you are squared away for this appointment. Good haircut, good uniform, proper use of customs and courtesy, etc. Chances are the Commander and First Sergeant will want to know why you are coming to see them, so they will most likely be prepared for the conversation and so you should be as well. Rehearse why you want to be a Warrant Officer and why you will be an awesome one. Keep your focus on the positive aspects, such as you're ready for more responsible, not on on issues such as a need for more money.

"Sir, I appreciate your time and consideration in this matter. I have decided I would like to become a Warrant Officer and I would like to request a letter of recommendation from you to support this effort. I have prepared a draft for your review in hard copy and electrons. I would greatly appreciate your recommendation and would sincerely appreciate anything you could do to improve the letter of recommendation."

Understanding your relationship with the Commander and his/her personality can go a long way in developing how you will approach the Commander. Other leaders within the Company might provide you a letter of recommendation that the Commander could use as a foundation for his/her letter. For example, you could provide letters from your platoon sergeant, platoon leader, or motor officer or First Sergeant. The key is to find a balanced approach.

Once you have a good letter from the Commander chances are he/she can then assist you in obtaining your other letters of recommendation.

If you do not have a Senior Warrant Officer in your unit you must be prepared to seek one out. This may require contacting senior leaders in your unit and asking them if they know of a Warrant that you can speak with. You need to be prepared to be interviewed by this Warrant Officer. Take this action seriously. Prepare for this meeting just as you prepared to meet with your Commander.

Chapter 5

Department of the Army (DA) Photo

The DA Photo is Defined as your **"virtual hand shake" with the board.**

The impact of the photo certainly depends on the discretion of the individual board member, but there is no doubt that while a good photo may not help you on a DA board; a poor photo can certainly hurt you. You will not appear in front of the selection board. Don't confuse the DA Selection board with local convening boards where an appearance is usually mandated. NCOs applying from NG or AR units check your local guidance.

Board members expect to see a sharply dressed Soldier with good military bearing, a clean hair cut and correctly worn decorations. Anything less is a negative discriminator.

It is your responsibility to correctly wear all your authorized awards and decorations and wear a clean, pressed and fitted uniform.

The old style Green A's had a wear out date of 4th quarter 2014 per ALARACT Message 202/2008. Ensure you wear the new (Blue) Army Service Uniform (ASU). Why?

- You are getting a clothing allowance

- You want to look like a future leader

- You endorse the Army Vision

- You are in touch with regulation updates

- It's mandatory for wear to your Warrant Officer Graduation! (Think Positive!)

- Upon Graduation you get a One-Time Clothing Allowance to cover expenses and it's required for Officers to own a set.

Selection boards see your current Department of the Army Photograph Management Information System (DAPMIS photograph, or DA photo) when considering selections.

Board members use your DA photo in their decision process.

Many board members view your DA photo as your personal statement of professionalism to the board.

Army Regulation 640-30 states that DA photos are valid for five years. C4IM baseline mission allows Soldiers to have ONE DA photo every five years or per significant change (i.e. promotion). New unit patches, service stripes or awards lower than an ARCOM are NOT justifiable reasons for a new DA photo within one calendar year.

Try to arrange to have your DA photo taken in the same calendar year as the selection board meets. It sends a message to the board that you updated your records and you are a serious candidate. Take your DA photo as early as possible in the day. You don't want a 5 o'clock shadow to impact the board's opinion of you.

Check your Enlisted Record Brief (ERB) BEFORE having the DA photo taken. Cross walk all your awards and decorations. You want your uniform to match your ERB exactly.

Only authorized Visual Information activities may take official DA photos, as required by AR 640-30. Check the Post phone book for the nearest DA Photo Lab or check the installation website. This website will search for the nearest VI Photo Facility based on your Zip Code. Recommend you set the locator to "50 Miles" for the best results : http://www.defenseimagery.mil/community/facilities.html

A digital file copy WILL NOT be issued to you. You must log in and "accept" or "decline" your DA photo thru DAPMIS. Download a copy of your photo while you are logged in at the site.

Reshoots will only be done if images are damaged or if major discrepancies are identified, such as unacceptable levels of wavy or rippled patterns or stair-stepping in digital photographs.

IAW AR 64-30 (Sep 2008) Soldiers will only be granted re-shoots if there is an error caused by the photographer. (There are **No re-shoots** for mistakes made by Soldiers)

Natural wrinkles from wearing the uniform are acceptable and are not justification for a reshoot. That being said –

1. Get your uniform pressed at a dry cleaners familiar with Army uniforms

2. Carefully and accurately position your awards and decorations

3. Remove any temporary awards (permanent awards of unit citations are OK)

4. Don't guess, check the placement of everything using AR 670-1 and use a ruler

5. Check the jacket in the mirror, get a second opinion

6. Put your ASU back in the dry cleaning bag

7. Change at the Photo Lab

8. Take someone with you that knows how to wear the uniform properly.

☐ Make your DA photo appointment now. Applying for Warrant Officer selection is justification to take a photo.

☐ Make your photo as current as possible based on when the board meets.

☐ Get a good fitting **ASU** uniform for the photo. Portray that you endorse the Army's vision.

☐ Get a regulation or shorter haircut. (Males Only)

☐ Shave your mustache off. (Look at the Chain of Command board; those same Officers sit in these selection boards. You want to be taken serious? It will grow back.)

☐ Cross reference your Uniform to the awards and citations listed on your **ERB.**

☐ The evening before your DA photo, get a good night's rest.

☐ On DA photo day, arrive early, change at the photo lab, check everything in the mirror.

☐ Be respectful and listen to your photographer, they can make or break you.

☐ Have a Senior NCO carefully review your DA photo before you accept it thru DAMPIS.

☐ Accept the DA photo in DAPMIS. If you don't log into DAPMIS within 3 days, the system will automatically accept the photo as your DA Official Photo of record on the 4th day. Download a copy of your photo and add it to your packet.

For more DA photo tips and a link to AR 670-1, check out this site: https://g1arng.army.pentagon.mil/Programs/DAPhoto/Pages/default.aspx

DA PHOTO GUIDE

REFER TO AR 640-30 FOR FURTHER GUIDANCE ON WHAT
TO WEAR FOR YOUR OFFICIAL PHOTO

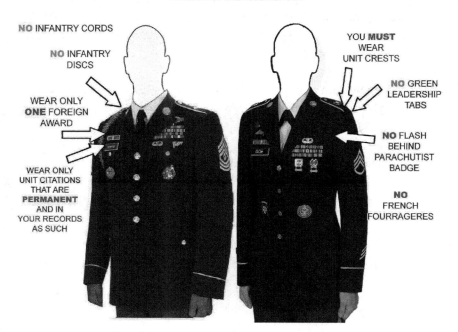

NO INFANTRY CORDS

NO INFANTRY
DISCS

WEAR ONLY
ONE FOREIGN
AWARD

WEAR ONLY
UNIT CITATIONS
THAT ARE
PERMANENT
AND IN
YOUR RECORDS
AS SUCH

YOU **MUST**
WEAR
UNIT CRESTS

NO GREEN
LEADERSHIP
TABS

NO FLASH
BEHIND
PARACHUTIST
BADGE

NO
FRENCH
FOURRAGERES

THIS IS A 3/4 LENGTH PHOTO, SHOES WILL NOT SHOW IN THE PHOTO
HOWEVER YOU **MUST HAVE** SOMETHING ON YOUR FEET OTHER THAN SOCKS

Wear U.S. insignia on the right collar so the bottom of the disk is centered between the outside point and inside edge of the collar, approximately 5/8 inch up from the notch, with the centerline of the U.S. insignia parallel to the inside edge of the lapel.

Wear regimental distinctive insignia centered ½ inch above the nameplate, or ¼ inch above any unit awards or foreign badges that are worn.

Wear foreign wings ½ inch above the nameplate, or ½ inch above any unit awards that are worn.

Wear unit citations centered on the right side of the uniform with the bottom edge ½ inch above the top edge of the nameplate.

Wear the nameplate 1 to 2 inches above the top button of the coat and centered horizontally on the wearer's right side

Identification badges are worn parallel to the waistline, with one inch between badges when two are worn on the same side.

Wear the distinctive unit insignia centered on the shoulder loops an equal distance from the outside shoulder seem to the outside edge of the button, with the base of the insignia toward the outside shoulder seem.

Wear badges ¼ inch above the ribbons, one above the other, with ½ inch between badges. In those instances where the coat lapel obscures ribbons, personnel may wear the badges alligned with the left edge of the ribbons.

Wear the ribbons centered on the left side, with the bottom row positioned parallel to the bottom edge of the nameplate. Ribbons are worn with either no space or 1/8 inch space between rows.

Marksmanship badges are worn with the upper portion ¼ inch below the bottom ribbon row. If more than 1 marksmanship badge is worn, space them at least 1 inch apart. When special skills badges are worn, place them to the right of marksmanship badges

DOE

NOTE - This is not an actual Official DA Photograph. This illustration is for training purposes only.

Women's Uniform

Additional information is contained in AR 670-1

Wear the distinctive unit insignia centered on the shoulder loops an equal distance from the outside shoulder seem to the outside edge of the button, with the base of the insignia toward the outside shoulder seem.

Wear the regimental distinctive insignia centered 1/8 inch above the top of the pocket, or 1/4 inch above any unit awards or foreign badges that are worn. When the coat lapel obscures the insignia, soldiers may wear the RDI aligned to the right edge of unit awards or the nameplate.

Wear badges ¼ inch above the ribbons or the top of the pocket, one above the other, with ½ inch between badges. In those instances where the coat lapel obscures ribbons, personnel may wear the badges aligned with the left edge of the ribbons.

Wear foreign badges 1/8 inch above the right pocket flap, or 1/2 inch above any unit awards that are worn.

Wear the ribbons centered 1/8 inch above the left breast pocket. Ribbon mounts will remain centered above the pocket even if the top ribbon row is offset.

Wear unit awards centered with the bottom edge of the emblem 1/8 inch above the right breast pocket flap

The nameplate is worn centered left to right on the pocket flap of the right breast pocket, and centered between the top of the button and the top of the pocket.

Marksmanship badges are worn centered on the pocket flap 1/8 inch below the top of the pocket. They are worn to the left of any special skills badges that are worn. When two badges are worn, they are to be equally spaced on the pocket flap with the upper portion of the badges approximately 1/8 inch below the top of the pocket, and with at least 1 inch between badges

Identification badges are worn centered between the bottom of the pocket flap and the bottom of the pocket, and centered from left to right. When two badges are worn on the same side, they are spaced equally from left to right on the pocket.

Men's Uniform

Additional information is contained in AR 670-1

NOTE - This is not an actual Official DA Photograph. This illustration is for training purposes only.

Trust the latest copy of DA 670-1, this stuff changes all the time!
http://www.apd.army.mil/pdffiles/r670_1.pdf

LEFT SIDE RIBBONS

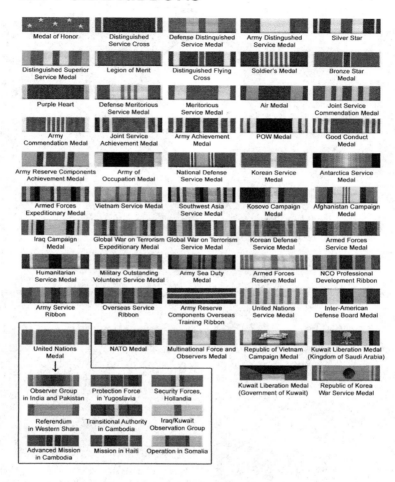

Medal of Honor	Distinguished Service Cross	Defense Distinquished Service Medal	Army Distingushed Service Medal	Silver Star
Distinguished Superior Service Medal	Legion of Merit	Distinguished Flying Cross	Soldier's Medal	Bronze Star Medal
Purple Heart	Defense Meritorious Service Medal	Meritorious Service Medal	Air Medal	Joint Service Commendation Medal
Army Commendation Medal	Joint Service Achievement Medal	Army Achievement Medal	POW Medal	Good Conduct Medal
Army Reserve Components Achievement Medal	Army of Occupation Medal	National Defense Service Medal	Korean Service Medal	Antarctica Service Medal
Armed Forces Expeditionary Medal	Vietnam Service Medal	Southwest Asia Service Medal	Kosovo Campaign Medal	Afghanistan Campaign Medal
Iraq Campaign Medal	Global War on Terrorism Expeditionary Medal	Global War on Terrorism Service Medal	Korean Defense Service Medal	Armed Forces Service Medal
Humanitarian Service Medal	Military Outstanding Volunteer Service Medal	Army Sea Duty Medal	Armed Forces Reserve Medal	NCO Professional Development Ribbon
Army Service Ribbon	Overseas Service Ribbon	Army Reserve Components Overseas Training Ribbon	United Nations Service Medal	Inter-American Defense Board Medal
United Nations Medal ↓	NATO Medal	Multinational Force and Observers Medal	Republic of Vietnam Campaign Medal	Kuwait Liberation Medal (Kingdom of Saudi Arabia)
Observer Group in India and Pakistan	Protection Force in Yugoslavia	Security Forces, Hollandia	Kuwait Liberation Medal (Government of Kuwait)	Republic of Korea War Service Medal
Referendum in Western Shara	Transitional Authority in Cambodia	Iraq/Kuwait Observation Group		
Advanced Mission in Cambodia	Mission in Haiti	Operation in Somalia		

Only permanent Unit Citations are worn for DA Photos.

RIGHT SIDE RIBBONS

Presidential Unit Citation	Joint Meritorious Unit Award	Valorous Unit Award	Meritorious Unit Commendation	Army Superior Unit Award.
Philippine Republic Presidential Unit Citation	Republic of Korea Presidential Unit Citation	Vietnam Presidential Unit Citation	Republic of Vietnam Gallantry Cross Unit Citation	Republic of Vietnam Civil Actions Unit Citation

Double-check the accuracy of your information.
Can you spot 3 things wrong with this photo?

DOE, JOHN Q.
000-00-0000
10 10 14
SSG, 35K30

A4508

Photo Source: Fort Knox Visual Information Lab
Clues to Question; Date: Photo is too old, badges not centered, uniform sleeve has wrinkled appearance.

Chapter 6

Waivers

Waiver Requests

Waiver	Approval Authority	Turn Around Time	Notes
AGE	DA G1	4–6 Weeks	1
AFS	DA G1	4–6 Weeks	1
APFT	DA G3	4–8 Weeks	1,2,3,4,5
Moral	HRC/DA G1	2–6 Weeks	1,6
Prerequisite	Proponent	2–4 Weeks	1
Medical	USAREC G3	2–4 Weeks	7
Tattoo	DA G1	4–6 Weeks	1, 8

Notes:

1. Example in Book and available at WOCs briefings or for download Warrant Officer Recruiting website.

2. DA Form 705 (APFT Score Card) must be included with application

3. BN CDR's LOR must state: "The applicant is physically capable of completing training and worldwide deployment"

4. Must have a Permanent Physical Profile

5. Permanent Physical Profile and physical must be dated within 12 Months

6. Must submit waiver with application.

7. Waiver request NOT prepared by the applicant

8. Waiver must include separation board proceedings indicating that the CDR retained the Soldier

Age Waiver—For 153A MOS—Is required if the applicant has reached their 33rd birthday prior to their packet being boarded.

For all other WO MOSs —Is required if the applicant has reached their 46th birthday prior to their packet being boarded.

Active Federal Service (AFS) Waiver—Is required if the applicant has more than 12 years AFS at time the DA61 is signed by applicant.

Moral Waiver—Is required if the applicant has had any legal infraction greater than a $250.00 speeding fine. This includes any negative UCMJ action.

Additional Waiver Examples—https://www.hrc.army.mil/ Search "Waiver".

Sample Prerequisite Waiver

DEPARTMENT OF THE ARMY

REPLY TO
ATTENTION OF

MEMORANDUM FOR Commander, U.S. Army Recruiting Command, ATTN: RCRO-SPA, Fort Knox, KY 40121-2725

SUBJECT: Request for Prerequisite Waiver

Mitigating circumstances:
1. (State the type of waiver you are requesting)
Example: (1) Request an age waiver
(2) Request an Active Federal Service Waiver
(3) Request a prerequisite waiver (state the prerequisite(s) you wish to waive).

2. Anyone can request a prerequisite, AFS or age waiver, but not everyone will get them approved. Give a detailed explanation why you feel this waiver should be approved. Please note that waivers are approved only in unusual circumstances. Prerequisite waiver requests that do not give adequate justification, Le. unusual skills, unique talents, special circumstances, etc. will probably be disapproved. With AFS waivers (required if you have 12 or more years AFS) or age waivers (required if you will be 33 or older for aviators or 46 for technicians, by the convene date of the board) the same principle applies and requests must be fully justified. Adequate justification might be: unusual circumstances, deployed for past year and unable to submit a packet, unusual skills, or unique talents. Asking for these waivers just because they are a part of the application will not result in approval.

Notes:
1). A separate waiver request must be submitted for each MOS that applicant does not meet the entire prerequisites for. Waiver should include why you feel that you should be accepted in the MOS without meeting all the requirements. Include any civilian experience, training or assignments that are similar to MOS you wish to apply for.

2). Make your request sound valid - for instance, an applicant stating they couldn't apply for the last 12 years because they were deployed... That doesn't sound valid because no one has been away from their duty station continuously over the last 12 years. You would need to include why you couldn't or didn't apply in between deployments. Another example is a 13 year request stating "I've been deployed for the last year... " does not explain why you didn't apply in the years leading up to the deployment.

3). Waiver request will not appear before the selection board once approved. Please use as much space as required to give all the information. A short and simple approach may result in a denied request.

4). Writing skills count. A properly written request ultimately may effect the approval of the request. Board members may interpret poor English, grammar and typographical errors as a lack of concern, sincerity or attention to detail from the applicant.

Self-Signed

81

Request for Other Waiver: Note 1

Waivers must give a written explanation of why you feel a waiver should be given. "Because" and "I just thought of it" type reasons are not heartfelt or convincing.

SUBJECT: Request for Prerequisite Waiver
Request for Age Waiver
Request for Active Federal Service (AFS) Waiver
(Select the appropriate one)

1. (State the type of waiver you are requesting) Example: Request a prerequisite waiver for MOS experience;

2. Anyone can request a prerequisite, AFS, or age waiver, but not everyone will get them approved. Give a detailed explanation why you feel this waiver should be approved. Prerequisite waivers that do not give adequate justification, i.e. unusual skills, unique talent, special circumstances, etc. will probably be disapproved. With AFS waivers (required if you have 12 or more years AFS) or age waivers (if you will be 33 or older for aviators or 47 or older for technicians, by the convening date of the board) the same principle applies and requests must be fully justified. Adequate justification might be: unusual circumstance, deployed for past year and unable to submit packet, unusual skills, or unique talent. Asking for these waivers just because they are a part of the application packet will not result in approval.

(Signature)
(Full Name)
(Rank)
(SSN)

NOTE: Waiver Requests must use the above signature block example.

NOTE: Use Times New Roman 12 –point font. Allow one inch for the left, right, top and bottom margins. Small deviation from 1 inch rule for top margins when using letterhead is allowed.

Sample Moral Waiver Memo

DEPARTMENT OF THE ARMY

REPLY TO
ATTENTION OF

MEMORANDUM FOR Commander, U.S. Army Recruiting Command, ATTN: RCRO-SPA, Fort Knox, KY 40121-2725

SUBJECT: Request for Moral Waiver

1. Nature of offense: Do not just list Article 92, Article 32, etc. Must request a moral waiver for any infractions listed on your enlistment contract.

   a. Date of offense: (Month and year)

   b. Place of offense: (City and State)

   c. Punishment imposed: (Fine amount, forfeiture amount, extra duty, letter of reprimand, etc.)

2. Mitigating circumstances:
*You will use this moral waiver request if you responded YES to block#26 on DA Form 61. If you responded NO, you do not need a moral waiver.

Moral waiver is not required for traffic fines of $250 or less. Do NOT include court cost).
Mitigating circumstances surrounding the charge: Four points to address:
(1) Explain the incident (what, where, when, how, etc..)
(2) Accepting responsibility for your actions
(3) The lessons learned
(4) How you now contribute to your unit, community and military service.

Notes:
1.) A separate moral waiver request must be submitted for each offense.
2.) Moral waiver request should give all the information possible related to the incident. Half answers and undisclosed information can cause a delay in processing. In some cases - the request will be returned to USAREC with a request for more information from applicant.
3.) This waiver request will not go before the selection board once approved. Please use as much space as required to give all the information. A short and simple approach may cause a returned request.
4.) Writing skills count. A properly written request may effect the approval of the request. HRC may interpret poor English, grammar and typographical errors as a lack of concern, sincerity or attention to detail from the applicant.

Joe E. Sample
SGT/E-5
111-22-3333

Request for Moral Waiver: Note 1 and 6

Use the standard MFR format from Chapter 4. *You will use this moral waiver request if you responded YES to block #26 on DA Form 61. If you responded NO, you do not need a moral waiver.

MEMORANDUM FOR Commander, U.S. Army Recruiting Command, ATTN: RCRO-SPA, Fort Knox, KY 40121-2725

SUBJECT: Request for Moral Waiver

1. Nature of offense: Do not just list Article 92, Article 32, etc. Must request a moral waiver for any infractions listed on your enlistment contract.

a. Date of offense: (Month and year)

b. Place of offense: (City and State)

c. Punishment imposed: (Fine amount, forfeiture amount, extra duty, letter of reprimand, etc.)

2. Mitigating circumstances:

Moral waiver is not required for traffic fines of $250 or less. Do NOT include court cost.

Mitigating circumstances surrounding the charge: Four points to address:

(1) Explain the incident (what, where, when, how, etc.)

(2) Accepting responsibility for your actions

(3) The lessons learned

(4) How you now contribute to your unit, community and military service.

Notes:

1.) A separate moral waiver request must be submitted for each offense.

2.) Moral waiver request should give all the information possible related to the incident. Half answers and undisclosed information can cause a delay in processing. In some cases the request will be returned to USAREC with a request for more information from the applicant.

3.) This waiver request will not go before the selection board once approved. Please use as much space as required to give all the information. A short and simple approach may cause a returned request.

4.) Writing skills count. A properly written request may effect the approval of the request. HRC may interpret poor English, grammar and typographical errors as a lack of concern, sincerity or attention to detail from the applicant.

Joe E. Sample
SGT/E-5
111-22-3333

Paragraph 2 - must cover "1.a", "1.b" and "1.c" in the example above.

Some applicants do not give a thorough explanation when they apply for a moral waiver. The waiver gets kicked back to the applicant with a request for more information. Kick backs can result in an applicant missing the submission dates and having to wait until the next cycle, which may not occur for another year.

Moral Waivers, USAREC FL 167 or Age, Active Service, Prerequisite or APFT Waiver Requests, USAREC FL 168-1, can be filled out on-line at:

http://www.usarec.army.mil/hq/warrant/WOpdownload_comapp.shtml

Moral Waiver Process

Approximate Time Line

- • Waivers without jail time can take 2 to 6 weeks to process.

- • Waivers with any jail time can take 1-2 months to process.

This process allows Soldiers to apply, with a very limited amount of paperwork, for Moral Waiver approval. If disapproved, the Soldier will be notified and the application process will be ended. If the Moral Waiver request is approved, the Soldier will then be responsible to complete a normal application packet and include a copy of the moral waiver approval memorandum. It will be placed in the same position the moral waiver request memorandum would have been according to the WO Application Checklist.

The entire packet must be submitted within 180 days of the approval of the Moral Waiver.

Interested Soldiers need to fill out and submit the following information:

Completed DA Form 61 exactly like the sample (including commanders comments in block 41).

Enlisted Records Brief (ERB).

Request for Moral Waiver exactly like the sample.

Any supporting documents including court papers, Article 15 paperwork, police records or other items related to the event.

Letters of recommendation are not allowed for the Moral Waiver requests unless it is someone related to the event. For example: Your commander cannot speak on your behalf because you are a great Soldier today if the Moral Waiver Request is for a juvenile offense. On the other hand, if the Commander is in direct relation to or has firsthand knowledge of an event (letter of reprimand, Article 15, etc...) then his/her letter can be included as related to the event in question.

Those applying for 153A - Rotary Wing Aviator, must also include a copy of their SIFT results score sheet.

To appeal your waiver disposition, please contact USAREC G3 Board Branch —via email at: http://www.usarec.army.mil/hq/warrant/mail or phone at: 502-626-0507 or DSN 536-0507.

Sample APFT Waiver Request

DEPARTMENT OF THE ARMY

REPLY TO
ATTENTION OF

MEMORANDUM FOR Commander, U.S. Army Recruiting Command, ATTN: RCRO-SPA, Fort Knox, KY 40121-2725

SUBJECT: Request for Army Physical Fitness Test Waiver

Mitigating circumstances:

1. State the type of profile to include your complete PULHES, the event(s) that you can no longer take, and what alternate event(s) your are allowed to take.

2. Give a detailed explanation why you believe this exception to policy should be approved in your case. Give an explanation of events that led up to the injury and how it happened. Explain your future expectations of your physical condition (i.e. come off profile after rehab, re-enlist, etc...).

NOTE: LEAVE PARAGRAPH 3 AS IS VERBATIM

3. I fully understand that applying for this waiver does not constitute an automatic approval. I further understand that I must be fully mission deployable in the Warrant Officer Specialty in which I am applying.

(SIGNATURE)
(FULL NAME)
(RANK)
(SSN)

APFT Waiver – Notes 1,2,3,4,5,

The revised AR 350-1 is dated 4 Aug 2011 (RAR) is online. Paragraph 3-12, i(3) states:

(3) Candidates enrolling in WOCS must pass the standard three-event APFT as an enrollment requirement; the alternate APFT is only authorized with HQDA, DCS, G–3/5/7 approval. The walk event on the alternate APFT is the only authorized alternate event used as an enrollment requirement. The Soldier must also be able to walk the 6.2 mile ruck march for WOCS with 48 lbs. or more in their rucksack within school time parameters. If a Soldier enrolling in WOCS fails the initial APFT, the Soldier will be denied enrollment but allowed one retest with a subsequent class. Soldiers failing the second APFT will be considered ineligible for enrollment and must reapply for WOCS selection. In other words, the only waiverable event is the 2 mile run. The only alternate event is the 2.5 mile walk. The pushup and sit up events cannot be waived under these guidelines. The effective date of the revised AR 350-1 is 4 Aug 2011 as stated above. Any waiver request for the pushup or sit up events, after 17 Jan 10, will be returned without action (denied).*Physical Profiles/ Body Fat Worksheets - AR 40-501, with a Rapid Action Revision date of 4 Aug 2011, paragraphs: 7-4(3); 8-20(2) &; 9-3b for USAR; and 10-10a for ARNG

Para 7-4 says that Permanent profiles "... will automatically be reviewed and verified by the privileged provider at the time of a Soldier's periodic health assessment or other medical examination". "Periodic "translates into annual (Yearly) in Para 8-20(2).

Effective immediately physicals and profiles must be no more than 1 year old in order to be current. Anything outside this window will not be processed. Body Fat Worksheet (DA Form 5500 or 5501 dated Aug 2006) calculations also must be within 12 months of the physical date for anyone exceeding the requirements of Table 2-1 (Males) or Table 2-2 (Females).

Sample Tattoo Memo

Only utilized if you are not in compliance with AR 670-1

DEPARTMENT OF THE ARMY
HEADQUARTERS, US ARMY RECRUITING COMMAND
1307 THIRD AVENUE
FORT KNOX, KENTUCKY 40121-2725

REPLY TO
ATTENTION OF:

RCRO-SP-B   22 OCT 2014

MEMORANDUM FOR Commander, U.S. Army Recruiting Command, ATTN: RCRO-SP,

Fort Knox, Kentucky 40121-2725

SUBJECT: Tattoo Policy Waiver Request for SFC SMITH, Thomas T., xxx-xx-0000

1. In accordance with AR 670-1, Para. 3-3e (dated 10 APR 2015), a check for tattoos or brands above the neckline, below the wrists, and on the hands was conducted for SFC Smith, Thomas T. The listing below identifies those tattoos or brands identified.

   a. Head (including on/inside the eyelids, mouth, and earsface): None
   b. Above the Army (short sleeve) PT Shirt neck line: None
   c. Hands (allowed one ring tattoo per hand IAW AR 670-1. Para 3-3c): None
   d. Below the wrist bone:

      (1) Right - 2.0" x 2.0", family symbol "MS" with "J" one side and "T" on the other.
      (2) Left - 2" x 1", "Mickey Mouse"

2. SFC Smith is or is not in compliance with Tattoo, Branding, and Body Mutilation Policy, AR 670-1, Para. 3-3c

3. SFC Smith does or does not require a tattoo waiver for warrant officer appointment.

4. SFC Smith has completed administrative separation proceedings IAW AR 670-1, Para. 3-3f (2)c and was retained by the Commander.

5. SFC Smith has been counseled IAW AR 670-1, Para. 3-3h, that he/she is prohibited from obtaining new tattoos which are in violation of AR 670-1, Para. 3-3c.

6. SFC Smith has been counseled that if he/she obtains any new tattoos which are in violation of AR 670-1, Para. 3-3b-c, he/she could be removed for consideration for warrant officer appointment

7. Recommend approval or Recommend disapproval of SFC Smith's tattoo waiver request.

8. Point of contact for this action is the undersigned at 917-342-xxxx or je.jones.mil@mail.mil.

Encl: JAMES E. JONES | Requires signature of
1. Photo, Right hand (Top)   LTC, AR | Commanders (O5 or above)
2. Photo, Left hand (Top)   Commanding

- Memo required if applicant has tattoos below the wrist/above the collar (in short sleeve PT shirt) that are <u>NOT documented correctly in iPERMS</u>

- Tattoo iPERMS compliance verified by the applicant's S1 on the application checklist

- **MUST** be accompanied by separation board proceedings (IAW AR 670-1 Para. 3-3f) indicating retained by Commander

- Sample memo located on downloads tab of Warrant Officer Recruiting website

Sample Tattoo Photos Enclosure-Arm

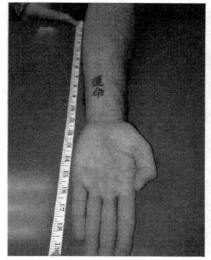 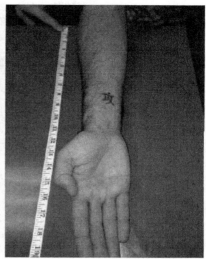

Encl 1   **Encl 2**

DA PAM 670-1 dated 15 September 2014, Para 3-3 provides guidance on tattoos/branding (words are interchangeably throughout the policy) and on the photos to be included with your tattoo waiver request. Based on photos previously received, the DA G1 has additional guidance:

1. Applicant should be in the IPFU (authorized PT uniform for applicants from other Services) when having their tattoo(s) photographed.

2. Color photos are required using a white or neutral color background.

3. Photos will depict tattoo location and size by showing the entire area below the elbow, below the knee, and/or above the t-shirt neck line using a ruler.

4. In order to show perspective, a full-length photo of the applicant showing their tattoo(s) is also required.

5. There are no specific camera settings required; however, all photos must be clear and visible.

BODY FAT CONTENT WORKSHEET *(Male)*
For use of this form, see AR 600-9; the proponent agency is DCS, G-1.

NAME *(Last, First, Middle Initial)*		RANK		NOTE: ¼" = .25
HEIGHT *(to nearest 0.50 inch)*	WEIGHT *(to nearest pound)*		AGE	½" = .50 ¾" = .75

STEP	FIRST	SECOND	THIRD	AVERAGE *(to nearest 0.50 in.)*
1. Measure abdomen at the level of the navel *(belly button.)* **Round down** to the nearest 0.50 inch. *(Repeat 3 times.)*				
2. Measure neck just below level of larynx *(Adam's apple.)* **Round up** to the nearest 0.50 inch. *(Repeat 3 times.)*				
3. Enter the average abdominal circumference.				
4. Enter the average neck circumference.				
5. Enter circumference value *(step 3 - step 4)*.				
6. Find the height in Table 3-1 *(Height Factor)*. Enter height in inches.				
7. Find the Soldier's circumference value *(step 5)* and height *(step 6)* in figure B-5 *(Percent Fat Estimation for Men)*. Enter the percent body fat value that intercepts with the circumference value and height. This is Soldier's Percent Body Fat.				

REMARKS

Common Errors:

- Physical not complete,
- Missing PULHES
- FULLY QUALIFIED Not checked off by physician

CHECK ONE
☐ Individual is in compliance with Army Standards;   ☐ is not in compliance with the standards.
☐ Recommended monthly weight loss is 3-8 lbs.

PREPARED BY *(Signature)*	RANK	DATE *(YYYYMMDD)*	APPROVED BY SUPERVISOR *(Printed Name and Signature)*	RANK	DATE *(YYYYMMDD)*

DA FORM 5500, JUN 2010   PREVIOUS EDITIONS ARE OBSOLETE.   APD PE v1.00ES

Statement of Understanding

REPLY TO
ATTENTION OF

_____   _____
                                                  Date

MEMORANDUM FOR Commander, U.S. Army Recruiting Command, ATTN: RCRO-SPA, Fort Knox, KY 40121-2725

SUBJECT: Statement of Understanding

1. I understand that if I am appointed as a warrant officer in the U.S. Army Reserves with concurrent active duty, that this appointment is contingent upon technical and tactical certification by successful completion of the appropriate warrant officer basic course unless I have been pre-certified by the warrant officer military occupational specialty (WOMOS) proponent. I understand that my application packet, to include all enclosures, may be converted to an electronic file and made available for review by qualifying officials at WOMOS proponent schools, Headquarters, Department of the Army, and other locations in order to determine my qualifications and competitive standing for appointment as a warrant officer.

2. I further understand that if I am appointed as a warrant officer in the U.S. Army Reserves without concurrent active duty, that this appointment is contingent upon technical and tactical certification by successful completion of the appropriate warrant officer basic course within 2 years of appointment unless I have been pre-certified by the WOMOS proponent or unless extended by Headquarters, Department of the Army.

3. FOR SISTER SERVICE APPLICANTS ONLY (Air Force, Coast Guard, Marines, Navy): I fully understand that if I am selected for the Warrant Officer Program, I will be required to attend Army Basic Training prior to attending Warrant Officer Candidate School if I have not successfully completed an Army Basic Training, Warrior Transition Course, Marine Basic Training, Air Force or Navy Special Operations Forces, or Air Force Security Police Training. This requirement applies to all ranks for both active and reserve components.

4. TATTOO, BRANDING, AND BODY MUTILATION POLICY: I understand that, if I am selected for the Warrant Officer Program, prior to starting the Warrant Officer Candidate School and prior to being appointed as a Warrant Officer, a determination will be made by the Commandant of the Warrant Officer Career College that I am in compliance with the Army's Tattoo, Branding, and Body Mutilation Policy, IAW AR 670-1.

5. I also understand that if I am eliminated from or fail to successfully complete the technical and tactical certification as specified above, I may be subject to discharge under regulations in effect at that time from the U.S. Army Reserves.

Self-Signed _____

_____

_____

NOTE: Statements of Understanding are on-line at:
http://www.usarec.army.mil/hq/warrant/WOpdownload_comapp.shtml

Common Issues:

- Memorandum in wrong format and/or not signed

Other Common Application Faults:

- Conditional Releases not complete

- ASVAB scores not converted

- Transcripts not included (if on DA 61 or required as a prerequisite)

- Typos on forms

Selection Board Application Updates and Corrections:

Caution: E-mail size with all attachments cannot exceed 5MB.

TIP: Scan in all documents into PDF format. If necessary, reduce the resolution to 150.

Send "New Packets" to: usarmy.knox.usarec.mbx.9sbn-new-warrant-packets@mail.mil

Updates for "Board Ready" packets to: usarmy.knox.usarec.mbx.9sbn-new-warrant-updates@mail.mil

Send any corrections for Status "R" Packets to: usarmy.knox.usarec.mbx.9sbn-new-warrant-corrections@mail.mil

IMPORTANT—ALL Warrant Officer application packet e-mails must contain the following in the subject line:

PRIMARY WO MOS - LAST NAME, FIRST NAME, MI - E-MAIL, NUMBER OF THE TOTAL NUMBER OF E-MAILS being sent. Example:

153A - JOHNSON, STEVEN M. - 1 OF 2, second e-mail subject line, 153A - JOHNSON, STEVEN M. - 2 OF 2. Also, be sure to title your PDF attachments in the following format: 1.pdf, 2.pdf, 3.pdf, etc... (Packet compiled in the order set in the checklist, then broken up and labeled in the manner shown.)

New packet submission e-mails that do not conform to this standard will experience significant delays and may be rejected from further processing.

Packet Submission (Effective Immediately)

All applications MUST be COMPLETE to be processed.
INCOMPLETE packets will be REJECTED without action.

For "New" applications, please allow 10 - 15 working days for processing, after submission, before inquiring about the status.

Applicants who do not require waiver approval and submit a 100% error free packet, by the respective cutoff date, are guaranteed to go to that board. Pending waiver approval or packet deficiencies can cause you to miss a board.

Check the WO Selection Board schedule for new packet submission cutoff dates.

Any applicant fully qualified/not selected for two consecutive boards will be considered not select/not competitive and may not reapply for one year from the date of the DA 61, IAW DA PAM 601-6, Ch2, para. 6.

Applicants may request an exception to the one year wait period when more pertinent qualifications have been acquired IAW AR 135-100 para. 2-5. All requests must be routed through the applicant's Company Commander or equivalent to the Warrant Officer Boards Branch OIC.

USAREC Form 1942 WARRANT OFFICER BOARD WAIT PERIOD EXCEPTION REQUEST
To submit supporting documents along with USAREC Form 1942, visit:
http://www.usarec.army.mil/hq/warrant/index.shtml
and click **"Application Processing"** for details.

NCOs will submit their most recent TEN YEARS of NCOERs and all of their Academic Evaluation Reports (1059s). NCOs who have less than ten years as an E-5 or above will submit all of their NCOERs. EX: 8 years of NCO service will submit 8 years worth of evaluations; 6 years of NCO service will submit 6 years worth of evaluations; 12 years of NCO service will submit 10 years worth of evaluations. Don't submit reports that extend beyond your last ten year period.

All Applicants: Warrant Officer applications must be 100% administratively complete at the time of submission and ready for immediate processing. Incomplete packets will be rejected and destroyed.

All applications must be submitted digitally (via e-mail) unless deployed.

Prior to submitting your application packet, please ensure you make a complete copy for your records.

Please check the Board Schedule page often as it is subject to change without notification.

Applicants twice not selected must send a complete new application after the one year wait period.

FAX:
Submitting your application via Fax <u>is NOT recommended</u>. Use the fax to PDF feature and dial **(502) 626-0938** as a last resort.
(**View quality will be diminished as a result.**)

Deployment Information
If you are currently deployed in support of OIF or OEF, USAREC is keenly aware of the challenges you face trying to put your Warrant Officer application together.

This page is designed to give you up-to-date information about resources in theater and policy changes positively affecting your ability to submit an application.

Email works best from theater.
usarmy.knox.usarec.mbx.9sbn-wo-team-questions@mail.mil

Policy Changes:

- Letters of Recommendation are good for 12 months.

- S-1 Letter can be substituted for the Milpo letter. (Our checklist will be better)

- Photos taken during contingency operations must be of good quality and have a clear background. (It is preferred that photos are taken against a wall with a clear backdrop if possible. No unit flags, vehicles, outside scenery etc.,) Remove headgear, tactical gear and weapons. Duty uniform only. (Traditional or Multi-Cam patterns)

- Resume.

- Security Memorandum Change. Use the sample provided in this book if you cannot access JPAS.

- Rotating through SWA, Contact our multi-functional recruiter located in Kuwait   Camp Virginia (PSB Tent#3)   DSN: 318-430-12149

- Army Personnel Testing sites in SWA for personnel desiring to take the Selection Instrument for Flight Training (SIFT).

http://www.usarec.army.mil/hq/warrant/download/APT_Sites_Iraq.pdf

MAIL:
Only deployed personnel may mail in their application packet.

NOTE: Digital submission (e-mail) is faster, more secure, and preferred.
US Army Recruiting Command
ATTN: RCMRB-SORB-WO
1307 Third Avenue
Fort Knox, KY
40121-2725

Chapter 7

Most Common Errors on Applications

DA Form 61

Block 1 - must check Warrant Officer - Army Reserve
Block 2 - AR 135-100
Block 3 - WO1

<table>
<tr><td colspan="4" align="center">APPLICATION FOR APPOINTMENT
For use of this form, see AR 135-100, AR 145-1, AR 351-5, and AR 601-100; the proponent agency is DCSPER</td></tr>
<tr><td colspan="4" align="center">DATA REQUIRED BY THE PRIVACY ACT OF 1974</td></tr>
<tr><td>AUTHORITY:</td><td colspan="3">Title 10 United States Code, Section 3012 (Title 5 United States Code, Section 552a)</td></tr>
<tr><td>PRINCIPAL PURPOSE:</td><td colspan="3">To obtain an appointment as a commissioned or warrant officer in the Regular Army or Army Reserve, or to obtain selection to attend the US Army Officer Candidate School.</td></tr>
<tr><td>ROUTINE USES:</td><td colspan="3">Basis for determination of qualifications and background information for eligibility for consideration for appointment as a Regular Army or Army Reserve commissioned/warrant officer or for selection for attendance at the US Army Officer Candidate School.</td></tr>
<tr><td>DISCLOSURE</td><td colspan="3">Disclosure of information requested in DA Form 61 is voluntary. Failure to provide the required information will result in non-acceptability of the application.</td></tr>
</table>

1. TYPE OF APPOINTMENT FOR WHICH APPLICATION IS SUBMITTED		2. GOVERNING REGULATION OR CIRCULAR *(Specify appropriate section(s) if applicable)* **AR-135-100**
	COMMISSIONED OFFICER - REGULAR ARMY	3. GRADE FOR WHICH APPLYING *(Reserve appointments only)* **WO1**
	COMMISSIONED OFFICER - ARMY RESERVE	4. SOURCE OF APPLICATION *(ROTC only)*
	WARRANT OFFICER - REGULAR ARMY	DMG DATE DESIGNATED:
X	WARRANT OFFICER - ARMY RESERVE	SCHOLARSHIP - ENTER 1, 2, 3 OR 4 YEARS:
	OFFICER CANDIDATE SCHOOL	5. ONLY FOR APPLICANTS FOR APPOINTMENT AS WARRANT OFFICERS
6. BRANCH AND SPECIALTY PREFERENCES		*(List choice by MOS code and title)*
Regular Army and Officer Candidate applicants and all ROTC graduates:		a. MOS CODE b. MOS TITLE
In numerical sequence, indicate 10 branch preferences other than CA and SS.		

All Warrant Applicants Must Follow the Above Example.

Block 24 must be checked No, 25 checked and 26 must be checked 'No'

24. ARE YOU NOW, OR HAVE YOU EVER BEEN A CONSCIENTIOUS OBJECTOR?	☐ YES	☒ NO *(If yes, attach affidavit)*

25. ☒ I UNDERSTAND THAT, IF I AM SELECTED FOR APPOINTMENT, I WILL BE EXPECTED TO ACCEPT SUCH ASSIGNMENTS AS ARE IN THE BEST INTEREST OF THE SERVICE REGARDLESS OF MY MARITAL STATUS AND/OR RESPONSIBILITY FOR DEPENDENTS; AND IT IS MY RESPONSIBILITY TO MAKE APPROPRIATE ARRANGEMENTS FOR THE CARE OF MY DEPENDENTS SHOULD I BE REQUIRED TO PERFORM DUTY IN AN AREA WHERE DEPENDENTS ARE NOT PERMITTED.

26. HAVE YOU EVER, UNDER EITHER MILITARY OR CIVILIAN LAW, BEEN INDICTED OR SUMMONED IN TO COURT AS A DEFENDANT IN A CRIMINAL PROCEEDING, *(including any proceedings involving juvenile offenses, article 15, UCMJ, and any court-martial)* REGARDLESS OF THE RESULT OF TRIAL, OR CONVICTED, FINED, IMPRISONED, PLACED ON PROBATION, PAROLED OR PARDONED, OR HAVE YOU EVER BEEN ORDERED TO DEPOSIT BAIL OR COLLATERAL FOR THE VIOLATION OF ANY LAW, POLICE REGULATION OR ORDINANCE? *(Exclude traffic violations involving a fine or forfeiture of $100 or less).*

☐ YES ☒ NO   IF YES, ATTACH REQUEST FOR WAIVER LISTING THE DATE, THE NATURE OF EACH ALLEGED OFFENSE OR VIOLATION, THE NAME AND LOCATION OF THE COURT OR PLACE OF HEARING, AND THE PENALTY IMPOSED OR OTHER DISPOSITION OF EACH CASE AND FURNISH COPY OF COURT ACTION OR DETAILED STATEMENT IN AFFIDAVIT FORM AS TO THE OUTCOME OF EACH CASE.

27. ACTIVE MILITARY SERVICE *(Indicate tour with each organization separately - show ROTC Camps in Item 39)*

	a. ORGANIZATION *(US Armed Forces, USCG, NOAA, US Public Health Service, Peace Corps)*	b. DATES *(Day, Month, Year)* FROM	TO	c. BRANCH/MOS *(As appropriate)*	d. PRIOR SERVICE NO. *(If applicable)*	e. HIGHEST GRADE AND COMPONENT
ENLISTED	US Army	25 Jun 92	Present	27D30	NA	E-6/RA

NOTE: If Block 26 is checked 'YES' then a Request for Moral Waiver must be completed. Waivers need more processing time prior to being board ready so you must submit the packet earlier. Block 27 should have one line covering all of service except for breaks in service. Blocks 27f and 27g must have ETS followed by DOR. Block 28 should have Reserve time in one line except for breaks in service.

Block 41—APFT statement completed and Commander's statement and/or Commander's Signature.

NOTE: No "for" signatures are authorized for Commander without Assumption of Command Orders (AOC). Add the AoC orders to your packet.

Block 42—Put in the current date and add your signature.

40. MAIN CIVILIAN EMPLOYMENT

a. NAME AND ADDRESS OF EMPLOYER	b. JOB TITLE	c. MONTH AND YEAR	
Kelly Temporary Services Grand Rapids, MI 48722	Secretary/Typing	FROM 0292	TO 0692

b. PRINCIPAL DUTIES *(Describe briefly)*
Typed letters, kept personnel files updated, answered inquiries

41. REMARKS *(Experience, proficiencies and special abilities not shown elsewhere in this application. Those required to enter primary entry specialties, see Para 1-27d,e, AR 601-100). (If more space is required, attach additional sheet)*

I certify that (Applicant's Name) successfully passed the APFT consisting of pushups, situps, and the two mile run with a score of _____ on _____; the verified height is _____ and verified weight is _____.

JOHN Q. DOE
CPT, AG
Commanding

Note 1: If you exceed the ht/wt tables of AR 600-9, you must include a Body Fat Worksheet (DA Form 5500-R or 5501-R)
Note 2: Ensure APFT is as recent as possible. If close to the six month expiration, then retest.

42. THE INFORMATION CONTAINED HEREIN IS TRUE TO THE BEST OF MY KNOWLEDGE AND BELIEF.	DATE Current Date	SIGNATURE OF APPLICANT Applicant's Signature Here

USAPPC V2.00

Example of Correctly Completed DA Form 61

APPLICATION FOR APPOINTMENT

For use of this form, see AR 135-100, AR 145-1, AR 351-5, and AR 601-100; the proponent agency is DCSPER

DATA REQUIRED BY THE PRIVACY ACT OF 1974

AUTHORITY: Title 10 United States Code, Section 3012 (Title 5 United States Code, Section 552a)

PRINCIPAL PURPOSE: To obtain an appointment as a commissioned or warrant officer in the Regular Army or Army Reserve, or to obtain selection to attend the US Army Officer Candidate School.

ROUTINE USES: Basis for determination of qualifications and background information for eligibility for consideration for appointment as a Regular Army or Army Reserve commissioned/warrant officer or for selection for attendance at the US Army Officer Candidate School.

DISCLOSURE: Disclosure of information requested in DA Form 61 is voluntary. Failure to provide the required information will result in non-acceptability of the application.

1. TYPE OF APPOINTMENT FOR WHICH APPLICATION IS SUBMITTED

COMMISSIONED OFFICER - REGULAR ARMY	
COMMISSIONED OFFICER - ARMY RESERVE	
WARRANT OFFICER - REGULAR ARMY	
X WARRANT OFFICER - ARMY RESERVE **ALL applicants must select this block**	
OFFICER CANDIDATE SCHOOL	

2. GOVERNING REGULATION OR CIRCULAR (Specify appropriate section(s) if applicable)
AR 135-100

3. GRADE FOR WHICH APPLYING (Reserve appointments only) WO1

4. SOURCE OF APPLICATION (ROTC only)
DMG   DATE DESIGNATED:
SCHOLARSHIP - ENTER 1, 2, 3 OR 4 YEARS:

5. ONLY FOR APPLICANTS FOR APPOINTMENT AS WARRANT OFFICERS (List choice by MOS code and title)

6. BRANCH AND SPECIALTY PREFERENCES

Regular Army and Officer Candidate applicants and all ROTC graduates: In numerical sequence, indicate 10 branch preferences other than CA and SS.

USAR applicants: If applying for a specific Reserve vacancy, indicate ONLY the branch of the vacant position; all other applicants may enter more than one branch.

a. MOS CODE	b. MOS TITLE
351L	Counterintelligence Technician
	If qualified, may list up to 3 MOSs. List MOSs in order of preference. Listing more than 1 MOS requires extra processing time because proponents must review.

PERSONAL DATA

7. NAME (Last, first, middle)(Explain variations from birth certificate in Item 41)
WHO, You Are

8. GRADE E-6

9a. SOCIAL SECURITY NUMBER 000-00-0000

PREFER-ENCE	BRANCH	SPECIALTY
	AD	
	AG	
	AR	
	AV	
	CA	
	CM	
	EN	
	FA	
	FI	
	IN	
	MI	
	MP	
	OD	
	QM	
	SC	
	SS	
	TC	
	AN	
	CH	
	DE	
	JA	
	MC	
	MS	
	SP	
	VC	

10. BRANCH (MOS if enl or wo) 351P

11. TOTAL YRS ACTIVE SERVICE 7

12. MARITAL STATUS M

13. NUMBER OF DEPENDENTS UNDER 18 YEARS OF AGE 2

9b. SELECTIVE SERVICE NUMBER

14. DATE OF BIRTH 7 Apr 75

15. PLACE OF BIRTH (City, county, state) Radcliff Hardin Kentucky

16. SEX M

17. COMPLETE MILITARY ADDRESS (If presently on active duty) (Include ZIP Code)
HHC, III Corps
Fort Hood, TX 76544
PHONE AND/OR AUTOVON NUMBER
EMAIL ADDRESS (AKO)
(817)288-1111
DSN 738-1111

18. PERMANENT ADDRESS (Include ZIP Code)
407 Keith Street
Elizabethtown, KY 42701
PHONE (Include area code) (502)765-6868

19. CURRENT MAILING ADDRESS (If difference from Item 18) (Include ZIP Code)
419A Nicholson Road
Fort Hood, TX 76544
PHONE (Include area code) (817)526-1111
EMAIL ADDRESS

20. US CITIZEN X YES ☐ NO
a. NATIVE X YES ☐ NO
b. ☐ NATURALIZATION ☐ DERIVED ☐ IMMIGRANT
c. APPLICANT'S CERTIFICATE NO. (If item b. checked) (Date, place, court)

21. CIVILIAN EDUCATION (See page 3 for additional requirements for professional personnel)

a. HIGH SCHOOL GRADUATE X YES ☐ NO

b. NAME AND LOCATION OF HIGH SCHOOL Orchard View High School, Muskegon, MI 49442

c. NAME AND LOCATION OF EACH COLLEGE OR UNIVERSITY ATTENDED (Include USMA, USNA, USAFA, USCGA, and USMMA)	(1) DEGREE	(2) SEMESTER CREDITS EARNED	(3) YEARS ATTENDED	(4) DATE GRADUATED OR WILL GRADUATE			(5) MAJOR SUBJECT
				DAY	MONTH	YEAR	
University of Maryland	BS	120	4	31	05	1999	Business Mgmt
Central Texas College	AA	60	2				Management

d. SPECIAL EDUCATIONAL HONORS, SCHOLAR-SHIPS, ETC.

e. IF YOU HAVE EVER BEEN EXPELLED FROM SCHOOL, OR PLACED ON PROBATION, EITHER FOR ACADEMIC OR DISCIPLINARY REASONS, EXPLAIN (Continue in Item 41 (Remarks))

22. HIGHEST LEVEL SERVICE SCHOOL ATTENDED

a. NAME OF SCHOOL	b. COURSE	c. DATES (Mo-Yr)		COMPLETED		d. IF NOT COMPLETED GIVE REASON
		FROM	TO	YES	NO	
US Army Soldier Spt Center Ft. Jackson, SC	BNCOC	10 04	12 04	X		

23a. FOREIGN LANGUAGES AND DEGREE OF PROFICIENCY
NA

b. ALAT SCORE (If applicable)
NA

DA FORM 61, JUN 81   EDITION OF 1 AUG 74 AND DA FORM 61-R, 26 SEP 75, PRIVACY ACT STATEMENT, ARE OBSOLETE.   USAPPC V2.00

Example of Correctly Completed DA Form 61 (back)

24. ARE YOU NOW, OR HAVE YOU EVER BEEN A CONSCIENTIOUS OBJECTOR? ☐ YES ☒ NO (If yes, attach affidavit)

25. ☒ I UNDERSTAND THAT, IF I AM SELECTED FOR APPOINTMENT, I WILL BE EXPECTED TO ACCEPT SUCH ASSIGNMENTS AS ARE IN THE BEST INTEREST OF THE SERVICE REGARDLESS OF MY MARITAL STATUS AND/OR RESPONSIBILITY FOR DEPENDENTS; AND IT IS MY RESPONSIBILITY TO MAKE APPROPRIATE ARRANGEMENTS FOR THE CARE OF MY DEPENDENTS SHOULD I BE REQUIRED TO PERFORM DUTY IN AN AREA WHERE DEPENDENTS ARE NOT PERMITTED.

26. HAVE YOU EVER UNDER EITHER MILITARY OR CIVILIAN LAW BEEN INDICTED OR SUMMONED IN TO COURT AS A DEFENDANT IN A CRIMINAL PROCEEDING (including any proceedings involving juvenile offenses, article 15, UCMJ, and any court-martial) REGARDLESS OF THE RESULT OF TRIAL, OR CONVICTED, FINED, IMPRISONED, PLACED ON PROBATION, PAROLED OR PARDONED, OR HAVE YOU EVER BEEN ORDERED TO DEPOSIT BAIL OR COLLATERAL FOR THE VIOLATION OF ANY LAW, POLICE REGULATION OR ORDINANCE? (Exclude traffic violations involving a fine or forfeiture of $100 or less).

☐ YES ☒ NO IF YES, ATTACH REQUEST FOR WAIVER LISTING THE DATE, THE NATURE OF EACH ALLEGED OFFENSE OR VIOLATION, THE NAME AND LOCATION OF THE COURT OR PLACE OF HEARING, AND THE PENALTY IMPOSED OR OTHER DISPOSITION OF EACH CASE AND FURNISH COPY OF COURT ACTION OR DETAILED STATEMENT IN AFFIDAVIT FORM AS TO THE OUTCOME OF EACH CASE.

27. ACTIVE MILITARY SERVICE (Indicate tour with each organization separately - show ROTC Camps in Item 39)

	a. ORGANIZATION (US Armed Forces, USCG, NOAA, US Public Health Service, Peace Corps)	b. DATES (Day, Month, Year) FROM	TO	c. BRANCH/MOS (As appropriate)	d. PRIOR SERVICE NO. (If applicable)	e. HIGHEST GRADE AND COMPONENT
ENLISTED	US Army	25 Jun 99	Present	35L3P	NA	E-6/RA
WARRANT OFFICER						
COMMIS-SIONED						

f. DATE CURRENT ACTIVE DUTY TOUR TERMINATES   ETS: 17 Oct 2015   g. DATE OF LAST ADL PROMOTION   DOR: 1 Aug 2005

28. RESERVE OR NATIONAL GUARD SERVICE (Not on active duty)

	a. ORGANIZATION (US Armed Forces, USCG, NOAA, US Public Health Service, Peace Corps)	b. DATES (Day, Month, Year) FROM	TO	c. BRANCH/MOS (As appropriate)	d. PRIOR SERVICE NO. (If applicable)	e. HIGHEST GRADE AND COMPONENT
ENLISTED	US Army Reserve	2 Feb 91	24 Jun 92	11B10	NA	E-4/USAR
WARRANT OFFICER						
COMMIS-SIONED						

29. SOURCE OF CURRENT COMMISSION (If applicable)

ARNGUS: ☐ OCS ☐ DIRECT APPOINTMENT ☐ OTHER

USAR: ☐ ROTC ☐ ROTC (ECP) ☐ ROTC (SMP) ☐ OCS

☐ DIRECT APPOINTMENT

30. AWARDS (Do not list theater or service medals)

MSM-2, ARCOM-4, AAM-2 (Achievement Awards Only)

31. HAVE YOU EVER APPLIED AND NOT BEEN SELECTED FOR: a. ROTC ☐ YES ☒ NO   b. OCS ☐ YES ☒ NO

c. APPOINTMENT IN RESERVE COMPONENT (USAR/ARNG)	YES	NO	d. APPOINTMENT IN REGULAR ARMY	YES	NO
AS A WARRANT OFFICER		✗	AS A WARRANT OFFICER		✗
AS A COMMISSIONED OFFICER		✗	AS A COMMISSIONED OFFICER		✗

e. IF ANSWER IS "YES", EXPLAIN FULLY

32. ARE YOU NOW OR HAVE YOU EVER BEEN IN THE MILITARY SERVICE OF OR BEEN EMPLOYED BY A FOREIGN GOVERNMENT (If yes, give dates, country and type of service or employment)   No

33. HAVE YOU EVER RESIGNED OR BEEN ASKED TO RESIGN IN LIEU OF ELIMINATION PROCEEDINGS; BEEN DISCHARGED IN LIEU OF ELIMINATION, FURLOUGHED (other than regular furlough or leave), OR PLACED ON INACTIVE STATUS WHILE SERVING IN THE US ARMED FORCES; OR, HAVE YOU EVER RESIGNED OR BEEN ASKED TO RESIGN FROM A POSITION WHILE IN PRIVATE OR GOVERNMENT EMPLOYMENT? (If yes, state circumstances; if more space is required, continue on separate sheet).

☐ YES ☒ NO

USAPPC V2.00

DA Form 160-R

Block 9 - must check block 'a' and type a number 6 in the YEARS space.

Blocks 10a & 10b must have MOS and locations listed (Dream Sheet).

Block 14 must have Applicant's Signature

9. I hereby volunteer to enter on active duty, for the period indicated below, in my branch or any of the following branches that I may be qualified for; and if accepted for active duty in another branch, I request transfer to that branch: *(Check as appropriate)*

☒ a. FOR A PERIOD OF ___6___ YEARS ☐ b. FOR AN INDEFINITE PERIOD

c. OTHER BRANCHES *(List in order of preference)*

10. I understand that if accepted for active duty I may be assigned to any command, including an overseas command, to fill any Army-wide vacancy. However, I would like to be considered for one of the three duty assignments and areas of assignment listed below in the order of my choice.	CHOICE NO. 1	CHOICE NO. 2	CHOICE NO. 3
a. DUTY ASSIGNMENT	270A	270A	270A
b. AREA ASSIGNMENT	Germany	Fort Knox, KY	Fort Hood, TX

11. If it is possible, I prefer to enter on active duty during one of the three periods indicated below in order of preference:

PREFERENCE NO. 1 *(Month and Year)* ASAP	PREFERENCE NO. 2 *(Month and Year)* ASAP	PREFERENCE NO. 3 *(Month and Year)* ASAP

12. Upon receipt of active duty orders, I will require the time indicated below to settle my affairs for entry on active duty. *(Check appropriate box)*

☐ 60 DAYS ☐ 30 DAYS ☐ 10 DAYS ☒ AVAILABLE ON DATE OF RECEIPT OF ORDERS

13. REMARKS *(If more space is needed, continue on separate sheet)*
Include information you consider essential in making your assignment, i.e. enrolled in the Exceptional Family Member Program or Army Married Couples Program.

14. SIGNATURE OF APPLICANT

Applicant's Signature

DA FORM 160-R, JAN 96   DA FORM 160, APR 77, IS OBSOLETE   USAPPC V1.00

TIP: In Block 10.b, pick locations the Army would actually assign you to. Fort Knox, Campbell, Hood, Bliss or overseas to Germany. Just because its called a "Dream Sheet" doesn't mean you should list fantasy assignments. Keep it realistic!

Warrant Officer Packets and Sample Applications can be downloaded at:
http://www.usarec.army.mil/hq/warrant/WOpdownload_forms.shtml

Chapter 8

Selection Instrument for Flight Training (SIFT)

Extracted from DA briefing titled: *Finding the "Right Stuff"*

OBJECTIVES:

1. Develop an operation ready computer-based, web administered aviator selection battery that corrects six identified deficiencies of the current test

- Review and revise the selection strategy to fit the current selection situation
- Revise job and task analyses to fit current missions and training goals
- Map resulting Knowledge, Skills, Attributes (KSA)s onto domains of observable behaviors
- Develop a computer-based, web administered selection test to replace AFAST

2. Lay groundwork for aviator classification and Unmanned Aerial System (UAS) operator selection

3. Facilitate the transition of the final product into operation

- Coordinate with and support Aviation Personnel Proponency Office in securing authorization and funding for fielding and operation of the test battery.

Task 1: REVIEW OF SELECTION & TEST STRATEGIES

Several pilot selection batteries have demonstrated reasonable validity for predicting training criteria—so validity is not a highly differentiating factor.

- Much less effort and success in predicting pilot performance beyond training.

- US Navy is currently administering selection battery online (APEX).

Domains used in Aviator Selection:

1. Cognitive Ability: Most batteries measure specific cognitive abilities, but general intelligence, g factor, typically accounts for much of the variance.

2. Aviation/Helicopter Knowledge

3. Aviation Interest

4. Relevant Experience

5. Psychomotor Skills (e.g., tracking; complex coordination)

6. Personality (Normal range)

Task 2: JOB ANALYSIS

Highest Rated Knowledge, Skills, Abilities, and Other Characteristics:

1. Situational Awareness

2. Helicopter Operation

3. Psychomotor Ability

4. Information Processing

5. Decision Making

Task 3: PREDICTOR MEASURES FOR VALIDITY TEST

Recommended Predictor Measures: Cognitive Ability:

All cognitive subtests from Navy ASTB

Perceptual Speed & Accuracy: Newly-developed (PSA)

Hidden Figures/Simple Drawings/Cockpit Displays

Personality/Temperament: Assessment of Individual Motivation (AIM; White &Young), Test of Adaptive Personality (TAP; Kilcullen)

Motivation/Attitude: Newly-developed (AAI), Army Aviation Identification scale (Kilcullen)

Task Prioritization: Popcorn Test

Task 4: CRITERION MEASURES FOR VALIDITY TEST

1) Academic Grades

2) Flight Grades

3) Behavioral Summary Scale (BSS) Ratings

(Instructor & Evaluator 7-point Ratings):

- Stress Tolerance -Problem Solving
- Initiative (Inst. Only) -Integrity (Inst. Only)
- Adaptability -Situational Awareness
- Work Ethic -Communication
- Openness to Feedback -Overall Potential

Behavioral Summary Scale (Example)

1. Stress Tolerance: Maintains composure in challenging and threatening situations; able to function well when presented with a large number of tasks to perform.

①————②	③———④———⑤	⑥————⑦
Needs Improvement	**Satisfactory**	**Outstanding**
• Becomes flustered when faced with many tasks. • Does not remain calm when challenged. • Shows frustration when presented with stressful situations.	• Usually functions well when faced with many tasks, but may occasionally get flustered. • Usually remains calm. • Occasionally shows frustration.	• Performs extremely well during overload situations. • Always remains calm. • Manages frustration by developing constructive solutions.

2. Adaptability: Adjusts easily to changing situations or conditions; quickly adapts and changes priorities when necessary.

①————②	③———④———⑤	⑥————⑦
Needs Improvement	**Satisfactory**	**Outstanding**
• Has difficulty adapting to mission changes. • "Locks in" on a single strategy.	• Usually able to adapt to mission changes. • Usually able to change strategy when necessary.	• Very effectively adapts to mission changes. • Very effectively changes strategy when necessary.

Task 5: PROTOTYPE VALIDATION

Completed with 240 flight students (June 2006)

Criteria for Recommending Predictors:

- Incremental validity over ASTB Cognitive Scales

- Administration time (4-hour limit)

- Logistical/administrative issues

Task 6: SIFT RECOMMENDATIONS

- Based on incremental validities

Includes:

- ASTB Cognitive Scales (without "Aviation/Nautical Info")

  - Math - Verbal Test (MVT)

  - Mechanical Comprehension Test (MCT)

  - Spatial Apperception Test (SAT)

- Army Aviation Information Test

- Perceptual Speed and Accuracy Test (2 subtests)

  - Hidden Figures and Simple Drawings

Results

Army Aviation replacement for AFAST

- Improved predictive validity ($225k/student)

- Computer-based (easily modified)

- Internet deliverable (APEX)

- Collaboration with Navy and Air Force

- Numerous products developed

- Foundation for Classification & UAS selection

Future Developments

- ARI will conduct validation beyond training

- ARI continues to collect criterion measures

- ARI R&D FY 07

  - Classification Instrument for Army Aviation

  - Selection Instrument for Unmanned Aviation Systems

TIP: Military Flight Aptitude Tests, 6th Edition by COL (R) Solomon Wiener is available on-line and has a great deal of SIFT-like pre-test quizzes and offers in-depth knowledge for future military aviators. Below is the web-link:

http://www.usarec.army.mil/hq/warrant/download/MilitaryFlight.pdf

Master the Military Flight Aptitude Tests,
by Peterson's Publishing, 8th Edition
SKU: 978-0-7689-3605-6

The book "Master the Military Flight Aptitude Tests" is also recommended. This book contains three full length sample tests, reviews of instrument comprehension, cyclic orientation, spatial apperception, and in-depth reviews of each question type.

Frequently Asked Questions (FAQs) about the SIFT

What does the SIFT measure?

The SIFT is a measure of multiple aptitudes. It assesses mathematical skills and aptitude, the ability to extract meaning from written passages, familiarity with mechanical concepts and simple machines, the ability to perform mental rotations to determine the orientation of aircraft in 3-dimensional space, and the ability to quickly recognize patterns within objects and groups of images. The SIFT also measures an examinee's knowledge of aviation terminology, familiarity with aircraft components and function, knowledge of basic aerodynamic principles, and a grasp of basic flight rules and regulations. Performance on this part of the battery can be improved by study, and examinees with aviation experience will typically do well.

All components of the SIFT have proven to be excellent predictors of training performance. That is, individuals who enter the flight program with high levels of cognitive aptitude and have background knowledge of aviation concepts are more likely to both achieve higher grades in aviation training and successfully complete the training program. By including multiple subtests that measure different constructs shown to predict success in aviation training, we can account for the more variance in training outcomes and help ensure that aviation programs make more efficient and accurate selection decisions.

How well does the SIFT predict training performance and attrition?

At present, the validity of the SIFT is still being assessed by Army personnel. However, similar test batteries used for aviation selection in the Navy and Air Force typically yield validity coefficients of approximately 0.40 between selection test scores and training performance (e.g., academic grades, flight grades). Validity coefficients range from 0 (the test does not predict grades in training at all) to 1 (the test predicts training grades perfectly). These validities compare favorably with industry selection testing standards. In addition, these tests have been a valuable resource for predicting attrition, or the student's probability of completing aviation training.

How long does the SIFT take to administer?

Total time required to take the SIFT may vary from individual to individual. All together, checking in at the exam site, exam setup, an optional exam break, and completing the SIFT may take up to 3 hours, though many individuals can often complete the exam in approximately 2 hours.

What if I don't answer all of the questions on the test before time expires?

The time limits and number of questions for the SIFT subtests are as follows:

- Simple Drawings (SD) – 2 minutes, 100 questions

- Hidden Figures (HF) – 5 minutes, 50 questions

- Army Aviation Information Test (AAIT) – 30 minutes, 40 questions

- Spatial Apperception Test (SAT) – 10 minutes, 25 questions

- Reading Comprehension Test (RCT) – 30 minutes, 20 questions

- Math Skills Test (MST) – 40 minutes, test length varies

- Mechanical Comprehension Test (MCT) – 15 minutes, test length varies

The recommended strategies vary between different components of the test:

Simple Drawings and Hidden Figures: Work quickly and don't guess. The SD and HF subtest scores are derived from the number of problems that you answer correctly, with a portion of the number of problems answered incorrectly being deducted from your score. In the majority of cases, examinees will not be able to answer all questions presented. Responding as quickly and as accurately as possible without randomly guessing as time is about to expire will, in most cases, work in the favor of the examinee.

Army Aviation Information Test, Spatial Apperception Test, and Reading Comprehension Test: Work quickly and guess at items you haven't reached if time is about to expire. The AAIT, SAT, and RCT include a fixed number of questions for each subtest. On these subtests, any items left unanswered will be scored as incorrect. It is therefore to the examinee's advantage to rule out poor answer choices on remaining questions and make educated guesses if time is about to expire.

Computer Adaptive Subtests (Math Skills Test and Mechanical Comprehension Test): Work quickly and don't guess. Due to the nature of adaptive tests, the number and difficulty of questions presented to different examinees may vary on the MST and MCT. Scores generated by examinees who fail to complete a sufficient number of items on any SIFT adaptive subtest before time expires may have a penalty applied to their scores. Therefore, examinees are expected to work as briskly as possible without losing accuracy. The severity of the score penalty will increase as the number of questions answered decreases. This penalty will never be applied to scores on adaptive subtests that automatically terminate before time has expired.

On the adaptive subtests, examinees are advised against randomly guessing as time is about to expire. The current time limits for each subtest have been established to allow as many examinees as possible to finish the test without time expiring. If an examinee has worked diligently and quickly on a given subtest, random guessing will, in most cases, be more detrimental to scores than the penalty received for not completing the entire test.

Is there a paper-based version of the SIFT?

The SIFT is available only in a web-based format. The system is operated on a secure server that is monitored and controlled.

What are the current SIFT minimum score requirements?

The current minimum qualifying score to apply for the Army's Aviation Program is 40 (possible scores range from 20 to 80, with a mean of 50 and standard deviation of 10). As the SIFT is validated, the minimum score may change to correspond with the Aviation Branch / U.S. Army Recruiting Commands' accessions requirements. Contact your local education center for current information.

How will I find out my SIFT scores? Is there any way to find out my scores immediately?

Your results (pass or fail) will be generated immediately after completing the test. You will be instructed to see the Test Control Officer (TCO) / Test Examiner (TE) to obtain your score letter. The score letter must be signed by the TCO / TE to be valid.

How many times can I take the SIFT? Can I retake the SIFT to get a better score?

If you attain a passing, or minimum qualifying, score you are no longer authorized to retake the SIFT. Additionally, if you fail to attain a minimum qualifying score on your first attempt, you may retake the SIFT no earlier than the 181st day following the previous attempt. If you fail to attain a minimum qualifying score on your second attempt, you are no longer authorized to retake the SIFT and are not qualified for the Army's Aviation Program.

Which subtests make the greatest contribution to my final SIFT score?

The formula utilized to compute your SIFT score is proprietary information and will not be released by APT. However, examinees should note that the formula used to calculate the SIFT score is compensatory, meaning that poor performance on a given subtest may often be offset by high performance on another. However, examinees are advised to perform as well as possible on all given subtests.

Where is the nearest SIFT testing location?

Locations that commonly administer the SIFT include:

- Post-servicing Education Centers

- Military Entrance Processing Stations (MEPS)

- Military Academies / ROTC Programs

You will need to schedule your SIFT exam at the location at which you intend to test. For military service members, contact your local servicing education center. For WOFT applicants, contact a recruiter for assistance in scheduling the SIFT.

What type of identification do I need to bring to the testing site?

You should bring some form of photo identification (i.e., driver's license, military ID card, passport) and verification of your social security number (i.e., social security card).

Is the SIFT offered in any language other than English?

No. At present, the SIFT is administered in English only.

How much does it cost to take the SIFT?

There is no charge to take the SIFT.

Can I use a calculator on the test?

No, the math problems on the exam are designed to be completed without the use of a calculator, but a few formulas are provided. Each examinee is provided scrap paper on which to compute problems.

What should I bring with me on the day of the test?

You will need to bring some form of photo identification (i.e., driver's license, military ID card, passport) and verification of your social security number (i.e., social security card).

Electronic devices (e.g., smart phones, cameras, etc.) are not permitted in the testing room. Examinees must stow these items in their automobiles or leave them with the exam proctor before proceeding into the testing room.

In addition, personal belongings (e.g., book bags) should not be brought into the testing room.

Paper and pencils will be supplied for you at the testing facility.

I have seen study guides for military aviation tests in bookstores. Would these guides help me study for the SIFT?

Army Personnel Testing does not endorse any commercial study guides, but the guides might be helpful for examinees who want to acquire testing strategies, review and practice math principles and problems, familiarize themselves with military history and aviation terminology, and practice pacing on timed tests.

Who can I contact if I have additional questions about the SIFT?

usarmy.knox.hrc.mbx.tagd-army-personnel-testing@mail.mil.

Source of FAQs: US Army Personnel Testing, HRC Fort Knox, KY

SIFT Test Break Down

The SIFT Test consists of seven separate sections. Some sections relate to Aviation Knowledge and some sections are general tests of intelligence and cognitive ability (General Knowledge and Problem Solving Abilities). The thought process involved in developing this test seems to be that those who do well on the SIFT will also be successful Army Aviator candidates. The SIFT Test is entirely computer based. Pencil and scrap paper are provided to assist in solving problems and making calculations. The time limit and the number of questions vary for each of the seven sections. There is also a 15 minute break after completing section three on Army Aviation Information Test (AAIT). There are a set number of questions for the first five sections. Sections six and seven have varied numbers of questions from one candidate to another.

The SIFT combined similar sections from the AFAST, ASVAB, and AFOQT into one test. Total test time is 3 hours, however some candidates report they have completed testing in about 2 hours.

The Seven SIFT Sections Defined

Simple Drawings: The candidate is shown five basic pictures and asked to identify the one picture that is odd or out-of-place. You have to decide which one is not like the others. For example, in the series "D D d D D"", lower case "d" is not the same. Be sure to move quickly through this section as you are given 2 minutes to answer 100 questions.

Hidden Figures: This section is similar to the Air Force Officer Qualifying test (AFOQT) hidden figures test. You are given 5 minutes to identify 50 shapes. This section requires training your brain to recognize the shape within a multitude of objects.

Army Aviation Information: This section requires the candidate to be familiar with aviation terms, concepts of helicopter flight, aerodynamics, flight controls, and general helicopter components and their functions as well as theoretical and practical aspects of flight. Several candidates who did well recommended the free download of the FAA Helicopter Flying Handbook FAA-H-8083-21A, especially the chapters dealing with aerodynamics, flight controls, weight and balance, basic and advanced flight maneuvers. If possible read through the entire handbook. There were additional questions related to Army helicopters. It's recommend you study up on them and what their roles are. This section is the first to let you flag a question and return back later. Devote plenty of study time towards this section until you understand the concepts and mechanics of flight. This section gives you half an hour to answer 40 questions.

Spatial Apperception: The pictures are similar to others used in standard military flight sample tests. Candidates are required to study cockpit attitude indicators and compare them to images of aircraft in flight. You'll be asked to identify diving, banking left, banking right, climbing etc. The purpose of this section is to test the candidate's ability conceptualize a 3D aircraft image and select the corresponding attitude image. Recommend you review various flight training study books, sample tests and flight simulator programs to familiarize yourself. You will have 10 minutes to determine attitude of 25 images.

Reading Comprehension: This section is similar to the ASVAB. You read a paragraph and then answer a question(s) based on what you read. You answer the questions by selecting from various possible answers. Several answers may be close to being right but only one will be correct. The section evaluates the candidates' comprehension and ability to eliminate incorrect answers in a timed event.

Math Skills Test: The test is the first section to use an adaptive question type format to mix up the SIFT test. Each candidate will receive various amounts of questions, plus the computer will assign additional questions in the areas it determines you are weakest in. (If you do poorly in probabilities, expect more probability questions). You will be shown math related questions ranging from word problems (time/distance or work/amount), geometry equations, basic algebra, averages, and probability problems. Recommend refreshing your basic algebra, basic geometry, logic, fractions, and terms such as mean, median, mode and so forth. The time limit for this section is 40 minutes.

Mechanical Comprehension: This section is also similar to what is shown in the standard ASVAB. It's the second (and last) section to use the adaptive question format. Understand the use of levers and pulleys and how they relate to force applied and exerted, specific gravity, gears, buoyancy, work, and velocity. You should also familiarize yourself with advanced topics as Bernoulli's Principle of Fluid Dynamics, Ohms Law, Principles of Electricity, Newton's Three Laws of Motion and similar concepts and how to solve problems with scientific formulas. This section of the test is allotted 15 minutes of test time.

BEGIN SAMPLE TEST
VERBAL ANALOGIES

Measures your ability to complete the analogy and make the proper word associations.

1. Initiate is to begin as conclude is to:
A. abbreviate.
B. induction.
C. end.
D. scorn.
E. agree.

2. Wood is to rot as fruit is to:
A. fresh.
B. spoiled.
C. mature.
D. torn.
E. smell.

3. Cloud is to eye as concert is to:
A. loud.
B. head.
C. music.
D. ear.
E. venue.

4. Wifi is to internet:
A. as on-ramp is to freeway.
B. as asphalt is roadway.
C. as pipe is to steel.
D. grass is to lawn.
E. rocks are to gravel.

5. Tadpole is to frog as:
A. dog is to puppy.
B. shell is to hermit crab.
C. horn is to rhinoceros.
D. savings is to 401K.
E. meteorite is to crater.

ARITHMETIC REASONING

Measures ability to use arithmetic to solve problems.

1. A locomotive speeds along the tracks at 90 MPH. If ½ inch equals 10 miles on the map, how far has the locomotive traveled on the map in 80 minutes?

A. 5.0 inches

B. 5.5 inches

C. 5.75 inches

D. 6.0 inches

E. 6.5 inches

2. A shipping container is 12 feet long, 9 feet high and 8 foot wide. 2 boxes measuring 4 foot on each side, are placed in the container. How many cubic foot of space remain?

A. 634 cu. ft.

B. 742 cu. ft.

C. 864 cu. ft

D. 832 cu. ft.

E. 736 cu. ft.

3. A helicopter can only lift 3000 pounds of cargo. If cases of bullets weigh 8 pounds apiece, rifles 15 pounds apiece and mortar shells 40 pounds apiece, which load comes closest to the helicopter's load capacity without going over it?

A. 38 cases of bullets, 164 rifles, 6 mortar shells

B. 6 cases of bullets, 9 rifles, 70 mortar shells

C. 319 cases of bullets, 25 Rifles, 2 mortar shells

D. 264 cases of bullets, 13 rifles, 17 mortar shells

E. 50 cases of bullets, 150 rifles, 10 mortar shells

4. A man took 3 hours to go grocery shopping. He spent 20 minutes reading magazines, 45 minutes drinking coffee, and 10 minutes driving each way. What percentage of time was actually spent grocery shopping?

A. 59 percent

B. 53 percent

C. 51 percent

D. 47 percent

E. 42 percent

5. If a car drives 185 miles in 2.5 hours, how many miles will it travel in 30 minutes?

A. 35 miles

B. 36 miles

C. 37 miles

D. 38 miles

E. 39 miles

WORD KNOWLEDGE

Measures your range of vocabulary. Choose the word that is most similar in meaning to the numbered word.

1. Tenacious
A. selfish
B. rude
C. stubborn
D. annoying
E. angry

2. Resuscitate
A. attempt
B. rebound
C. refrain
D. enlighten
E. revive

3. Zealous
A. enthusiastic
B. jumpy
C. agree
D. consent
E. annoyed

4. Obligatory
A. owe
B. required
C. legal
D. intentional
E. accidental

5. Obfuscate
A. steal
B. destroy
C. remove
D. duplicate
E. obscure

MATH KNOWLEDGE

Measures your abilities to solve equations using mathematical terms and principles.

1. 3/5 x 1/12 x 5/7 equals
A. 5/140
B. 1/28
C. 15/420
D. 3/8
E. 1/8

2. Solve for a in the equation 4a+15=31
A. 3
B. -3
C. 4
D. -4
E. 5

3. In the decimal number 3,916.842 the 2 represents:
A. ones
B. tenths
C. hundredths
D. thousandths
E. decimal point.

4. Multiply the radical expressions (2√3) (3√6) and solve.
A. 6√18
B. 5√9
C. 5√18
D. 2√3
E. 18√2

5. Simplify the factors of (x+3) (x+4)
A. 2x7
B. 2x12
C. $x^2 + 7x + 12$
D. x-1
E 2x-12

INSTRUMENT COMPREHENSION

Measures your ability to visualize an inflight aircraft's position using an Artificial Horizon dial and Compass dial. Directions: Using the provided instrument dials you should be able to determine if the aircraft is climbing, diving, banking left or right, and it's heading. Be able to select the aircraft that best represents what the dials indicate.

Artificial Horizon: Referring to the three Artificial Horizon dials A, B, and C, notice the small aircraft silhouette in the center. It always remain stationary. The black line represents the horizon and the pointer will indicate the aircraft's degree of bank.

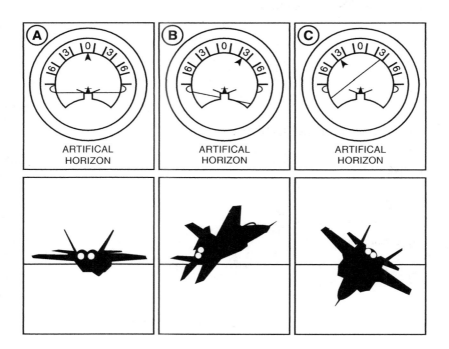

Refer to Dial A. When the aircraft's wings are level, the horizon line will be straight across the dial and the pointer will indicate "0".

Refer to Dial B. If the aircraft were to climb and simultaneously make a left bank turn, the horizon line will dip below the aircraft silhouette and the pointer will indicate the degree of bank, in this case 30 degrees. Note the pointer will appear opposite of how the aircraft banks, as it remains perpendicular to the horizon line.

Refer to Dial C. Notice the horizon line is above the aircraft silhouette, symbolizing a dive, and the aircraft is banking 30 degrees to the right. The greater the distance the horizon line is from the aircraft silhouette, the greater the rate of climb or dive.

Compass: On the compass dials 1,2, and 3, the arrow indicates the direction the aircraft is heading. Dial 1 shows an aircraft heading South, Dial 2 shows it heading East, and dial 3 shows it heading Northeast.

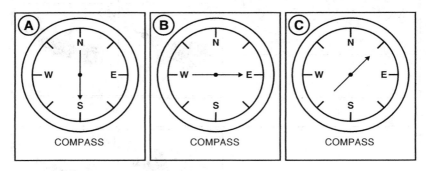

Using the provided Artificial Horizon and Compass Dials determine which of the four aircraft is flying in the position shown. For reference, you are always heading North in level flight at the same altitude as the aircraft you are observing. East is on the right side of the page and West is on your left.

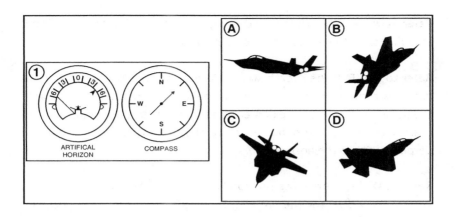

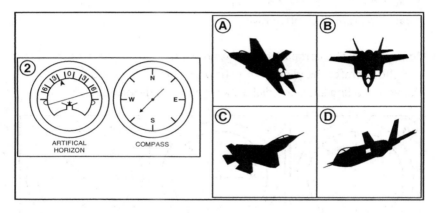

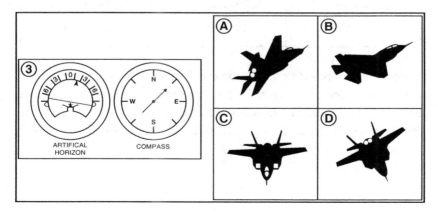

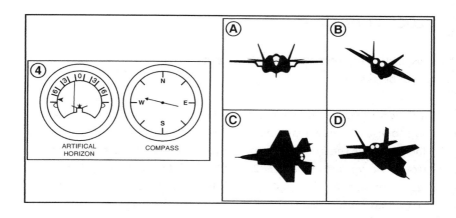

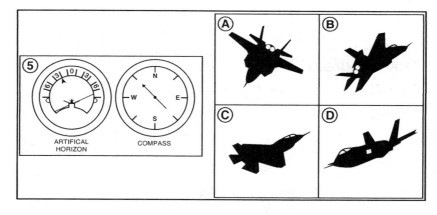

BLOCK COUNTING

This part of the test measures your ability to "see into" a 3-dimensional pile of blocks.

Directions: You are shown a stack of 11 same sized blocks and you will have to visualize how many blocks come in contact with the designated block. Look at the Trial Diagram for Block T1. Following the directional arrows, T1 contacts blocks 1, 2, and 3. So T1=3. Now see Block T2. It clearly contacts blocks 2,3,4,5, and 9. But not so clearly, as indicated by the dashed lines, it also touches 6, 7, and 8. So T2 = 8.

Trial Diagram
T1 = 3
T2 = 8

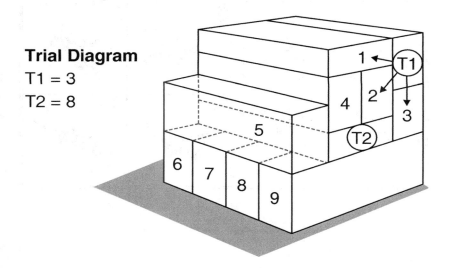

Now refer to the Test Diagram and determine how many blocks contact Blocks B1 through B5.

Test Diagram

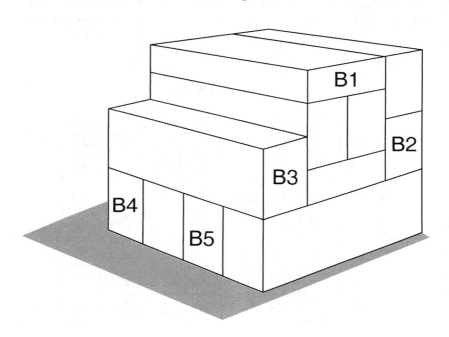

Answer

Block	A	B	C	D	E
B1	3	4	5	6	7
B2	5	6	7	8	9
B3	2	3	4	5	6
B4	1	2	3	4	5
B5	4	5	6	7	8

TABLE READING

Measures your ability to read a table correctly. Using the XY Table diagram you'll see that X values are along the top of each column and Y values run along the left side of each row. **Directions:** Given an X and Y value, your task is to determine where they intersect. Example: The intersect of X +3 and Y -3 is 28. Find the five X and Y intersects on the chart below the table diagram and record your answer as A through E.

X Value

	-3	-2	-1	0	+1	+2	+3
+3	16	17	18	19	20	21	22
+2	17	18	19	20	21	22	23
+1	18	19	20	21	22	23	24
0	19	20	21	22	23	24	25
-1	20	21	22	23	24	25	26
-2	21	22	23	24	25	26	27
-3	22	23	24	25	26	27	28

Y Value (along left side)

	X	Y	A	B	C	D	E
1.	-1	-2	21	22	23	24	25
2.	0	+1	19	21	24	27	28
3.	+3	-1	18	20	22	24	26
4.	-3	0	16	17	18	19	20
5.	+2	-3	27	25	23	21	19

AVIATION INFORMATION

Measures your knowledge of Aviation Terms and helicopter concepts. Match each sentence with the correct term to complete it accurately.

1. The forward force of aircraft thrust is opposed by:
A. lift
B. drag
C. weight
D. gravity
E. velocity

2. What helicopter component converts stationary control inputs from the pilot into rotating inputs which can be connected to rotor blades or control surfaces?
A. flapping hinge
B. drag hinge
C. pitch horn
D. control rod
E. swash plate

3. One of the four fundamentals of flight which all maneuvers are based on is:
A. climbs
B. landings
C. hovers
D. takeoffs
E. lifts

4. An imaginary line drawn halfway between the upper and lower surface of the airfoil is known as the:
A. Blade Span
B. Chord line
C. Chord
D. Mean Camber Line
E. Airfoil

5. The drag generated by the airflow circulation around the rotor blades as it creates lift is:
A. profile drag
B. parasite drag
C. induced drag
D. profile drag
E. total drag

GENERAL SCIENCE

Measures your scientific aptitude.

1. Which of the following fluid properties is not typically required to calculate a solution to a fluid dynamics problem?
A. viscosity
B. flow velocity
C. pressure
D. density
E. temperature

2. The process where particles tend to move from a region of greater concentration to an area of lesser concentration is called:
A. osmotic pressure
B. capillary action
C. active transport
D. diffusion
E. osmosis

3. The plant process of losing water vapor through the stoma or leaves is known as:
A. photosynthesis
B. respiration
C. transpiration
D. sweating
E. dehydration

4. Which of the following amplitude measurements would not appear as a Sine Wave?
A. A/C current
B. Car Battery
C. Radio Signal
D. Audio Signal
E. Modulated Signal

5. The moons Charon, Nix, Hydra, Kerberos and Styx obit which planet or dwarf planet in our solar system?
A. Saturn
B. Uranus
C. Venus
D. Jupiter
E. Pluto

HIDDEN FIGURES

Directions: Measures your skill at finding one of the five figures within a complicated drawing. Each of the five figures is lettered. The <u>complete</u> figure will be hidden within the drawing block and will remain in the same position and size.

The lettered figures are:

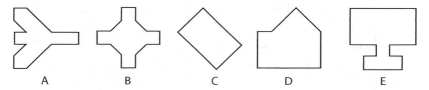

A   B   C   D   E

Which one of the five figures is contained in drawing Trial A?

Trial A

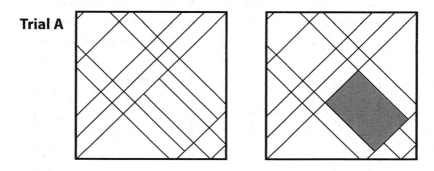

Figure C is contained in Trial A. So C is the answer. The drawing on the right is exactly like Trial A except Figure C was greyed in to show that all of it appears within it. Notice that the <u>complete</u> figure is the same size and in the same position as it appears in the instructions.

Directions: Determine the lettered figure within each drawing.

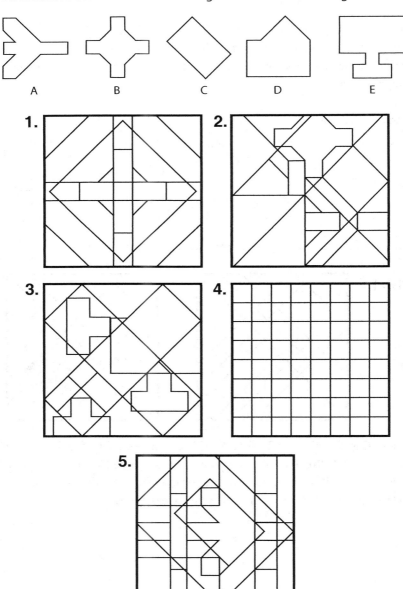

A   B   C   D   E

1.   2.

3.   4.

5.

SELF-DESCRIPTION INVENTORY

Measures your personal traits and attitudes.

Sample: I like heavy metal music.

Does this test statement describe you? Indicate your response using the scale below. Usually your first initial response (gut response) will be the most accurate.

A: Strongly Agree
B: Agree
C: Neutral (Neither agree nor disagree)
D: Disagree
E: Strongly Disagree

If you like heavy metal music agree by selecting A or B, depending on how much you like it. If you don't like it choose D or E. If you equally like all types of music choose C.

Directions: Read the following statements and decide how best it depicts you.

There is no right or wrong answer to each statement.

1. I like to help out others.
2. I bring enthusiasm to projects I'm involved in.
3. I like to have routine in my life and at work.
4. I like to come up with creative solutions to problems.
5. I usually finish listening to others before responding.
6. My friends would call me first if they needed help.
7. I take criticism well.
8. I am on social media more than 3 hours a day.
9. When I'm in a bad mood people know not to bother me.
10. I like to point out mistakes others have made.

SAMPLE QUESTION ANSWERS

Verbal Analogies
1. C
2. B
3. D
4. A
5. D

Block Counting
B1 = A
B2 = C
B3 = E
B4 = D
B5 = B

Arithmetic Reasoning
1. D
2. E
3. D
4. B
5. C

Table Reading
1. C
2. B
3. E
4. D
5. A

Word Knowledge
1. C
2. E
3. A
4. B
5. E

Aviation Information
1. B
2. E
3. A
4. D
5. C

Math Knowledge
1. B
2. C
3. D
4. E
5. C

General Science
1. A
2. D
3. C
4. B
5. E

Instrument Comprehension
1. B
2. D
3. D
4. C
5. A

Hidden Figures
1. B
2. A
3. D
4. E
5. C

Self-Description Inventory
There is no right or wrong answer for these items.

Everything I came across in the section on Helicopter Knowledge was covered in the free to download FAA publications available at:

Helicopter Flying Handbook FAA-H-8083-21
http://www.faa.gov/regulations_policies/handbooks_manuals/
aircraft/media/faa-h-8083-21A.pdf
and Rotorcraft Flying Handbook
http://www.faa.gov/regulations_policies/handbooks_manuals/
aircraft/media/faa-h-8083-21.pdf

Also highly recommended was Paul Cantrell's free site:
http://www.copters.com/helo_aero.html

Check out the Aerodynamics links for lots of useful study information.

Also be sure to check out the "SIFT Study Guide: Test Prep and Practice Test Questions for the Army SIFT "

by Accepted Inc. (Author)

ISBN-13: 9780991316502
ISBN-10: 0991316509

Finally, remember to bring proper documentation to the test. It seems like something that anyone who thinks they have the stuff to become a Warrant Officer should know to do without being told. However, when tested, 2 of 5 testees did not have the proper paperwork on them. You need the Request for Examination form and proof of your social security number (driver's license with social security card, or a military ID). Be sure that your ID is current! Outdated ID cannot be used to authenticate yourself. One testee had his military dependent's card confiscated because it was out-of-date. Finally, you may need additional documentation. One applicant was attempting to transfer from the USMC and needed a letter from the Commandant of the Marine Corps, which he did not have on him. In short, if you don't know for sure what you need to bring, ask. No matter what, bring proof of your social security number.

SIFT Requirement

The Aviation Branch developed a replacement for the Alternate Flight Aptitude Selection Test (AFAST). The test is the Selection Instrument for Flight Training (SIFT), and implemented on 1 October 2012. The first Accessions Board to select 153A packets with SIFT results included occurred on January 2013.

Any Warrant Officer packets for MOS 153A, Rotary Wing Aviator, MUST have a qualifying SIFT score in their packet after 1 October 2012.

The link below is about the SIFT and discusses the test development process: http://www.dtic.mil/cgi-bin/GetTRDoc?AD=ADA481060

Recommendation on a Successful Process

- Spend the time to get good letters of recommendations.

- Use highly influential people that personally know the applicant.

- Close all loops in the packet. It represents the applicant and the recruiter.

- Make sure all forms have legible signatures and branch identified.

- Make sure that the Body Fat Sheet matches the UR FL 136

- Get several people to review the packet to make sure it is complete.

Warrant Officer Aviator Packet Checklist

11. USAREC FL 136, Scanned into PDF (SIP)
12. UF 609-R-E (SIP)
13. College Degree/ College Transcripts/ HS Diploma/ HS Transcript (SIP)
14. DA Form 61 (SIP)
15. DD FORM 1966
16. SF 86
17. UF 1104
18. 680 ADP (SIP)
19. DA 5500/DA 5501 (SIP)
20. Copy of all Waivers and Grade Determination for Enlistment
21. Full Length Photo (SIP)
22. Letters of Recommendation (Minimum of 3, MAX of 6)
23. Typed and Hand Written Statements "Why I want to be an Army WOFT Aviator" (SIP)
24. DA Form 705(Must score a 60 or higher in each event (SIP)
25. Prior Service DD 214, DMDC Report and NGB Form 22
26. UF 1227 Clearance Eligibility Questionnaire (SIP)
27. Resume (Optional)
28. All Documents must be scanned into the proper section of the ERM.

Chapter 9

WOFT (Civilian) Enlistment Program Procedures

153A - Rotary Wing Aviator

**WOFT (Warrant Officer Flight Training) PROGRAM IS FOR CIVILIAN APPLICANTS ONLY

References:

- AR 601-210 (RA and USAR) Program, Chapter 9-10

- UR 601-91 Officer Candidate School and Warrant Officer Flight Training Program

- DA Pam 611-256-2 Alternate Flight Aptitude Selection Test (AFAST) Information Pam

- AR 135-100 Appointment of Commissioned and Warrant Officer of the Army

- AR 40-501 Standards of Medical Fitness

All Current USAREC Messages Pertaining to the WOFT Program

Basic Qualifications:

- Meet basic enlistment eligibility requirements IAW AR 601-210

- Be at least 18 years old at the time of RA Enlistment and not passed 33rd birthday at the time of selection. Age waivers will be considered on a case by case basis.

- No age adjustment for Prior Service Applicants for the WOFT Program.

- Passing SIFT Test

- GT Score of 110 or Higher. (No Exceptions)

- High school diploma. If the applicant has a GED he/she must complete 15 semester hours of college level courses.

- High School seniors may apply.

- Must be a U.S. Citizen. (No Exceptions)

- All applicants must meet HT/WT standards IAW AR 600-9.

- Any applicant that does not meet these standards must have a DA 5500 (male) or DA5501 (female) indicating that the applicant is within Body Fat standards.

- Pass a Class 1 Flight Physical that is approved by The US Army Aero-Medical Center (USAAMC), Fort Rucker, AL. All Flight Physicals are forwarded to the USAAMC for review and approval. (It is recommended that the Recruiter conduct a timely follow-up to ensure that the physical has been forwarded from issuing facility to Fort Rucker). Any questions concerning physicals at Fort Rucker should be directed to (334)598-8955.

Service Obligation

- A three year active duty service obligation is required upon enlistment for WOFT. Upon completion of Warrant Officer Candidate School there is a six year service obligation

- If applicant does not complete the Warrant Officer Candidate School they are still obligated for the remaining of their enlistment option.

Moral Waiver Procedures

- All WOFT applicants must meet the following standards:

- WOFT appointment eligibility (AR 135-100 and UR 601-91)

- Waivers are not processed by USAREC waivers section. WOFT appointment moral waivers must be forwarded to HRC for review.

- All packets requiring moral waivers should be processed and boarded at the Battalion prior to the packet review by G-3 Special Programs.

- After the packet is complete the moral waiver will be forwarded to HRC.

- Documents needed in order to process a waiver are USAREC Form 1037 and USAREC Form 1227.

Boards

- Battalion Boards will consist of a panel of three Commissioned Officers; one must be an Aviator Officer.

- Exceptions will be granted if there are no Aviator Officers assigned to the Battalion.

- Area of emphasis:

    - Neatness/ Grooming
    - Enthusiasm/ Motivation
    - Maturity
    - Decisiveness
    - Self expression
    - Confidence
    - Composure
    - Attitude towards the military
    - Personal affairs in order

- At a minimum, 2 of the 3 board members must recommend for WOFT.

- HQ USAREC Board (Selection) DA Centralized Selection Board consisting of three or more officers. Applicant's application is boarded and the most competitive applicants are selected based upon available training seats and the needs of the Army.

- HQ USAREC will notify the Recruiting Battalion of selected and non-selected applicants.

- Board results are posted to the G3 Web page shortly after the release, usually 48 hours after the board convenes.

- Applicants are automatically re-boarded a second time if non-selected on their first look. (The following month).

Recommendation on a Successful Process

- Spend the time to get good letters of recommendations.

- Use highly influential people that personally know the applicant.

- Close all loops in the packet. It represents the applicant and the recruiter.

- Make sure all forms have legible signatures and branch identified.

- Make sure that the Body Fat Sheet matches the UR FL 136

- Get several people to review the packet to make sure it is complete.

Packet Checklist

1. USAREC FL 136, Scanned into PDF (SIP)
2. UF 609-R-E (SIP)
3. College Degree/ College Transcripts/ HS Diploma/ HS Transcript (SIP)
4. DA Form 61 (SIP)
5. DD FORM 1966
6. SF 86
7. UF 1104
8. 680 ADP (SIP)
9. DA 5500/DA 5501 (SIP)
10. Copy of all Waivers and Grade Determination for Enlistment
11. Full Length Photo (SIP)
12. Letters of Recommendation (Minimum of 3, MAX of 6)
13. Typed and Hand Written Statements "Why I want to be an Army WOFT Aviator" (SIP)
14. DA Form 705(Must score a 60 or higher in each event (SIP)
15. Prior Service DD 214, DMDC Report and NGB Form 22
16. UF 1227 Clearance Eligibility Questionnaire (SIP)
17. Resume (Optional)
18. All Documents must be scanned into the proper section of the ERM.

Aviator Warrant Applicant Reference List

The intent of this reading list is to provide the Aviation Warrant Officer applicant with materials that may aid in the understanding of some of the subtests in the SIFT. This is NOT a required reading list nor does it include all possible reference sources.

1. Advisory Circular (AC) 61-13B, Department of Transportation, Federal Aviation Administration, Basic Helicopter Handbook. Government Printing Office, Superintendent of Documents, Washington, DC 20402.

2. Field Manual (FM) 1-51, Department of the Army, Rotary Wing Flight

3. St. John, Clark, Airline Pilot Employment Test Guide. California: Aviation Book Company, 1973. Aviation Book Company, PO Box 4187, Glendale, CA 91202.

4. Saunders, G.H., Dynamics of Helicopter Flight, New York: John Wiley & Sons, Inc., 1975. John Wiley & Sons Inc., 3rd Avenue, New York, New York 10016.

5. Tower, Merrill E., Flight Facts for Private Pilots. Aero Publications, 1971. Aero Publications, 329 W. Aviation Road, Fallbrook, CA 92028.

6. Misenhimer, T. G., Aeroscience, California: Aero Products Research, Inc., 1976. Aero Products Research, 11201 Hendry Avenue, Los Angeles, CA 90045.

Information On What To Expect After Selection Into The Warrant Officer Program

Those selected for the Warrant Officer Program will be notified by Department of the Army (DA) about 90 days after the board adjourns. DA establishes a reporting date to Ft Rucker, AL based upon MOS requirements. Military Entrance Processing Station (MEPS) will then publish your orders with authorized travel time to Ft Rucker. Upon arrival, you will be given your basic issue and time to resolve any military related problems, i.e. pay, uniform, etc. You will be paid as an E5, or your current pay grade if higher, and begin wearing the WOC brass. (Please see next page on Information on Discharge from Current Service and Enlistment into the Army).

Selectees will attend the six week, four day Warrant Officer Candidate School (WOCS) similar to basic training or boot camp. Visit the Warrant Officer Career Center (Http://leav-www.army.mil/wocc/) on the web for a welcome packet and more information on the candidate school. This course is designed to evaluate leadership and management skills. Soldiers will be appointed as a Warrant Officer One (WO1) upon successful completion of WOCS. Soldiers who fail to successfully complete WOCS will serve the remainder of their four-year enlistment based upon the needs of the Army. All Warrant Officers have an initial obligation of six years, which will be served on active duty as an Army Reserve Officer. Warrant Officers remain on active duty in the Army Reserve until promotion to CW3, normally between the seventh and eighth year of Warrant Officer service. Upon promotion to CW3, the Warrant Officer is integrated into the Regular Army.

Information On Discharge From Current Service And Enlistment Into The Army

(Once Selected For The Warrant Officer Program)

NOTE: During the Discharge and Enlistment process, you must ensure that you arrange to enlist into the Army the next day after separation from your parent service. If you have a day or more break in service, or if you enlist on the same day as separation, you will not receive your correct pay and allowances until this discrepancy is corrected. The process of correcting this discrepancy could take 3-6 months.

Warrant Officer (WO) selectees will receive instructions from Warrant Officer Accessions, Human Resource Command (HRC) 90 days after selection and will report back to an Army Recruiter with those instructions. The recruiter will complete the DD Form 1966 (enlistment contract) and SF 86 (no other forms are required) and schedule WO selectee for processing based on the instructions from HRC. The recruiter will then schedule the WO selectee into the Army Recruiting and Accession Data System (ARADS) for enlistment into the Army.

WO selectees do not require a physical because a physical was taken as part of the application process. WO selectees' copy of the physical will have the physical category. WO selectee must enlist in the Army for a period of 4 years on the day scheduled. MEPS will administer the oath of enlistment and issue orders using AR 600-8-105 to assign Aviation WO selectee to HHC, Warrant Officer Career Center, Ft Rucker, AL. All other WO selectees will be reassigned to their first WO assignment with TDY enroute at Ft Rucker, AL for the Warrant Officer Candidate School (WOCS) and TDY enroute at their basic technical course (wherever the school is located). Movement of family members is authorized to the location where the WO selectee is to be permanently assigned after training.

Chapter 10

When You Are Selected

How do I find out if I've been selected?

Do NOT phone the Warrant Officer Career College or Recruiting Command

ARNG - Notification through state headquarters. Check with your state.

Effective immediately: Notifications are available at this site:

http://www.usarec.army.mil/hq/warrant/WOgeninfo_boardresults.shtml

Due to a recent DOD mandate regarding website information, USAREC will no longer post an unofficial selection list at the conclusion of each Warrant Officer Selection Board.

To view selection board results, you will need to access the Army's Human Resource Center's (HRC-A) website. SEE ABOVE. You will need your CAC card or Army Knowledge Online (AKO) account username and password to do so.

Individual applicants may check the selection status of their application by using the "Application Status" feature on the website.

The process of notifying and placing candidates on orders may take up to 90 days after the board results are published. If you are a newly-selected candidate, wait at least 90 days before contacting Human Resources Command about assignment instructions.

I'm selected –Yoo-hoo! Now what?

Read the "Welcome Letter", "Orientation Packet", "1st WOC Student Letter" and "Warrant Officer Candidate Standing Operation Procedure (WOC SOP)". http://usacac.army.mil/cac2/WOCC/wocs.asp

The WOCS Website

Your first step is to review the WOCS web site:
http://usacac.army.mil/cac2/WOCC/

At the WOCS website you will find multiple sources of information to include a checklist to ensure you arrive with the correct uniforms and equipment; Security Clearance information for individuals that have not completed their Secret level clearance; and course information to try and limit the number of surprises for candidates when arriving.

 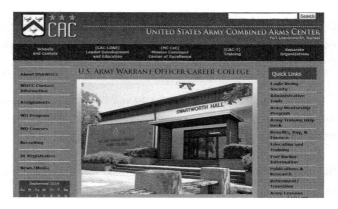

DEPARTMENT OF THE ARMY
UNITED STATES ARMY WARRANT OFFICER CAREER CENTER
FORT RUCKER, ALABAMA 36362-5000

REPLY TO
ATTENTION OF:

ATSW-Z

1 February 2008

MEMORANDUM FOR ALL WARRANT OFFICER CANDIDATES

SUBJECT: Warrant Officer Candidate School (WOCS) Welcome and Orientation

1. Congratulations on your selection to attend WOCS! I am confident that WOCS will be a challenging and rewarding experience for you. The program is designed to ensure you are adequately prepared to be an Army Warrant Officer as well as to help you realize what you are capable of achieving under physically and mentally demanding conditions. The daily training, mentoring, and feedback regimen in a task saturated environment will help you develop the leadership skills and attributes the Army expects its Warrant Officers to possess. Upon your completion of the program and appointment as a Warrant Officer, you will have a justifiable sense of accomplishment and pride in knowing that you are truly prepared to serve as an Army officer.

2. Prior to reporting to WOCS, there are some things you can do to prepare mentally and physically to ensure your success.

   a. Resolve to exceed the leadership challenges you will encounter during the program—the stronger your motivation to successfully complete the program, the better you will do.

   b. Ignore rumors you may hear about WOCS; it is true that WOCS is transforming just as the rest of the Army is transforming, but the goals of WOCS remain the same.

   c. In-as-much as possible, resolve personal and family matters before you report.

   d. Get into top-notch physical condition before you arrive to enable you to do your best in daily physical training and to adjust to the higher temperatures and extremely high humidity that are prevalent during much of the year.

3. Again, congratulations on your selection for WOCS! All of us at WOCS look forward to helping you gain the tools you will need to serve our country effectively as a Warrant Officer in the US Army.

2 Encls
1. Pre-Reporting Checklist
2. Orientation Packet

MARK T. JONES
Colonel, Aviation
Commandant

Orders:

Once selected, you can expect to receive notification Request For Orders (RFO) of your Warrant Officer Candidate School class date emailed 90 days after selection. Your local Reassignment / LEVY section will receive notification of your upcoming class on or about the same date you receive you email notification. The Reassignment / LEVY section will publish your orders.

Don't call or email the Warrant Officer Recruiting Team about your orders for at least 90 days after the release of selection board results.

For **153A aviators**, there are additional locations for information dealing with follow on training at the Fort Rucker Flight Training School. Soldiers with CAC or AKO access can get additional information from Bravo Company 1-145th Regiment's web site: http://www.militarymediainc.com/ruckerguide/command.html

For Interservice transfers - please review the MEPS information page.

If you have problems while in route to training, can not make the report date and/or you need further assistance, please call the S1 section of Headquarters and Headquarters Company and inform the leadership. After hours contact (334) 255-1371 or DSN 558-1371

The U.S. Army Human Resources Command (HRC) contact numbers are also helpful if you need answers and only seem to get the runaround.

Email: askhrc.army@us.army.mil

Phone Number: 1-888-ARMYHRC
DSN Phone Number: 983-9500
Address: Human Resource Service Center
Fort Knox, KY 40121

HRC Frequently Asked Questions:

If you have concerns because of upcoming deployment, conflicting school dates with other DA select programs (Drill Sergeant, NCO academy, Recruiting, ETC.) PCS or family issues, you can find information on how to change a class date on the HRC WOCS sites:

https://www.hrc.army.mil/
Once in the site log in with your CAC or AKO user name and password, then add WOCS to the search line, and lastly click on WOCS FAQs.

Information at this site is updated frequently so check back often for updates.

1. **When is my class date?** School dates are determined by HRC not the selection board. Soldiers will be scheduled in the next available class. An email will be generated by ATRRS at that time and sent to the your email address. If a request for a specific class date is submitted with your application it will not be acknowledged.

2. **When will I receive my RFO?** You will receive a Request for Orders (RFO) within 30 to 90 days after your selection designating school dates and ultimate duty assignment from your future career manager.

3. **Can I request a class date change?** Yes, for the following reasons:

> a. **Medical deferments**—Request must be submitted by 4187 through your local chain of command to Reserve Appointments and Accessions Branch, HRC. Request for deferment must contain justification to include the following: Name, SSN, Warrant Officer MOS soldier has been selected for, class number and date soldier is scheduled for, and requested deferment date. It must include a note from a doctor stating what the medical problem is and date soldier will be physically ready to attend school. If request is approved, a new class date will be determined and an amended Request for Orders will be issued.

b. **Compassionate deferments**—Request must be submitted by 4187 through your local chain of command to Reserve Appointments and Accessions Branch, HRC. Request for deferment must contain justification to include the following: Name, SSN, Warrant Officer MOS soldier has been selected for, class number and date soldier is scheduled for, and requested deferment date. If request is approved, a new class date will be determined and an amended Request for Orders will be issued.

c. **Deployment deferments**—A Soldier's chain of command (COC) may request deferment from school for the purpose of deployment by submitting a request to HRC for consideration. Deferment requests must be received not later than 60 days prior to deployment or school date, whichever is soonest.

4. If I am currently deployed, how will I be scheduled for training?

If you are currently deployed and selected for WOCS/WOFT, the COC must return the Soldier from theater in order to meet the scheduled class date. To keep a Soldier deployed and not returned for school, the Soldier's COC must submit a request to HRC for consideration.

5. How do I decline WOCS acceptance?

If you have been selected and no longer desire attendance to WOCS and appointment as a Warrant Officer you may decline by sending an email to the WO Reserve Appointments and Accessions Branch at usarmy.knox. hrc.mbx.opmd-raawo@mail.mil. Email must state name, WO MOS and reason for declination.

What To Expect After Selection Into The Warrant Officer Program

Those selected for the Warrant Officer Program will be notified by Department of the Army (DA) about 90 days after the board adjourns. DA establishes a reporting date to Ft Rucker, AL based upon MOS requirements. Military Entrance Processing Station (MEPS) will then publish your orders with authorized travel time to Ft Rucker. Upon arrival, you will be given your basic issue and time to resolve any military related problems, i.e. pay, uniform, etc. You will be paid as an E5, or your current pay grade if higher, and begin wearing the WOC brass.

Selectees will attend the six week, four day Warrant Officer Candidate School (WOCS) similar to basic training or boot camp. Visit the Warrant Officer Career Center (http://leav-www.army.mil/wocc/) on the web for a welcome packet and more information on the candidate school. This course is designed to evaluate leadership and management skills. Soldiers will be appointed as a Warrant Officer One (WO1) upon successful completion of WOCS. Soldiers who fail to successfully complete WOCS will serve the remainder of their four-year enlistment based upon the needs of the Army. All Warrant Officers have an initial obligation of six years, which will be served on active duty as an Army Reserve Officer. Warrant Officers remain on active duty in the Army Reserve until promotion to CW3, normally between the seventh and eighth year of Warrant Officer service. Upon promotion to CW3, the Warrant Officer is integrated into the Regular Army.

Information On Discharge From Current Service And Enlistment Into The Army (Once Selected For The Warrant Officer Program)

NOTE: During the Discharge and Enlistment process, you must ensure that you arrange to enlist into the Army the next day after separation from your parent service. If you have a day or more break in service, or if you enlist on the same day as separation, you will not receive your correct pay and allowances until this discrepancy is corrected. The process of correcting this discrepancy could take 3-6 months.

Warrant Officer (WO) selectees will receive instructions from Warrant Officer Accessions, Human Resources Command (HRC) 90 days after selection and will report back to an Army Recruiter with those instructions. The recruiter will complete the DD Form 1966 (enlistment contract) and SF 86 (no other forms are required) and schedule WO selectee for processing based on the instructions from HRC. The recruiter will then schedule the WO selectee into the Army Recruiting and Accession Data System (ARADS) for enlistment into the Army.

WO selectees do not require a physical because a physical was taken as part of the application process. WO selectees' copy of the physical will have the physical category. WO selectee must enlist in the Army for a period of 4 years on the day scheduled. MEPS will administer the oath of enlistment and issue orders using AR 600-8-105 to assign Aviation WO selectee to HHC, Warrant Officer Career Center, Ft Rucker, AL. All other WO selectees will be reassigned to their first WO assignment with TDY enroute at Ft Rucker, AL for the Warrant Officer Candidate School (WOCS) and TDY enroute at their basic technical course (wherever the school is located). Movement of family members is authorized to the location where the WO selectee is to be permanently assigned after training.

Chapter 11

Orientation Packet

WOCS Orientation Packet
1. PURPOSE.

The purpose of this packet is to provide information to help you prepare for Warrant Officer Candidate School (WOCS).

2. COURSE OVERVIEW

a. Report in the Army Combat Uniform (ACU) to Headquarters & Headquarters Company (HHC), U.S. Army Warrant Officer Career College (WOCC), building 5901 on Skychief Street. We encourage you to arrive by 1500 or earlier if possible on your report date. Bring the enclosed Pre-Reporting Checklist with all applicable documents required to begin training. HHC Cadre or the Candidate Duty Officer will provide in-processing instructions and assign you a room in the billets. On report day, the class will have formation in the HHC area for WOCS orientation. You will be issued a Warrant Officer Candidate Standing Operating Procedure (WOC SOP); study it and pay close attention during the orientation. Additional information is available at: http://usacac.army.mil/organizations/cace/wocc/courses/wocs

b. TAC Officers and other cadre members at the WOCC educate, train, and evaluate each candidate in the following areas: leadership, academics, and performance in the garrison and field environment. Moreover, TAC Officers advise, counsel, develop, and make recommendations concerning the progress of each candidate. They demand maximum performance and strive to set the example for all candidates to follow. In order to graduate WOCS, candidates must pass all course requirements.

3. ENROLLMENT/COURSE PREREQUISITES

You must:

a. Meet all application and selection prerequisites outlined by the Warrant Officer Procurement Program and the Selection Board.

b. Meet the medical fitness standards for WOCS in AR 40-501, Chapter 2. The three-event APFT will be administered on day three. If you fail the APFT you will not be enrolled in WOCS training. The only authorized alternate event is the walk, and then only with HQDA, DCS G-3/5/7 approval. In addition, you will be required to participate in foot marches and carry a rucksack with a prescribed weight.

c. Meet the height and weight screening criteria of the Army Weight Control Program. If you exceed weight standards, you will be measured for percentage of body fat. If you exceed body fat standards you will be removed from the program in accordance with AR 350-1 & AR 600-9.

d. Possess an initial issue of serviceable clothing as outlined in AR 670-1 and AR 700-84. See Appendix A (Males), Appendix B (Females) and Appendix C (All).

4. SECURITY CLEARANCE REQUIREMENTS

The Joint Personnel Adjudication System (JPAS) is the Army system of record for security clearance eligibility and access. You must have a SECRET clearance upon your arrival at HHC. We recommend you check with your unit security officer to ensure the correct access is granted in JPAS. **If you do not meet security clearance requirements you will be returned to your home station.**

5. CONDUCT AND APPEARANCE

You are required to present a neat, professional appearance IAW AR 670-1 and DA Pam 670-1. Mustaches are not permitted in WOCS. If you have any tattoos, ensure that they comply with AR 670-1, paragraph 3-3, 3(g); DA Pam 670-1, paragraph 3-3; and ALARACT message 082-2014.

6. DINING FACILITY

You will use the Consolidated Dining Facility. Your class will march as a unit to and from the dining facility.

7. FINANCES

a. It is your responsibility to insure your financial matters are in order before your arrival. A report of indebtedness or bad checks may result in your removal from training until the problem is resolved. Recurring problems of this nature may result in elimination from the course.

b. Do not waste money purchasing unauthorized items. You will be given ample time to purchase required items after your arrival. The average course costs have been $300 to $400 for alterations, laundry and class/personal items. The taxi fee from Dothan airport to Fort Rucker is around $60. Once training begins, you will be limited to $350 on hand. You are authorized to have personal checks, traveler checks, and ATM cards during the course.

8. MILITARY CLOTHING

Verify that you have the military clothing required for the course.

Do not waste money buying all new uniforms if your old ones are serviceable IAW AR 670-1; however, if you have missing or unserviceable items, purchase replacements from your local Military Clothing Sales Store (MCSS). The Fort Rucker MCSS may not have all the basic issue items required. Appendix A and B list all military clothing requirements for males and females. If you report from Basic Training with ill-fitting uniforms (too large, too small, etc.) contact the HHC cadre for direct exchange.

a. The ACU with tan boots is the daily duty uniform.

b. If you are Reserve Component, CTA 50-900 (paragraph 8b and table 3) authorizes you to receive two additional sets of ACUs through your unit supply prior to your arrival.

c. If you are attending WOCS in a TDY or ADT status wear the unit patch of your current or last unit. All others wear the Aviation Center patch.

d. If you are an inter-service transfer or have six months or more break in service you must report to HHC supply with a copy of your DD Form 214 in order to receive basic clothing issue from Fort Rucker MCSS. If you meet this criterion you are authorized to have patches and name tapes issued at the government expense. Recommend you report early to allow time to receive the basic clothing issue prior to the start of your class.

e. Sign in wearing the ACU with patrol cap. Soldiers who are authorized to wear the maroon/tan beret and black jump boots will only wear these items to the graduation.

f. Wait until you get to HHC to mark your equipment to ensure it is marked IAW WOCS policy.

g. You will wear the Army Service Uniform (ASU) for WOCS graduation. **The Army Service Uniform is a graduation requirement; those who do not possess it will not graduate this course.**

9. PRIVATELY OWNED VEHICLES

On the second day of in-processing you will park your POV in the designated class area, where it will remain for the duration of your time in WOCS. Store valuable personal items in a designated area, not in your POV. Every Sunday you will be allowed to start and idle your vehicle to prevent battery and engine problems.

10. PRIVATELY OWNED WEAPONS (POW)

We recommend that you leave any POW at your place of residence. If you have a POW with you, report it immediately to the HHC cadre (XO or Operations Officer). If it is after duty hours, have the Candidate Duty Officer notify HHC cadre by phone. You will register your weapon with the military police and store it in the arms room until you complete the course. Do not store any privately owned weapons (shotgun, rifle, or handgun) in your POV. Ensure you receive a briefing on how you are to draw your weapon from the arms room after the course.

11. MEDICAL

a. Ensure your annual Periodic Health Assessment (PHA) is current in the Army's Medical Protection System (MEDPROS) and will not expire while attending WOCS.

b. Notify the Warrant Officer Recruiting Team or HHC cadre if your medical status changes after selection for WOCS. You must provide HHC cadre a copy of any approved HQDA DCS G-3/5/7 waiver during in-processing. If you receive a profile while in training, you will be required to have an updated DD Form 2808 prior to continuing training. If you are assigned to HHC while on medical or administrative hold you will be required to perform duties within the limits of your profile.

12. STATIC ITEMS

Static items are not authorized. A static item is anything that duplicates an item that you display for inspections, or an inspected item that is hidden for the purpose of evading inspection. You may be eliminated from the course for possession of a static item after the course begins. You will have ample opportunity to store extra items in a security room on your first day of active training, so do not throw duplicate items away. Avoid having items that may be considered "static" by waiting until arrival at HHC to purchase required items.

13. UNAUTHORIZED ITEMS

You are not permitted to use certain clothing items, equipment and products in WOCS; items considered to give you an unfair advantage over others. Appendix E contains a list of unauthorized items.

14. ALCOHOLIC BEVERAGES AND TOBACCO USE

You may neither consume nor possess alcoholic beverages or tobacco products while assigned to WOCS. This restriction applies from the date of sign-in to date of departure, regardless of your status (i.e., wait status, active class, admin/medical hold, or holdover). Violation of this restriction can result in your immediate elimination.

15. MAIL

If you request a mailbox it will be issued when you in-process.

16. TELEPHONES AND CELLULAR PHONES

You are not authorized to use military phones for personal business. Personal cellular phones are authorized during scheduled times while in-processing. Once training begins, you will not have telephone privileges until your class earns those privileges (usually after the first two weeks). At HHC, you are encouraged to call or email your family members to inform them of your safe arrival and to advise them of your new address (once you receive your P.O. Box assignment). Do not store cellular phones in your POV.

17. AKO ACCOUNT

You must have an AKO account. Register in advance at www.us.army.mil. We recommend that you renew your password one week prior to your arrival so it will not expire during your time in WOCS. A computer lab is available at HHC for your use. Prior to training, upload all documents required to your personal folder in AKO (Senior TAC essay, autobiography, awards, lease, marriage certificate, etc.).

18. MOVING DEPENDENTS

You will be in a TDY and return status while at WOCS regardless of MOS (Aviators are IAW ALARACT Message 044/2014 dated 21 Feb 14) and movement of your dependents will not be authorized. Moving your family at your own expense may create undue hardship and is not reimbursable.

19. WARRANT OFFICER NETWORK (WO Net)

https://www.milsuite.mil/book/community/spaces/apf/warrant_
officer_network_(wo_net)/warrant_officercareer_college/content.

You may join the WO Net on the Army Professional Forums by creating a "MilBook" account and identify yourself as a candidate to gain access. The Warrant Officer Career College through the "MilBook website" has an area within the WO Net for your WOCS class to collaborate with each other prior to the start of WOCS. Once you have gained authorization or access to the

"MilBook" website, you will click on the following menus: Army Professional Forums > Warrant Officer Network (WO Net) > Warrant Officer Career College > Content > Class number (ie, 14-xx) discussion group.

If you still have questions on items to bring, contact HHC for information. Phone 334-255-1287/1967 or DSN 558-1287/1967.

ENCLOSURE

WOCS Pre-Reporting Checklist

APPENDICES

Appendix A Inventory Form – Male Clothing Requirements

Appendix B Inventory Form – Female Clothing Requirements

Appendix C Inventory Form – Required Additional Items

Appendix D Inventory Form – Optional Items Appendix E Unauthorized Items

Appendix F Sample Report of Medical Examination

Appendix G MSAF Instructions

Warrant Officer Candidate School Pre-Reporting Checklist

Warrant Officer Candidate School Pre-Reporting Checklist

NAME (type or print)		SSN	
UNIT		DOR:	BASD (AC only)
COURSE TITLE **Warrant Officer Candidate School**		START DATE:	

Supervisor Initial	Soldier Initial	**PART I – PRE-EXECUTION (D-90 to D-1)**
		Unit verified the Soldier has a valid WOCS ATRRS seat and date?
		Candidate has all course information, read the entire welcome packet (at http://usacac.army.mil/cac2/wocc/wocourses.asp) and viewed all links related to WOCS?
		Possesses required clothing/equipment IAW WOCS orientation packet?
		Soldier successfully passed physical fitness requirement on standard 3-event APFT administered within 30 days of scheduled departure for WOCS? Only alternate event is walk, which must be approved by exception to policy through Army G-3. Must score 60 points in each event (receive a "GO" in the authorized alternate event). Approved exceptions will not preclude participation in foot marches or carrying a rucksack. (Bring DA Form 705, APFT Scorecard)
		Soldier meets height and weight standards of AR 600-9?
		Adequate cash/traveler checks/Government Credit Card?
		15 copies of individual orders received? (PCS for Aviation.)
		School mailing address/telephone numbers received for family?
		Soldier's transportation requirements completed?
		Valid Common Access Card (CAC) and ID tags (1 pr)
		Personnel Data Sheet?
		MSAF requirements completed? See instructions at Appendix 7 to WOCS Orientation Packet.
		If corrective lenses are required, Soldier has a set of military prescription eyeglasses.
		DL Phase 1 Candidates only: Soldier has completed WOCS Phase 1 DL NLT 14 days prior to scheduled arrival at WOCS. Students will only have 90 days to complete DL phase upon enrollment. Ensure you print your grades within 5 days of completion and be prepared to turn them in upon arrival at WOCS.

Unit POC List:

Commander	Work phone	Home phone
First Sergeant	Work phone	Home phone
ARNG/USAR Unit Tech/AGR	Work phone	Home phone
Unit FAX	Unit Email	

Equipment Qualifications (if applicable)

YES / NO	Soldier has current military and civilian vehicle operator license(s) through end of course?
	List special equipment qualifications (e.g., bus driver. Bring DA Form 348):
	Completed the Army Accident Avoidance Course at https://www.lms.army.mil (Use "Catalog Search" to register for the online course)? Bring your certificate.

Page 1 of 2

Checklist - 1

Soldier Initial	PART II – REQUIREMENTS
	Joint Personnel Adjudication System (JPAS) verification of SECRET level access (no printout is required). Soldiers are required to complete ALL security submissions, e.g., e-QIP, fingerprints, etc., prior to reporting to WOCS. Soldiers who do not possess a SECRET Clearance will not be enrolled in WOCS.
	Handcarry all three pages of the approved DD Form 2808, Report of Medical Examination (Chapter 2, AR 40-501). The Report of Medical Examination must be no more than 24 months old from the date signed by the examining physician as of the projected WOCS graduation date for technical MOS candidates, and 18 months for aviation candidates. *A new physical examination is required if the physical will expire prior to the WOCS graduation date.*
	If you have a medical profile handcarry the DA Form 3349, Physical Profile, signed by your commander. Remember that you must be able to pass the standard 3-event APFT. No alternate events are authorized unless approved by exception to policy through Army G-3. Approved exceptions will not preclude participation in daily PT, road marches, or carrying a rucksack.

Handcarry the following records. All must have been screened and updated within 30 days of your departure for WOCS by the unit S-1 or supporting personnel office.

	Your Enlisted Record Brief (ERB), SGLI Election, Record of Emergency Data, DA 2-1, and/or ARNG/USAR Personnel Qualification Record. AC only, also your DA 61, Application for Appointment, pages 1-3.
	The following documents are essential for ensuring that the DD Form 214, Certificate of Release/Discharge from Active duty, issued prior to your receiving WO1 is complete and correct. Entries on DD 214 must be verified against copies the source documents. • Copies of orders for all awards, decorations, and qualification badges. • Previously issued DD Form 214 or DD Form 220, Active Duty Report • Proof of deployment if not annotated on your ERB • Initial enlistment contract(s) for AC Soldiers with a break in service; pages 4/1, 4/2, and 4/3 *For those who were in ARNG and USAR:* • Retirement Points Worksheet, previous DD 214, or NGB 22 for ARNG and USAR • A copy of the contract and orders bringing you into the ARNG/USAR • Copies of orders for all ADSW/ADOS periods and all amendments/extensions • AGR Title 10 or Title 32: Copies of orders bringing you into AGR with all amendments/extension
	ARNG/USAR may be required to provide copies of lease/mortgage agreement, marriage license/certificate or proof of court ordered child support in order to receive BAH entitlements

I have been counseled and have read all requirements applicable to the WOCS. Attendance at this course and class will not pose any known hardship on me and/or my family that would detract from, or prevent me from, successfully completing course requirements.

Candidate's Signature: _____ Date:_____

I have reviewed the above candidate's qualifications and potential to successfully complete this course; have counseled him/her on these requirements and hereby verify his/her readiness to attend same.

Commanding Officer (typed or printed name) _____

Signature _____ Date:_____

Unit commanders will ensure all candidates enrolled in WOCS meet course prerequisites. Candidates who report for training must have in their possession a completed pre-execution checklist signed by the candidate and the unit commander, along with other required documents. The commander can also certify the completion of prerequisite testing/evaluation (i.e., FAST test). The commander's signature certifies that the candidate meets the stated course prerequisites. Candidates reporting for training without the required supporting documents and a completed checklist signed by the candidate and unit commander will be returned to their unit.

Page 2 of 2

Checklist - 2

I have been counseled and have read all requirements applicable to the Warrant Officer Candidate Course (WOCS). Attendance at this course and class will not pose any known hardship on me and/or my family that would detract from or prevent me from successfully completing course requirements.

Candidate's Signature: _____ Date: _____

I have reviewed the above candidate's qualifications and potential to successfully complete this course;

have counseled him/her on these requirements and hereby verify his/her readiness to attend same.

_____

Commanding Officer (typed or printed name)
Signature_____
Date:_____

Unit commanders will ensure all candidates enrolled in WOCS meet course prerequisites. Candidates who report for training must have in their possession a completed pre-execution checklist, signed by the candidate and the unit commander. Unit commander can further certify the completion of prerequisite testing/evaluation (i.e., FAST test). Documentary evidence of security clearance, physical profile, and other non-routine prerequisites are required in addition to the pre-execution checklist. The unit commander's signature on the pre-execution checklist will suffice as certification that the candidate meets course prerequisites (as stated above) IAW all requirements of the course. Candidates reporting for training without the required supporting documents, and a completed checklist signed by the candidate and unit commander, will be returned to their unit. This checklist is a pre-enrollment requirement for the Warrant Officer Candidate School.

NOTE: Close to graduation you will review your draft DD 214. To become a Warrant Officer you will first be discharged from the Army. Your DD 214 is a permanent document and you have one chance to make any additions to it, such as adding awards. Bring your "Brag Book" with you and get it done right the first time. The S1 will want to see proof (certificates or orders) of any changes not reflected on your ERB.

Appendix A

WOCS Military Clothing Requirements
INVENTORY FORM - MALE PERSONNEL

Item	REQ	Additional Optional	O/H
Bag, Duffel, Nylon, OG	1 each	1 each	
Belt, Black, Web (brass tip)	1 each		
Belt, Riggers, Desert Sand 503	1 each	1 each	
Beret, Black, with flash (also maroon or tan if authorized to wear)	1 each	1 each	
Boots, Combat, Tan (must be 8-10 inch height; no zippers)	2 pair	1 pair-field	
Buckle, Belt (brass)	1 each		
Cap, Patrol ACU	2 each		
Cap, Synthetic Microfleece, Green (IPFU)	1 each	1 each	
Coat, Army Service Blue (AB 450)	1 each		
Coat, All Weather, Double-breasted, Black, w/liner	1 each		
Coat, ACU	4 each	2 each	
Drawers, White, Tan, or Brown, Jockey or Boxer	7 each		
Glove, Inserts, Cold, Foliage Green, Black or Tan	2 pair		
Gloves, Shell, Leather, Black or Foliage Green	1 pair		
Gloves, Black, Leather, Unisex, Dress	1 pair		
Jacket, Improved Physical Fitness Uniform (IPFU)	1 each	1 each	
*Rucksack, Large w/Frame	1 each		
Pants, IPFU	1 each	1 each	
Trunks, IPFU	3 each	2 each	
Shirt, Long Sleeve, IPFU	2 each	2 each	
Shirt, Short Sleeve, IPFU	3 each	2 each	
Necktie, Black (no clip on)	1 each		
Shirt, Long sleeve, White (ASU) AW 521	1 each		
Shirt, Short sleeve, White (ASU) AW 521	1 each	1 each	
Shoes, Dress, Black	1 pair		
Socks, Dress, Black	2 pair		
Socks, Boot, Black, Tan, or Green	7 pair		
Towel, Bath, Brown	4 each	2 each	
Trousers, ASU w/belt loops, AB 451	2 each		
Trousers, ACU	4 each	2 each	
Undershirt, Cotton, White	2 each		
Undershirt, Cotton, Tan	7 each		
**Washcloth, Cotton, Brown	4 each	2 each	

1. The above list shows military clothing items required to be displayed and/or accounted for throughout the course.
2. An asterisk (*) indicates an item you must obtain from your Central Issue Facility if you currently possess the item. If you are unable to obtain the item, you must bring a signed Memorandum from your commander stating the reason(s).
3. A double asterisk (**) indicates an item deleted from the FY12 clothing bag issue.
4. I have physically inventoried all required military clothing and annotated the correct quantities on hand.

WOC _____Class No. _____Signature _____Date:_____

NOTE: Less is Better! Every item on your list will be on display and will be used. ACU caps and Boots are rotated daily. Your 7 t-shirts will be worn, one per day of the week. TAC Officers have been known to unroll a T-Shirt one week, place a small piece of paper in it and roll it up and replace it in your display. At the following week's inspection if the paper is still in the t-shirt, you will be accused of cheating and placed on Commander's Probation. ROTATE YOUR CLOTHING AS REQUIRED!

Appendix B

WOCS Military Clothing Requirements
INVENTORY FORM - FEMALE PERSONNEL

Item	REQ	Additional *Optional*	O/H
Bag, Duffel, Nylon, OG	1 each	1 each	
Belt, black,1" web (brass tip)	1 each		
Belt, Riggers, Desert Sand 503	1 each	1 each	
Beret, black, with flash (also bring maroon or tan if authorized to wear)	1 each	1 each	
Boots, Combat, Tan (must be 8-10 inch height; no zippers)	2 pair	1 pair-field	
*Brassieres (sports brassieres authorized)	5 each	2 each	
Buckle, Belt (brass) 1 and 1/8"	1 each		
Cap, Patrol, ACU	2 each		
Cap, Synthetic Microfleece, Green (IPFU)	1 each	1 each	
Coat, Army Service Blue (AB 450)	1 each		
Coat, All Weather, Double-breasted, Black, w/liner	1 each		
Coat, ACU	4 each	2 each	
Glove, Inserts, Cold, Foliage Green, Black, or Tan	2 pair		
Gloves, Shell, Leather, Black or Foliage Green	1 pair		
Gloves, Black, Leather, Unisex, Dress	1 pair		
Jacket, Improved Physical Fitness Uniform (IPFU)	1 each	1 each	
Pants, IPFU	1 each	1 each	
*Rucksack, Large w/ Frame	1 each		
Trunks, IPFU	3 each	2 each	
Shirt, Long Sleeve, IPFU	2 each	2 each	
Shirt, Short Sleeve, IPFU	3 each	2 each	
Neck tab, Woman's Shirt, Black	1 each		
Shirt, Long sleeve, White (ASU) AW 521	1 each		
Shirt, Short sleeve, White (ASU) AW 521	1 each	1 each	
Shoes, Black, Poromeric (Oxfords)	1 pair		
Pumps, Black (purchased with annual clothing allowance)	1 pair		
Skirt, ASU, AB 450	1 each		
Slacks, ASU w/belt loops AB 451	1 each	1 each	
Socks, Boot, Black, Tan, or Green	7 pair		
Socks, Dress, Black	2 pair		
Towel, Bath, Brown	4 each	2 each	
Trousers, ACU	4 each	2 each	
**Underwear, Cotton, White	7 each		
Undershirt, Cotton, Tan	7 each		
**Washcloth, Cotton, Brown	4 each	2 each	

1. The above list shows military clothing items required to be displayed and/or accounted for throughout the course.
2. An asterisk (*) indicates an item you must obtain from your Central Issue Facility if you do not currently posses. If you are unable to obtain the item, you must bring a signed Memorandum from your Commander stating the reason you are unable to obtain the item.
3. A double asterisk (**) indicates an item deleted from the FY12 clothing bag issue.
4. I have physically inventoried all required military clothing and annotated the correct quantities on hand.

WOC _____ Class No. _____ Signature _____ Date: _____

NOTE: Less is Better! Every item on your list will be on display and will be used. ACU caps and Boots are rotated daily. Your 7 t-shirts will be worn, one per day of the week. TAC Officers have been known to unroll a T-Shirt one week, place a small piece of paper in it and roll it up and replace it in your display. At the following week's inspection if the paper is still in the t-shirt, you will be accused of cheating and placed on Commander's Probation. ROTATE YOUR CLOTHING AS REQUIRED!

Appendix C
REQUIRED ADDITIONAL ITEMS INVENTORY

ITEM	QUANTITY	ON HAND QTY
Serviceable Athletic/Running Shoes	1 pr	
All White Athletic ankle or crew length Socks	6 pr	
Eyeglass retaining strap (if wearing eyeglasses)	1 ea	
Shower Shoes	1 pr	
Staedtler Lumocolor Fine Tip Markers (for map marking)	2 ea	
Protractor (1:50,000 scale)	1 ea	
Boot care kit	1 ea	
Personal hygiene items	As needed	
Padlock (combination preferable)	1 ea	
Clear Double-Stick Scotch Tape	1 roll	
White 1" Medical Tape (Fort Rucker MCSS)	2 rolls	
3"x5" Cards, Ruled	1 pkg	
Soap (bar or liquid)	1 ea	
Eyewear, ballistic, Army Protective Eyewear List (APEL)-approved, black (Wiley-X, ESS, Oakley M-Frame, Revision Sawfly, Uvex) Note: If you were issued eye protection from your CIF or during RFI, bring them. If you were never issued eye pro, you will receive them from CIF. Also, bring prescribed optical inserts, if needed.	1 ea	
Safety whistle (pocket size)	1 ea	
Hearing protection (foam or Army-issued flange type)	2 pr	
Officer US and branch insignia for ASU (may purchase from Fort Rucker MCSS)	1 set	

1. I understand that I am required to possess these items during WOCS.

2. The required quantity is also the authorized quantity. Duplicate type items are considered "static" items and could be grounds for elimination from the program. Prior to purchasing any additional items, verify with your WOCS TAC Officer that you are authorized to possess them.

3. I understand that I may purchase required additional items prior to my arrival at Fort Rucker. However, waiting until I sign in at WOCS to purchase the listed items will ensure I have the correct items (e.g., color, type, etc.).

4. My signature below indicates I have physically inventoried all required purchase items (both required and authorized), that I am in compliance with the maximum authorized quantities, and that prior to purchasing additional items I will verify with my WOCS TAC Officer that I am authorized to possess them.

5. Required TA-50 will be issued at the Central Issue Facility during inprocessing.

Tips: Small "Children Sized" Toothbrushes work better in your display. White toothbrushes do not show toothpaste residue like red or blue ones do.

Neutrogena or Dove soap won't leave a residue in the showers.

Also make sure any item you bring is serviceable. All buttons securely attached, Velcro tabs work, no rips or holes especially in knee and elbow areas, ACUs with too much fading, sweat rings in hats and so forth.

Turn pockets inside out and trim loose threads and frayed seams with sharp scissors. Comb or pick out the fuzz in the hook side of the Velcro.

Appendix D

Note: These items are not required but can be useful during the course. You may decide to purchase either 1 item or as many as you think you may need during the course.

OPTIONAL ITEMS						
ITEM	**Qty**	**O/H**	**ITEM**	**Qty**	**O/H**
Baby wipes			Moleskin		
Sewing kit			Nonmilitary or modified issue boot inserts		
Civilian long underwear – black or Army brown (Seasonal)			Nonmilitary or modified issue boot socks		
Soldier's Manual of Common Tasks, Warrior Skills Level One			Pace count cord		
EM Nu black paint for subdued insignia			Pantyhose (females)		
Extra bootlaces			Small flashlight for field use		
Foot powder			Religious writings		
Gore-Tex/Polypro gloves (black) – no logos visible (Seasonal)			Spandex type athletic wear/underwear (Black or gray)		
Gore-Tex/Polypro socks (black) (Seasonal)			Waterproof bags, quart or gallon size (zip lock)		
Hand sanitizer (small bottles to fit in pockets)			Wire hangers	15ea	
Insect repellant			5" x 8" cards (plain on at least one side)	1 pk	
Laundry bag (extra)			Alarm clock (w/o radio) plug-in		
Letter writing material			Small mirror		
Map pens					
Gore-Tex jacket/ACU color or Army issued equivalent (Ensure your last name is sewn on left arm pocket). Due to unpredictable weather, it is highly recommended that you bring this item that you will be allowed to wear regardless of standardization of troop formation.	1 each				

At a minimum, the items on this list are required to ensure your success while at WOCS. Due a very limited storage space, you should bring only the items on this list.

*** All TA-50 will be issued at the Central Issue Facility. Do not bring your personal TA-50 items with the exception of the large rucksack with frame.

1. I understand that I may purchase authorized additional items prior to my arrival at Fort Rucker. However, waiting until I sign in at WOCS to purchase the listed items will ensure I have the correct items (e.g., color, type, etc).

2. My signature below indicates I have physically inventoried all purchase items (both required and authorized), that I am in compliance with the maximum authorized quantities, and that prior to purchasing additional items I will verify with my WOCS TAC Officer that I am authorized to possess them.

WOC _____ Class No._____

Signature _____ Date: _____

NOTE: Everything you bring is on display and becomes an INSPECTABLE item. This is one of those times where less is better.

Appendix E

UNAUTHORIZED ITEMS

1. The following list indicates those items which have been identified as unauthorized for possession or use while attending WOCS. Possession or use of unauthorized items may result in elimination from the school for attempting to gain an unfair advantage over fellow candidates or for failure to comply with course guidelines and standards.

2. If you have any questions concerning the use of any products or aids, ask your TAC Officer. If you are not authorized to use an item, it does not mean that you have to throw it away. Storage locations are available. Co-ordinate with your TAC Officer(s) to place all unauthorized items (except for flammables) in the security room or class amnesty box:

- Tobacco products (*)
- Cap stiffeners (*)
- Civilian clothes
- Commercial cleaning products, items, and waxes (not issued by supply) (*)
- Computer, e.g., PDA/ pocket PC
- Performance-enhancing and weight loss dietary supplements (*)
- Alcohol (*)
- Correction tape/liquid
- All-weather coat with sewn-in liner
- Knife with blade in excess of four inches (*)
- Pornography (*)

Note: **DO NOT** bring items marked with an asterisk (*) to school. WOCC will not provide storage for these items.

NOTE: We were allowed to store extra items in the security room, such as extra razors, hygiene stuff, medications, extra clothing and so forth and the TAC Officers would let us get stuff out at later dates. No need to throw away items that exceed what you have on hand.

One of the common items we stored in the Security rooms were irons. No matter how well you cleaned your iron, it would fail to pass inspection.

Appendix F

<table>
<tr><td colspan="2" rowspan="2">REPORT OF MEDICAL EXAMINATION</td><td>1. DATE OF EXAMINATION
(YYYYMMDD)
20121022</td><td>2. SOCIAL SECURITY NUMBER
555-55-5555</td></tr>
</table>

> Expiration date is 2 years from exam date. Must be valid through WOCS graduation.

> Verify SSN is correct

... STATEMENT

..., and 4346; and E.O. 9397.

...ination of medical fitness for enlistment, induction, appointment and retention for ...n will also be used for medical boards and separation of Service members from

ROUTINE USE(S): None.

DISCLOSURE: Voluntary; however, failure by an applicant to provide the information may result in delay or possible rejection of the individual's application to enter the Armed Forces. For an Armed Forces member, failure to provide the information may result in the individual being placed in a non-deployable status.

3. LAST NAME - FIRST NAME - MIDDLE NAME (SUFFIX) LEE, BRUCE M	4. HOME ADDRESS (Street, Apartment Number, City, State and ZIP Code) 1234 Hopkins Drive Apt #123, Columbia SC 29061	5. HOME TELEPHONE NUMBER (Include Area Code) (813) 555-5555

6. GRADE SFC	7. DATE OF BIRTH (YYYYMMDD) 19741015	8. AGE 38	9. SEX Female X Male	10.a. RACIAL CATEGORY (X one or more) American Indian or Alaska Native / Asian / Black or African American / White / X Native Hawaiian or Other Pacific Islander	b. ETHNIC CATEGORY Hispanic/Latino X Not Hispanic/Latino

11. TOTAL YEARS GOVERNMENT SERVICE a. MILITARY 12 b. CIVILIAN	12. AGENCY (Non-Service Members Only)	13. ORGANIZATION UNIT AND UIC/CODE HHC, 264TH (WYQSCB0)

14.a. RATING OR SPECIALTY (Aviators Only)	b. TOTAL FLYING TIME	c. LAST SIX MONTHS

15.a. SERVICE X Army / Navy / Marine Corps / Air Force	b. COMPONENT Coast Guard / X Active Duty / Reserve / National Guard	c. PURPOSE OF EXAMINATION Enlistment / X Commission / Re... / Separa...	Medical Board / Retirement / U.S. Service Ac... / ROTC Scholarship ...ram	Other	16. NAME OF EXAMINING LOCATION, AND ADDRESS (Include ZIP Code) 28th MSC 2800 Doolittle Dr. Ft Jackson, SC 29061

> Must have "X" in Commission or Other, with WOCS specified

CLINICAL EVALUATION (Check each item in appropriate column. Enter ... evaluate... Enter pertinent item ...m 73 and use additional

	Nor-mal	Ab-norm
17. Head, face, neck, and scalp	X	
18. Nose	X	
19. Sinuses	X	
20. Mouth and throat	X	
21. Ears - General (Int. and ext. canals/Auditory acuity under item 71)	X	
22. Drums (Perforation)	X	
23. Eyes - General (Visual acuity and refraction under items 61 - 63)	X	
24. Ophthalmoscopic	X	
25. Pupils (Equality and reaction)	X	
26. Ocular motility (Associated parallel movements, nystagmus)	X	
27. Heart (Thrust, size, rhythm, sounds)	X	
28. Lungs and chest (Include breasts)	X	
29. Vascular system (Varicosities, etc.)	X	
30. Anus and rectum (Hemorrhoids, Fistulae) (Prostate if indicated)	X	
31. Abdomen and viscera (Include hernia)	X	
32. External genitalia (Genitourinary)	X	
33. Upper extremities	X	
34. Lower extremities (Except feet)	X	
35. Feet (See Item 35 Continued)	X	
36. Spine, other musculoskeletal	X	
37. Identifying body marks, scars, tattoos		X
38. Skin, lymphatics	X	
39. Neurolog...	X	
40. Psychiat...	X	
41. Pelvic (F...		X
42. Endocrine	X	

> Ensure dental category is annotated.

35. FEET (Continued) (Circle category)
Normal Arch   Mild   Asymptomatic
Pes Cavus   Moderate
Pes Planus   Severe   Symptomatic

43. DENTAL DEFECTS AND DISE... (Please explain. Use dental form if completed by dentist. If dental examination not done by dental officer, explain in Item 44.)
X Acceptable
Not Acceptable   Class   II

SAMPLE

LAST NAME - FIRST NAME - MIDDLE NAME (SUFFIX)								SOCIAL SECURITY NUMBER		
LEE, BRUCE M								555-55-5555		

LABORATORY FINDINGS

45. URINALYSIS		a. Albumin		46. URINE HCG		47. H/H		48. BLOOD TYPE	
		b. Sugar							

TESTS	RESULTS	HIV SPECIMEN ID LABEL	DRUG TEST SPECIMEN ID LABEL
49. HIV			
50. DRUGS			
51. ALCOHOL			
52. OTHER			
a. PAP SMEAR			
b.			
c.			

Ensure LAB/HIV results are entered

MEASUREMENTS AND OTHER FINDINGS

53. HEIGHT	54. WEIGHT	55. MIN WGT - MAX WGT	MAX BF %	56. TEMPERATURE	57. PULSE
	lbs.				

58. BLOOD PRESSURE			59. RED/GREEN *(Army Only)*	60. OTHER VISION TEST
a. 1ST	b. 2ND	c. 3RD		
SYS.	SYS.	SYS.		
DIAS.	DIAS.	DIAS.		

61. DISTANT VISION		62. REFRACTION BY AUTOREFRACTION OR MANIFEST				63. NEAR VISION			
Right 20/	Corr. to 20/	By	S.	CX		Right 20/	Corr. to 20/	by	
Left 20/	Corr. to 20/	By	S.	CX		Left 20/	Corr. to 20/	by	

64. HETEROPHORIA *(Specify distance)*								
ES°	EX°	R.H.	L.H.	Prism div.	Prism Conv CT		NPR	PD

65. ACCOMMODATION		66. COLOR VISION *(Test used and result)*		67. DEPTH PERCEPTION *(Test used and score)* AFVT	
Right	Left	PIP	/14	Uncorrected	Corrected

68. FIELD OF VISION	69. NIGHT VISION *(Test used and score)*	70. INTRAOCULAR TENSION	
		O.D.	O.S.

71a. AUDIOMETER	Unit Serial Number						71b. Unit Serial Number							72a. READING ALOUD TEST	
Date Calibrated *(YYYYMMDD)*							Date Calibrated *(YYYYMMDD)*								
HZ	500	1000	2000	3000	4000	6000	HZ	500	1000	2000	3000	4000	6000	SAT	UNSAT
Right							Right							72b. VALSALVA	
Left							Left							SAT	UNSAT

73. NOTES *(Continued)* AND SIGNIFICANT OR INTERVAL HISTORY *(Use additional sheets if necessary.)*

SAMPLE

DD FORM 2808, OCT 2005   Reset   Page 2 of 3 Pages

LAST NAME - FIRST NAME - MIDDLE NAME (SUFFIX)							SOCIAL SECURITY NUMBER		
LEE, BRUCE M							555-55-5555		

74.a. EXAMINEE/APPLICANT (check one)				75. I have been advised of my disqualifying condition.				
X IS QUALIFIED FOR SERVICE				a. SIGNATURE OF EXAMINEE			b. DATE (YYYYMMDD)	
IS NOT QUALIFIED FOR SERVICE							20121023	

PHYSICAL PROFILE

P	U	L	H	E	S	X	PROFI...	...TIALS	DATE (YYYYMMDD)
1	1	1	1	1	1				

Physical must have block 74a checked, showing "IS QUALIFIED FOR SERVICE." If not, you must provide an approved Army G3 waiver of your profile before you are allowed enrollment in WOCS. If the PULHES contains any entry other than "1" you must have a waiver of your profile.

Your signature indicates your knowledge of your physical status and, if applicable, your need for a profile waiver.

QUALIFIED

77. SUMMARY OF DEFECTS AND DIAGNOSES (List diagnoses with item numbers) (Use additional sheets if necessary.)

SAMPLE

78. RECOMMENDATIONS - FURTHER SPECIALIST EXAMINATIONS INDICATED (Specify) (Use additional sheets if necessary.)

79. MEPS WORKLOAD (For MEPS use only)

WKID	ST	DATE (YYYYMMDD)	INITIAL	WKID			...IAL

Must be signed by an MD/Doctor/PA-C or equivalent, NOT a PA or Nurse Practitioner.

80. MEDICAL INSPECTION DATE	HT	WT	%BF	MAX WT	HCG	QUAL	DIS...

81.a. TYPED OR PRINTED NAME OF PHYSICIAN OR EXAMINER	b. SIGNATURE
82.a. TYPED OR PRINTED NAME OF PHYSICIAN OR EXAMINER	b. SIGNATURE
83.a. TYPED OR PRINTED NAME OF DENTIST OR PHYSICIAN (Indicate which)	b. SIGNATURE
84.a. TYPED OR PRINTED NAME OF REVIEWING OFFICER/APPROVING AUTHORITY	b. SIGNATURE

85. This examination has been administratively reviewed for completeness and accuracy.

a. SIGNATURE	b. GRADE	c. DATE (YYYYMMDD)

86. WAIVER GRANTED (If yes, date and by whom)	87. NUMBER OF
YES	ATTACHED SHEETS
NO	

DD FORM 2808, OCT 2005

Reset

Page 3 of 3 Pages

178

Appendix G

Multi-Source Assessment and Feedback (MSAF):

"I believe that multi-dimensional feedback is an important component to holistic leader development. By encouraging input from peers, subordinates, and superiors alike, leaders can better "see themselves" and increase self-awareness. A 360-degree approach applies equally to junior leaders at the squad, platoon, and company level as well as to Senior leaders. The ability to receive honest and candid feedback, in an anonymous manner, is a great opportunity to facilitate positive leadership growth."

—GEN Ray Odierno

1. Access MSAF (https://msaf.army.mil/) or Google search " MSAF"

2. Log in using your Common Access Card (CAC). CAC login required as of 1 Jul 11.

3. Under "Assess" click "Begin Your 360 Event"

4. It then asks if you are ready to begin your 360 Assessment...select "Begin"

5. Select "No" for the PME/CES Class question, then skip to question 2.

6. Select when you want the assessment to end (the date selected must allow the assessment to be completed prior to WOCS), then select "Next."

7. Select "Leader Behavior Scale" out of the 3 options, then click "Next"

8. You will be prompted to enter a minimum of 13 email addresses to create a group for your assessment. This searches the entire Army Directory. You can search by name (and even partial names), rank, and UIC. Once the person is found, check the box by their name and add "Add"

** You will be prompted to put 3 names in the supervisor position, 5 peers, and 5 subordinates.

** You may want to select more than 13 names in case some do not participate in the assessment...you are required to receive 13 RESPONSES in order to complete the event.

** When finished with each group, select "Next"

9. Review the Event Setup will allow you to go back and edit anything you need to. Once you are satisfied with your selections, select "Start My Event"

** There are quite a few instruction pages for how to properly conduct an assessment before being required to assess yourself.

10. Complete the leadership survey as per the directions on the screen. Once done, click "Finish"

** If you cannot complete the assessment all at once, ensure you click "Save & Exit"

11. Now... it's wait time. You must have at least 13 people respond in order to select "Finish my Event"

12. Once a minimum of 13 responses are received, select "Finish my Event," print out the final results, and bring them to WOCS per the pre-execution checklist.

13. **NOTE:** You will be requested to authorize the release of your MSAF results during WOCS. Releasing your MSAF results are optional.

However, when released, your MSAF results will be included in your student packet for cadre to access in order to ensure a 360-degree, multi-dimensional assessment is being performed.

MASF Assessment is a time consuming process so start early!

Student Personnel Data Record

STUDENT PERSONNEL DATA RECORD

STATUS:	DATA REQUIRED BY THE PRIVACY ACT OF 1974
	1. AUTHORITY: 10 USC 3012 2. PRINCIPLE PURPOSE: TO RECORD DATA PERTAINING TO STUDENTS 3. ROUTINE USES: EMERGENCY NOTIFICATION AND BACKGROUND INFORMATION FOR ASSIGNMENT 4. DISCLOSURE IS VOLUNTARY: REFUSAL TO FURNISH DATA WILL NOT ADVERSELY AFFECT STUDENT

NAME (LAST, FIRST, MIDDLE):		DOB:		CLASS #:	SECURITY CLEARANCE:	SEX: F / M
CURRENT ADDRESS:		HOME/CELL PHONE:	RELIGION:	RACE:		PHYSICAL DATE: YR MO

RANK/GRADE:	DOR:	BRANCH:	Enlisted MOS: P: S:	WO1 MOS:	COMPONENT (CIRCLE) RA AGR AR NG _____ State	SOURCE OF COMMISSION:
TDY enroute: Yes____ No___	TD Y and return: Yes___ No____	DATE ARRIVED:	BLOOD TYPE:	ALLERGIES:	MEDICATIONS:	HEIGHT: WEIGHT:
BASD:	TIS:	ETS:	HIGHEST MILITARY EDUCATION:		HIGHEST CIVILIAN EDUCATION:	

UNDER THE PROVISION OF THE "NATIONAL PRIVACY ACT OF 1974," I (CIRCLE ONE) DO / DO NOT GIVE CONSENT TO RELEASE ANY INFORMATION ON THIS CARD TO THIRD PARTIES.

DATE: _____   SIGNATURE: _____

FAMILY AND RELATIVES:

	NAME	ADDRESS	SEX	DOB	REMARKS
SPOUSE:					
DEP:					
DEP:					
DEP:					
DEP:					

YOUR PARENTS: _____ ADDRESS: _____ PHONE: _____

SPOUSE'S PARENTS: _____ ADDRESS: _____ PHONE: _____

VIP'S (GS-14 OR O-6 AND ABOVE)

NAME/RANK:_____
ADDRESS:_____
RELATIONSHIP: _____
BRANCH OF SERVICE: _____ ACTIVE / RETIRED

CLASS HISTORY

CLASS #	FROM	TO

POV (S):	MAKE	MODEL	YEAR	TAG	COLOR
1.					
2.					
3.					

FORWARDING/HOME/LEAVE ADDRESS	PERMANENT HOME OF RECORD/STATE OF RESIDENCE

Be prepared to fill out a standard Student Personnel Data Record form once you arrive at WOCS. Some of the information can be found on your ERB. Also have your family members and parent's addresses with you to help fill out the form. Remember, you are not allowed cell phones while attending WOCS, so go old school and print out the information on a piece of paper and bring it with you.

Warrant Officer Candidate School Pre-Reporting Checklist

NAME (type or print)		SSN	

UNIT		DOR:	BASD (AC only)

COURSE TITLE Warrant Officer Candidate School		START DATE:

1ST Line Leader Initial	Soldier Initial	PART I – PRE-EXECUTION (D-90 to D-1)
		Unit verified the Soldier has a valid WOCS ATRRS seat and date.
		Candidate in receipt of school/course information? Candidates will read the entire welcome packet (at http://usawocc.army.mil), and view all links related to WOCS prior to arrival.
		All required clothing/equipment IAW school/course information packet
		Soldier successfully passed physical fitness requirement on standard 3-event APFT administered within 30 days of scheduled departure for WOCS. No Alternate event is authorized unless approved by exception to policy through Army G-3. Must score 60 points in each event or receive a "GO" in the authorized alternate event. Approved exceptions will not preclude participation in road marches or carrying a rucksack weighing 40 pounds.
		Soldier meets standards of AR 600-9.
		Adequate cash/traveler checks/Government Credit Card?
		10 copies of individual orders received? (PCS for Aviation.)
		School Mailing address/Telephone numbers received? (for family)
		Transportation requirements completed?
		Current/valid identification card
		ID tags (1 pair)
		Army Values card/tag
		If applicable: Candidate requiring corrective lenses has a set of military prescription eyeglasses with military eyeglass strap.

Unit POC List:

Commander	Work phone	Home phone
First Sergeant	Work phone	Home phone
ARNG/USAR Unit Tech/AGR	Work phone	Home phone
Unit FAX	Unit Email	

Equipment Qualifications (if applicable)

YES / NO	Soldier has current military and civilian vehicle operator license(s) through end of course.
	List special equipment qualifications (e.g., bus driver. Bring DA Form 348):

Soldier Initial	**PART II – REQUIRED DOCUMENTS**
	Joint Personnel Adjudication System (JPAS) print out reflecting Secret or Secret level access. Individuals are required to complete ALL security submissions, i.e. EPSQ, fingerprints, etc., prior to reporting to WOCS. Individuals who have not received an Secret Clearance will NOT be allowed to attend WOCS. (Attach if applicable.)
	Approved appointment physical (Chapter 2, AR 40-501). Handcarry this with you. *The Report of Medical Examination (SF 88 or DD Form 2808) must be no more than 24 months old (from the date signed by the examining physician) as of your projected graduation date for technical MOS candidates, and 18 months for aviation candidates. If the physical will expire prior to your graduation date, complete a new physical.*
	If applicable, permanent profile attendees must have a copy of Profile (P2) results, with DA Form 3349 signed by his/her commander. Must be able to pass standard 3-event APFT. No alternate events are authorized unless approved by exception to policy through Army G-3. Approved exceptions will not preclude participation in road marches or carrying a rucksack weighing a minimum of 40 pounds.
All candidates, either PCS or TDY, MUST handcarry the following records/documents. All records must have been screened and updated within 30 days of your departure for WOCS by the unit S-1 or supporting personnel office/company.	
	a. Your complete personnel, updated Enlisted Record Brief, updated SGLI forms and DD 93 (Emergency Data Card).
	b. Copies of all orders for awards, decorations, and qualification badges issued during your current enlistment. If you have been issued a DD Form 214 (Certificate of Release or Discharge from Active Duty), bring it. *(These additional documents are essential to ensuring that the DD Form 214 issued prior to your Warrant Officer appointment is complete and correct. Entries on DD Form 214 must be verified against copies of the source documents.)*
	c. Enlistment contract with Place of Birth, (POB), Place of entry onto active duty, (PLEAD), and Home of Record, (HOR)

I have been counseled and have read all requirements applicable to the Warrant Officer Candidate Course (WOCS). Attendance at this course and class will not pose any known hardship on me and/or my family that would detract from or prevent me from successfully completing course requirements.

Candidate's Signature: _____ Date:_____

I have reviewed the above candidate's qualifications and potential to successfully complete this course; have counseled him/her on these requirements and hereby verify his/her readiness to attend same.

_____

Commanding Officer (typed or printed name)

_____Date:_____

Signature

Unit commanders will ensure all candidates enrolled in WOCS meet course prerequisites. Candidates who report for training must have in their possession a completed pre-execution checklist, signed by the candidate and the unit commander. Unit commander can further certify the completion of prerequisite testing/evaluation (i.e., FAST test). Documentary evidence of security clearance, physical profile, and other non-routine prerequisites are required in addition to the pre-execution checklist. The unit commander's signature on the pre-execution checklist will suffice as certification that the candidate meets course prerequisites (as stated above) IAW all requirements of the course. Candidates reporting for training without the required supporting documents, and a completed checklist signed by the candidate and unit commander, will be returned to their unit. This checklist is a pre-enrollment requirement for the Warrant Officer Candidate School.

Page 2 of 2 (2 Mar 2007)

NOTE: Close to graduation you will review your draft DD 214. To become a Warrant Officer you will first be discharged from the Army. Your DD 214 is a permanent document and you have one chance to make any additions to it, such as adding awards. Bring your "Brag Book" with you and get it done right the first time. The S1 will want to see proof (certificates or orders) of any changes not reflected on your ERB.

Army Knowledge On-line AKO Accounts:

If you don't have an AKO account these directions will help you in getting one.

All selected applicants from other services and civilians accepted into WOCS school are encouraged to review www.futuresoldiers.com website for more information about becoming an US Army Soldier and get an AKO account.

NOTE: It takes up to three days after you visit your MEPS before you can create your AKO account. If you have problems creating your AKO account and it has been three days since you visited the MEPS, contact the fsc@usarec.army.mil

To create your AKO account go to: https://www.us.army.mil

Click the "I Accept" button and follow the "How do I register for an AKO/DKO Account?" question.

Follow the directions displayed based on your status.

When prompted, enter your SSN, DOB, and PEBD (Pay Entry Basic Date). PED is the date you start getting paid in the U.S. Army. When you visited the MEPS, your Army Guidance Counselor gave you some paperwork called the Annex. Your PEBD is printed on your Annex as YYYYMMDD. Ensure you enter this as shown on the registration screen (MM,DD,YYYY).

Complete the remaining questions to finalize your account.

Family Readiness Group (FRG):

IF YOU ARE BRINGING YOUR FAMILY: Candidates authorized to move their dependents to Fort Rucker must do so PRIOR to their report date for WOCS. It is the individual's responsibility to request 10 days Permissive Temporary Duty (PTDY) for house hunting, from the losing command, and to settle their family prior to signing in to HHC. After signing in, candidates will NOT be authorized PTDY until completion of WOCS. Candidates who are intra-service transfers will be processed case-by-case due to the limitations and restrictions placed upon them by their losing branch of service. All personnel arriving to Fort Rucker, PTDY for house hunting, are required to first report to the Post Housing Office (located in Bldg 5700) to have their PTDY paperwork stamped. Officer Candidates are authorized on post quarters, if available.

Welcome Letter from the Family Readiness Group:

Dear Future Fort Rucker Family,

Welcome! We are excited that you are here (or soon will be) and look forward to working with you and your Family to make sure you have the information you need to better prepare you for your assignment to the home of Army Aviation. Families can choose to relocate to the Fort Rucker area while their Soldier is in training, while others choose to relocate after graduation from Warrant Officer Candidate School. Whatever your decision, know that we are here to assist you in any way we can.

Students of 1st WOC are not "permanently" assigned to the Warrant Officer Career College. Many students will complete their WOC training and move onto their next school and duty assignment. For other students, that assignment will be here at Fort Rucker – Flight School. Congratulations!!

Because of the dynamics and length of time for 1st WOC training, there is no student dedicated Family Readiness Group (FRG). In an effort to still provide information to spouses and provide a source to ask any questions you may have, the United States Army Aviation Center of Excellence (USAACE) Family Readiness Support Assistant (FRSA) will serve as a point of contact for information/questions/issues/concerns for Families of 1st WOC students.

The USAACE FRSA's office is located on 7th Avenue. Hours of Operation are Monday – Friday, 8:00 – 4:30pm. Phone: (334) 255-0960 or email: ruck.frgap@conus.army.mil.

The USAACE FRSA posts all current information about military resources / programs / scholarships, as well as Fort Rucker events / activities on the Fort Rucker Family Readiness Support Facebook page: www.facebook.com/fortruckerfamilies

Become a fan, and check it out!

On the day of graduation, if your Soldier will be attending Flight School, he/she will attend unit in-processing for B Co. 1-145th. The in-processing can take several hours depending on the number of graduating students attending Flight School. While the students are in-processing we offer the Families a "Warm Welcome" providing them information about housing (to include a tour, if desired), employment opportunities, and Army Community Service (ACS). The unit Commander also provides information about what Soldiers and Families of Flight School can expect. This event is open to all Families – moms/dads, spouses, children, etc. We look forward to meeting you!

USAACE FRSA
(334) 255-0960
Ruck.frgap@conus.army.mil
www.facebook.com/fortruckerfamily
"Leave no Family Behind"

WOCS Curriculum:

Phase 1 of WOCS is available as either distributed learning (dL) or resident training. Attendance at the Phase 1 (Resident) course is MANDATORY for all Soldiers in the grade of E-1 through E-4 and for E-5's that are not WLC/PLDC graduates.

Phase 1 dL. There is only one Phase 1 dL class scheduled, covering the entire training year. Once you have been enrolled in ATRRS for Course 911-09W (DL), you must access the training at: https://blackboard3.leavenworth.army.mil by logging in with your CAC or AKO user name and password. Supplemental instructions for WOCS Phase 1 dL students:

1. NCOs who are fully qualified/selected (FQS) and fall into one of the following categories are required to complete the Phase 1 dL.

   a. US Army E-5 WLC/PLDC graduates and Army E-6 or higher.

   b. USMC E-5 or higher with WLC/PLDC operational leadership training.

   c. US Navy E-7 or higher (E-5 and E-6 must request a waiver to be enrolled in Phase 1 dL. Proof of operational leadership schooling/experience must be provided to the Commandant, WOCC).

   d. US Air Force E-7 or higher (E-5 and E-6 must request a waiver to be enrolled in Phase 1 dL. Proof of operational leadership schooling/experience must be provided to the Commandant, WOCC).

2. Soldiers (E-1 thru E-4) that have completed WLC/PLDC are PROHIBITED from enrollment into Phase 1 dL. Soldiers promoted or advanced to the grade of E-5 solely to attend WOCS will be disenrolled from the Phase 1 dL and enrolled in the next Phase 1 resident course.

Phase 1 dL is a MANDATORY non-resident course that must be completed not later than two weeks prior to attending resident WOCS Phase 2 training at Fort Rucker or ARNG Regional Training Institute (RTI) locations.

WOCS Course Dates Phase 1 Resident:

Phase 1 Resident. (E5 non-graduate from PLDC/WLC and all E1 to E4. All others ineligible to complete Phase 1 dL) should be enrolled in corresponding Phase 2 class. Example: Student enrolled in Phase 1 (resident) class 06-013 should also be enrolled in Phase 2 class 06-013.

Course Scope:

WOCS provides the basic skills necessary to prepare the Warrant Officer Candidate to become an effective Army Warrant Officer. WOCS incorporates a high stress environment, designed to challenge the Candidate from day one. Additionally, it is used to evaluate and develop the Candidate's potential as a Warrant Officer. WOCS consists of two phases:

a. Phase 1 is available as both dL and Resident. Attendance at the resident phase is mandatory for all in the grade of E1 through E4 prior to entry into the program; non-PLDC/WLC (or equivalent) graduates in the grade of E5; and all prior service Air Force, Navy, or Coast Guard personnel who have not completed Army or Marine Corps basic training. All others will complete phase 1 through dL.

b. The WOCS curriculum is redesigned to provide two different versions of the program; one version is approximately six weeks and four days long and the other is approximately four weeks long. Both versions are tough and demanding. The version a Candidate attends depends on the Candidate's background and experience.

(1) Candidates who are Sergeants (E-5s) who haven't attended the Warrior Leader Course (WLC), previously known as the Primary Leadership Development Course, and those in lower grades attend the 6-week, 4-day version of the course.

(2) All other Army NCOs attend the 4-week resident version after completing a distributive Learning (DL) phase. The DL phase consists of refresher courses aligned with the WLC and contains the same material the Candidates in the long version cover during the first 11 days of the 6-week, 4-day version. Students access the DL material through Army Knowledge Online (AKO). They may complete the DL phase anywhere they can access AKO.

(3) The phase of WOCS (Phase 2) that all Candidates complete in residence consists of academic classes on subjects relevant to the Course of Education such as:

Leadership

Officership

Ethics

History

Oral and Written Communications

These are all topics that are important in helping Candidates develop into effective Warrant Officers. Throughout all resident training, training, advising, and counseling (TAC) Officers mentor candidates and provide them feedback on the effectiveness of their leadership and Officership skills.

WOCS Phase I Prerequisite:

b. Phase 2 is attended as Resident training by all candidates. The listed pre-requisites apply to all candidates.

Information For Course 911-09W (DL)

Back to Course Listing   New Search

School: 020
Course: 911-09W (DL)
Course Title: WARRANT OFFICER CANDIDATE
Academic Hours: 69
Military Career Development Crs Completion (Resident):
Military Career Development Crs Completion (DL):

Location: 5302 OUTLAW STREET, FT RUCKER, AL
Phase: 1

DL Academic Hours: 69

View Course Prequisites

● Class Schedule ○ Nonconducted Classes ○ Cancelled Classes ○ Rescheduled Classes   View

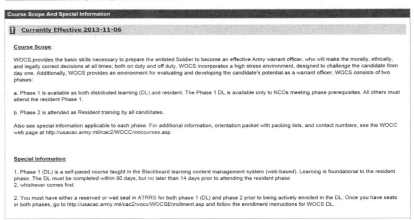

Class Schedule

FY: 2014   **School:** 020   **Course:** 911-09W (DL)   **Phase:** 1   **Course Length:** 1 Weeks 3.0 Days
Course Title: WARRANT OFFICER CANDIDATE
Class Maximum: 100   **Class Optimum:** 100   **Class Minimum:** 1

Class	Prereqs	Report Date	Start Date	End Date	Capacity	Class Type	Street	City	State	Zip
001	View	01 Oct 2013	02 Oct 2013	30 Sep 2014	2315	Internet				

Classes that have been nonconducted or cancelled or rescheduled have been excluded

Click to Show Historical Scope and Special Information Sets

Course Scope And Special Information

🛈 **Currently Effective 2013-11-06**

Course Scope:

WOCS provides the basic skills necessary to prepare the enlisted Soldier to become an effective Army warrant officer, who will make the morally, ethically, and legally correct decisions at all times; both on duty and off duty. WOCS incorporates a high stress environment, designed to challenge the candidate from day one. Additionally, WOCS provides an environment for evaluating and developing the candidate's potential as a warrant officer. WOCS consists of two phases:

a. Phase 1 is available as both distributed learning (DL) and resident. The Phase 1 DL is available only to NCOs meeting phase prerequisites. All others must attend the resident Phase 1.

b. Phase 2 is attended as Resident training by all candidates.

Also see special information applicable to each phase. For additional information, orientation packet with packing lists, and contact numbers, see the WOCC web page at http://usacac.army.mil/cac2/WOCC/wocourses.asp

Special Information:

1. Phase 1 (DL) is a self-paced course taught in the Blackboard learning content management system (web-based). Learning is foundational to the resident phase. The DL must be completed within 90 days, but no later than 14 days prior to attending the resident phase 2, whichever comes first.

2. You must have either a reserved or wait seat in ATRRS for both phase 1 (DL) and phase 2 prior to being actively enrolled in the DL. Once you have seats in both phases, go to http://usacac.army.mil/cac2/wocc/WOCSEnrollment.asp and follow the enrollment instructions for WOCS DL.

WOCS Phase II Prerequisite:

Find more information on class schedules at:
https://atrrs.army.mil/atrrscc/ and type in a School Code of "20" and click on ATRRS Search.

Prerequisites For Course 911-09W

| Back to Course Information | New Search |

Prerequisites Set(s)

Title	Effective Start Date	Effective End Date	Valid Fiscal Year(s)
▶ UPDATE	2012-10-05	N/A	2013 2014 2015 2016 2017 2018 2019

Verifiable Prerequisites

Prerequiste Item	Value(s) or Range	Constraint
Must meet height weight std IAW AR 600-9	YES	Required
Civilian Education Level	C - TWELFTH GRADE	Required
Course Security Clearance	F - SECRET	Required

Prerequisite Courses

The Student must satisfy any one of the following Prerequisite Course Solution Sets:

Students Must:
   Have a Reservation, or be Attending, or be Graduated from course: 911-09W Phase : 1 (WARRANT OFFICER CANDIDATE) *.

Or

Students Must:
   Have a Reservation, or be Attending, or be Graduated from course: 911-09W (DL) Phase : 1 (WARRANT OFFICER CANDIDATE) *.

* The prerequisite course class must end on or before the report date of the class for which the student is enrolling.
Note: This rule does not apply if the prerequisite course is self-paced training such as correspondence or web.

Text Prerequisites

1. Must have been selected to attend WOCS.

2. Must be U.S. Citizen for Military Intelligence or Civil Affairs MOSs.

3. Must possess a current SECRET security clearance, or TOP SECRET clearance when required by the accession MOS, valid through the projected WOCS graduation date.

4. Pass a standard 3-event APFT administered within 30 days prior to departure from losing command for WOCS. Individuals with a permanent profile approved by HQDA G3 may take the alternate walking event, but must have a copy of the approved HQDA G3 waiver in their possession to be enrolled.

5. Have in possession a current appointment physical or flight physical (DD 2808 or SF 88) valid through projected graduation date. The Report of Medical Examination must be no more than 24 months old from the date signed by the examining physician as of the projected WOCS graduation date for non-flight MOS candidates, and 18 months for aviation candidates.

School: 020
Course: 911-09W
Course Title: WARRANT OFFICER CANDIDATE

Phases of Training. Candidate training is divided into three distinct phases, each of which emphasizes different aspects of leadership development. Although you may have already completed the Junior Phase, you're being provided this information now because understanding all three phases will help you see the big picture and more accurately evaluate the relevance of the phase you're in at a particular time.

1. Junior Phase. The Junior Phase for E-5s (WLC graduates) and above is the DL module. The Junior Phase of the 6-week course emphasizes Candidates' ability to function in a mentally and physically demanding, fluid environment. The phase is a period of anxiety and insecurity for Candidates; it's a time to adapt to a new, disciplined environment. Candidates must quickly learn new rules and policies and demonstrate that they can maintain a positive attitude in the face of hardship, stress, and adversity. During this phase, TAC Officers evaluate Candidates' attitudes, educate them about desired Officer leadership traits, and teach and evaluate them in the following areas: qualities of moral integrity; ability to maintain strict discipline; physical and mental toughness; reaction speed; assertiveness; grasp of command responsibilities; ability to rapidly respond; persistence in the face of difficulties; mission accomplishment; and ability to lead others to develop these qualities and understand these responsibilities and requirements.

2. Intermediate Phase. E-5s (WLC graduates) and above begin this phase when they start resident training; Candidates who complete the Junior Phase in residence enter the Intermediate Phase on APX the 12th day of training. During this phase, the Army values and desired Officer attitudes are still communicated, trained, and instilled.

Emphasis is placed on required direct leadership level skills and actions. Efforts to train Candidates to build teams and solidify team cohesion are intensified. The class takes on a unique identity. This phase serves as a period of transition in which Candidates are allowed to move closer to the self discipline that will be required of them as Officers—the "test" is not over, it has just changed. This phase includes field leadership opportunities for Candidates during a 5-day field leadership exercise (FLX). (**NOTE:** For RTI Candidates, the FLX occurs during the Senior Phase.)

3. Senior Phase. Resident Candidates enter the Senior Phase APX two weeks after entering the Intermediate Phase; for RTI Candidates, the Senior Phase is the 15 days active duty for training (ADT) following the inactive duty for training (IDT) weekends. During the Senior Phase,

Candidates are faced with greater responsibility, and Cadre Officers have greater expectations of the soon-to-be Warrant Officers. During the other phases, Candidates have progressed from a state of "external discipline" to one of "self discipline"; they have progressively had to do more and more on their own. Now, emphasis is placed on developing a Candidates' Officer-ship and mentorship skills. Additionally, during this phase, efforts are directed at helping Candidates complete the program on a motivational high note.

4. Senior Status. After successfully completing the FLX, exam 2-2, and the TA-50 serviceability review, you enter Senior status unless you're on a punitive probation. "Senior status" is not the same as "Senior Phase"; you may be in the Senior phase of training without having Senior status. You may also qualify for Senior status and then lose that status. The following guidance applies to Senior status with exceptions noted for Candidates who are in Senior phase but not in Senior status or who lose Senior status. (The Primary TAC will provide additional guidance.)

a. When you qualify for Senior status, you change your insignia to the non-subdued insignia. If you enter the Senior phase but do not qualify for Senior status, continue to wear subdued insignia. If you qualify for Senior status and then lose Senior status eligibility, you revert to the subdued insignia.

b. As a Senior status Candidate, you will not harass junior or intermediate phase Candidates. Additionally, you will not visit their floors unless you receive directions and specific guidance for the visit from your Primary TAC.

c. In Senior status, you will be afforded certain courtesies by junior and intermediate Candidates: they will assume the position of attention when talking to you, address you as "ma'am" or "sir," and salute you as they would salute their Senior Officers in a non-training environment, e.g. at a normal distance applying common sense as to when saluting is appropriate.

d. The only privileges you receive in Senior status are the ones listed in (1) through (3) below plus any additional privileges the Primary TAC chooses to add such as extended time for personal phone calls; the Primary TAC's decision to award additional privileges will be based on your class' performance and its esprit de corps. Do not assume you have other privileges such as relaxed standards for maintaining your room and equipment or that your class has relaxed standards for maintaining common areas. To the contrary, your room and equipment and your class' common areas must always meet standards, and the training team will spot check to ensure compliance. If you fail to meet standards, you may lose privileges, receive probation, and/or be placed on probation.

(1) You will be excused from running in the Company area.

(2) You are granted the Senior reception pass (See the WOC SOP). http://usacac.army.mil/cac2/WOCC/repository/WOC_SOP_FY11.pdf

Senior reception passes are requested and grant you approval to go to restaurants in the local area, ie Daleville, Dothan, Ozark, Enterprise.

(3) You may be released early from common areas by class leadership if your class has cleaned the area to standards prior to the end of the scheduled cleaning period. Common area standards do not change. If your class doesn't maintain its common areas to standards, it may be placed on intermediate status.

Below is a proud photo of Class 10-001 Rising Eagles, Blue Class, Indiana Regional Training Institute looking good!

Chapter 12

What Are TAC Officers

Training, Advising, and Counseling (TAC) officers are assigned to mentor and evaluate Warrant Officer Candidates attending WOCS at Fort Rucker and at Army National Guard Regional Training Institutes.

TAC officers, along with class room instructors, continuously evaluate every candidate's potential to become a Warrant Officer. Not only do the TAC Officers evaluate the candidates to determine if they have the "Right Stuff" to become WO1's they also judge the candidate for drive, will power and fortitude to successful fill the Army's needs for CW2s-CW5. Candidates are evaluated on five areas:

- Academic
- Performance
- Physical Fitness
- Leadership
- Readiness (includes appearance, attitude, personal performance, equipment maintenance, compliance with SOP and team work).

"The current focus emphasizes officer roles and responsibilities more, and individual activities less. Candidates are required to meet high standards for maintaining their personal living areas; however, the standards are based on the need to maintain a clean and orderly living environment rather than what many in the past perceived as arbitrary specifications designed to heighten stress levels.

There are experiential learning events throughout the program, particularly warrior tasks and battle drill related activities that provide leadership opportunities while emphasizing lessons relevant to the Operating Environment (OE). These activities culminate in a Field Leadership Exercise (FLX) that draws heavily on recent lessons learned. This capstone event provides candidates expanded opportunities to apply flexible, adaptive leadership principles in stressful, sometimes ambiguous, situations to reinforce and build upon previous classroom theory studies and discussion. "

(Source WOCS website)

Mentoring

Actual one-on-one mentorship rarely occurs until the senior phase, when the pace is a bit slower. Senior Warrant Officers attending the Warrant Officer Staff Course or the Warrant Officer Senior Staff Course are invited to have dinner with the WOCS candidates. The candidates are grouped by Branch and the Senior Warrants answer questions, provide advice and all participate in a free flowing conversation. It's usually the first time since arriving at WOCS that the candidates have a normal conversation with a Senior Warrant Officer. Most of the Senior Warrants really enjoy the opportunity to pass some "lessons learned" down to the candidates.

Mentoring comes in various forums throughout the WOCS course that may not be so apparent: Evaluations, Inspections, Class discussions, Individual assessments or through On-the-Spot Corrections.

Our class expected quite a bit more "Officership" and mentorship than we received. I imagine we received more mentorship, only it was unrecognizable at the time because we were exhausted from performing so many push-ups and sit ups.

Prioritizing

TIP: WOCS is about prioritizing activities, time management and attention to detail. These are the Officer skills that will take you to graduation and help you with a successful Warrant Officer career.

TAC Officers are well aware that today's Army is at war, and the candidates undergoing WOCS today may be called on tomorrow to perform their duties and lead Soldiers in combat. The stress applied while undergoing WOCS is embedded into the curriculum to give the TAC Officers insight as to how the candidate will react when they are physically, emotionally, and mentally drained.

The TAC Officers enforce uncompromising schedules, excessive tasks (both individual and group) with complicated standards coupled with virtually instantaneous corrective discipline. Each and every minuscule event of your waking day is evaluated against the WOC SOP standards and Mondays through Friday include academic standards. Academically if you fail a second retest you are sent packing. You are held accountable for your short falls and lack of class team work. Simultaneously, your lifelines and vices are removed.

NOTE: No caffeine, alcohol, texting, email, tobacco, spouses, phone calls, computers, junk food or sodas are allowed, at least for the first 2 weeks. It will take your body 10 or more days to acclimatize.

All this evaluation is done with one goal prominently in sight. Can you, the candidate, prioritize the day's activities and multi-task in an environment of chaos, confusion and fatigue, and make the correct decisions that demonstrate you have the required skill set to successfully graduate and become a Warrant Officer after 6-8 weeks of intense training?

WOCS Success Tips:

Mentally prepare yourself for the training. Arrive with a clear mental image of why you want to succeed and don't lose sight of it. I kept a WO1 rank in my WOC wallet and would rub the rank during the low points of the course. WOCS is not like basic training. **On average, 30% of candidates will not graduate with their class.**

Read, understand, and follow EVERYTHING in the WOCS SOP.

Show up in the best physical shape possible. The training will physically punish you. You will be sore and Sundays are the only day your body can recover. **Over the counter pain relievers are only allowed with TAC Officer approval.**

Wean yourself off tobacco, junk food and caffeine BEFORE reporting in. Drink more water, cut out sodas and eat balanced meals.

Arrive 1–2 days early and closely observe formations and Dining Procedures at the WOCS Dining Facility.

When you are assigned a room, look around carefully. The posted Room Occupancy Cards (ROC) and Room Discrepancy Cards (DIS) passed the final Phase Inspection for the previous class and should be used as examples to fill out yours. Also check for rulers marked for the correct spacing of hangers in your display.

TIP: Post ROC Cards Immediately Upon Room Assignment! (Don't forget the Vacant Rooms on your floor.)

TIP: Some 3X5 cards are written in all caps, some in upper and lower case. Some have ¼ inch margins, others have 1 inch margins. ALL HAVE THE SMALL LINE AT THE BOTTOM CUT OFF! Follow the WOCS SOP example exactly for each card.

Make some friends and help each other out.

Your whole class must come together.

Example 1: Candidate Smith receives fewer demerits on her display than anyone else. The class examines her display and applies her tips to make their displays better. Candidate Smith spot checks each Squad Leader's display and they pass the lessons learned on to their squads.

Example 2: Post a sentry when on break. The sentry looks out for approaching TAC Officers and calls out the greeting of the day.

Example 3: Don't leave the room if your roommate is looking like a soup sandwich.

Realize the TAC Officers will choose the least experienced individuals to be the Class Leaders. You must help them out and they must let you help them out. If you have to, whisper the correct facing movements to them during formations.

TIP: You can survive as a class or drown as individuals.

Refresh yourself on Drill and Ceremony (D&C) before arriving. We conducted several evaluations where every candidate led a squad through 18 D&C movements on a 10X10 square without stepping out of bounds. Each day formations, marching, and issuing of commands are evaluated.

Example: "Forward, March!" is correct, whereas "Ford, Harch!" will result in "corrective" PT.

When Marching, road guards must use Safety Vests or you risk "Safety Violations". Double time across roads when marching. TACs have spies EVERYWHERE!

TIP: Celebrate the small successes and don't dwell on the failures.

Always salute and give the greeting of the day, plus the phrase of the day, as soon as you spot a TAC Officer, even if they are 100 yards away. If you are uncertain of the time, check your watch:

0001-1159 is morning

1200-1759 is afternoon

1800 to 0000 evening.

The phrase of the day is posted daily and also located in Appendix H of the WOC SOP.

If alone, "Sir, Candidate (Last Name), Army Values, Good Morning, Sir!"

If with others, "Sir, elements of Red Class, Army Values, Good Morning Sir!"

If with other classes" "Sir, elements of 1st Warrant Officer Company, Army Values, Good Morning Sir!"

DAILY GREETING DEFINITION: (Phase of the Day)

Training Day #

1. **LEADERSHIP** Influencing people by providing Purpose, Direction and Motivation.

2. **BE, KNOW, DO** Clearly and concisely states the characteristics of an Army leader.

3. **ARMY VALUES** Guide you, the leader, and the rest of the Army.

4. **LOYALTY** Bear true faith and allegiance to the U.S. Constitution, the Army, your unit, and other soldiers.

5. **DUTY** Fulfill your obligations.

6. **RESPECT** Treat people as they should be treated.

7. **SELFLESS SERVICE** Put the welfare of the nation, the Army, and subordinates before your own.

8. **HONOR** Live up to the Army's values.

9. **INTEGRITY** Do what is right, legally and morally.

10. **PERSONAL COURAGE** Face fear, danger, or adversity (physical or moral).

11. **DIRECT LEADERSHIP** Face-to-face, first line leadership.

12. **ORGANIZATIONAL LEADERSHIP** Influences many. Done indirectly, generally through more levels of subordinates than do direct leaders.

13. **STRATEGIC LEADERSHIP** Responsible for large organizations and influence many. They establish force structure, allocate resources, communicate strategic vision, and prepare their commands and America's Army as a whole for their future roles.

14. **LEADER ATTRIBUTES** A person's fundamental qualities and characteristics.

15. **MENTAL ATTRIBUTES** Include will, self-discipline, initiative, judgment, self-confidence, intelligence, and cultural awareness.

16. **PHYSICAL ATTRIBUTES** Includes health fitness, physical fitness, and military and professional bearing.

17. **EMOTIONAL ATTRIBUTES** Help leaders to make the right ethical choice. Includes the ability to use self-control, to remain balanced and to be stable in the face of adversity.

18. **LEADER SKILLS** Includes interpersonal, conceptual, technical, and tactical.

19. **INTERPERSONAL SKILLS** Affect how you deal with people. Includes: coaching, teaching, counseling, motivating, and empowering.

20. **CONCEPTUAL SKILLS** Enables you to handle ideas. Requires sound judgment and reasoning analytically, critically, and ethically.

21. **TECHNICAL SKILLS** Job related abilities including basic soldier skills.

22. **TACTICAL SKILLS** Ability to solve problems dealing with the arrangement of forces and capabilities on the battlefield.

23. **LEADER ACTIONS** Bring together everything you believe and everything you know how to do to provide purpose, direction, and motivation.

24. **INFLUENCING** Guiding others toward a goal.

25. **OPERATING** What you do to accomplish a goal. Including planning and preparing, executing and assessing.

26. **IMPROVING** Leaving an organization better than you found it.

27. **COUNSELING** Conducted to make subordinates better members of the team, maintain and improve performance, and prepare for the future.

28. **DISCIPLINE** To train or develop by instruction and exercise especially in self-control

29. **PROFESSIONALISM** The conduct, aims, or qualities that characterize or mark a professional person

30. **SET THE EXAMPLE** Leader, Demonstrator, and Mentor (Role Model)

31. **OFFICERSHIP** Is the practice of being a warrant/commissioned Army leader, accountable to the President of the United States for the army and its mission. Officers swear an oath of loyalty and service to the Constitution. Grounded in Army Values (Role Model)

32. **WARRIOR ETHOS** Soldier's Creed; Mission first; A soldier will never do.

33. **THE CONSTITUTION** The basic principles and laws of our nation.

34. **ARMY STRONG** There is nothing on this green earth that is stronger than the US Army. Because there is nothing on this green earth that is stronger than a US Army Soldier. (Army's Ad Campaign)

35. **CLASS MOTTO** Self explanatory

36. **CLASS NAME** Self explanatory

Example Squad Greeting for Training Day 11 at 09:45 to a male TAC Officer: "Sir, Elements of Red Class, Good morning, Direct Leadership, Sir."

Categories for Elimination:

1. Compassionate or Hardship.

2. Medical/Physical Conditions

3. Failure to Progress.

4. Academic Deficiencies.

5. Leadership Development Deficiencies.

6. Policy Violations. WOCS policy, policy letters, etc. or guidance from Cadre Officers

7. Processing Setback/Recycle Actions.

8. Honor Code Violations.

9. Disciplinary Reasons.

10. Misconduct.

11. Failure to Meet Security Requirements.

12. Administrative Recall.

13. Lack of Physical Stamina.

14. Lack of Adaptability.

15. Falsifying or Omitting Facts or Information on Application

16. Failure to Maintain Height/Weight Standards.

17. Voluntary Resignation.

18. Failure to Report for WOCS (Changed Mind)

A Typical WOCS Training Day:

0500—Wake up.

0530—First Formation.

0530-0635—Warm Ups and conduct physical training, afterwards a 3+ mile run and end with 5 pull ups.

0600—The company stops momentarily to salute the flag.

0635-0730—Personal hygiene time. Shave, shower, dress, prepare laundry for turn in, gather class books, prepare room and locker for inspection, and clean common areas.

0728—Class formation.

0730—Squad leaders perform a uniform inspection.

0730-0815—March to the dining facility for breakfast. Dining rights enforced.

0815-1230 March to General Studies Branch/Academics.

TIP: During breaks in class write memorandums for inspection shortfalls, leave the subject blank, and fill it in after you return to the room and find out the results.

1215—March to lunch.

1230-1330—Lunch. Dining rights enforced.

1330-1720—March back to General Studies Branch for more class room training.

1630—March back to WOCS for evening formation/retreat.

1705—Move to Parade Field for 30-45 minutes of PT for WOC SOP violations.

1730-1820—Admin Time.

1805-1900—Dinner. Dining rights enforced.

1830—Pickup Laundry.

1900-2245—Candiate Leadership designs and implements schedule to accomplish specified tasks. Personal time. Assess TAC evaluation and replace display items "displaced" as a result of TAC Officer Inspections.

It's not uncommon to return to the room and find 40-50 pair of shoes knotted together across adjoining door knobs, bunk beds reassembled in the showers, specks of dust on desks circled by sharpie markers, laundry bags suspended from the ceiling tiles, and entire wall lockers emptied onto bunks. It's possible to exceed 2000 demerits on just one inspection.

TIP: You must read and comprehend the WOC SOP before placing any display item out. The SOP has directions on how to lace your shoes, ground your items, place your socks in the drawer with "Smiles to the Aisles", how to tie your laundry bag, and which electric socket to plug your desk lamp in to.

If the standard is 12 inches, 11 7/8 inches is a NO-GO.

TIP: Measure everything!

2015-2115—Mandatory study hour. Wall lockers closed tight, seated at your desk, studying for tomorrow's class or test.

2115-2215—Common area cleanup.

2215-2230—Personal hygiene time.

2230-2245—Form up in hallway at 2230 at "Attention" and recite the Soldier's Creed, and sing the Army and Class song.

2245-0500—Lights out. Sleep. No working on displays, no writing memos.

The pace increases as you become more familiar with the standards, however the inspection demerits do slack off after a few weeks. You can only hand write so many memorandums before the novelty wears off.

HEADS UP: The first month we did not have a hot shower. It was commonly believed the TAC Officers turned the hot water off. After the 5th memorandum requesting a work order to "Fix" the hot water, it was restored. Coincidently the "Fix" occurred the same day our class won the WOCS Olympics.

TIP: Have your Morale Officer start spitting out Memorandums requesting all manner of things as soon as your class hits the ground. We had to request things like hot water in the showers, access to the Day Room on Sunday's and the washing machine privileges. You can try for Caffeine Rights, but it might take 1-2 weeks before your class has earned them. Most memos will not get approved at first, but each one that does feels like a major victory, so keep churning them out.

In Summary, What's WOC's like?

PT, Rush, Rush, Rush, Stencil, Align and Measure, Clothes Rolled and Folded to Perfection, Drink Water, Greeting of the Day, Organized Lockers, Boots and Shoes and Shower Shoes Grounded, Studying, Testing, Getting Smoked for No Reason, Getting Smoked for Any Reason, Inspections, Writing Memos, TAC Officers Everywhere, Singing, Cadence, Earning Colors, Pull-ups, Running, Marching, Earning Privileges - Losing Privileges, More PT, Carwash, Sweat, Caffeine and Desert Rights, Fun, Teamwork, Graduation!!!

"Mister" or "Chief"?

Let's clear up the confusion here. What do you call a Warrant Officer? For some folks out there this is a sensitive subject. Some want to be called "Chief" and others want to be called "Mister."

Most Technical Warrants are addressed as "Chief" or "Sir". Technical Warrant Officers almost without exception are prior military and had a minimum of 3-5 years experience in their MOS prior to being selected. All are considered the Technical Expert in their field and usually specialize in the same equipment or weapon systems throughout their career. They generally will start at the Unit level. As they get promoted they will steadily advance to assignments at the Brigade and Division Headquarters.

Aviator Warrants, for the most part, prefer to be addressed as "Mister" or "Sir". Aviator Warrant Officers are a mix of prior Military and Civilian Applicants. No feeder MOS is required. Most Aviator Warrant Officers will start off as co-pilots to a more Senior Warrant Officer until such time as they've proven themselves to Command the Aircraft. They also will fill a multitude of additional duties within their Aviation Unit and their assignments will likewise progress similar to the Technical Warrant Officers. Aviator Warrant Officers also get Flight Pay in addition to their normal pay. The most often reason I've heard that Aviator Warrants prefer "Mister" is because on the helicopter, the title "Chief" refers to the Crew Chief, who is an NCO. No Aviator Warrant Officer wants to be referred to by a NCO title, especially in front of peers and subordinates.

As a Warrant Officer don't get hung up on the titles. Quite a few old timers and RLOs still call a WO1 a "Wobbly One', referring to an inexperienced helicopter pilot, regardless whether or not the WO1 is an Aviator. Do your job, do it well and you will earn their respect. "Nuff Said!"

Chapter 13

Showing up to School

Warrant Officer Candidate School—WOCS

Currently the three biggest delays in starting WOCS are:

1. Physical expiring prior to graduation—you must ensure your physical will carry you through your WOCS graduation. (Aviators–18 Months and Technicians–24 Months) If you are close—it will be strongly advised to get an updated physical prior to arrival. Candidates with physicals that do not cover complete attendance through Warrant Officer Candidate School may result in denied enrollment.

2. Security Clearance Issues—make sure you don't show up with surprises for the Security Office at Ft. Rucker. If the Ft. Rucker Security Manager cannot verify your clearance - you will not start WOCS. The only form accepted after 9 April 05 will be the Joint Personnel Adjudication System (JPAS) printout. It is your responsibility to ensure you carry a copy with you to Ft. Rucker.

3. Physical fitness—your arrival date is not a surprise, therefore the APFT you'll take within the first week should not be a surprise either. Make sure you are mentally and physically fit—remember this is an Officer producing program; the APFT grading standards are strictly enforced.

Course Focus:

Warrant Officer Candidate School (WOCS) continues to evolve to better align its philosophy and activities to meet the needs of an Army at war. The driving force is the desire to produce Warrant Officers better qualified to operate effectively in the demanding operational environment.

The current focus emphasizes Officer roles and responsibilities more, and individual activities less. Candidates are required to meet high standards for maintaining their personal living areas; however, the standards are based on the need to maintain a clean and orderly living environment rather than what many in the past perceived as arbitrary specifications designed to heighten stress levels.

There are experiential learning events throughout the program, particularly warrior tasks and battle drill related activities that provide leadership opportunities while emphasizing lessons relevant to the OE. These activities culminate in a field leadership exercise (FLX) that draws heavily on recent lessons learned. This capstone event provides candidates expanded opportunities to apply flexible, adaptive leadership principles in stressful, sometimes ambiguous, situations to reinforce and build upon previous classroom theory studies and discussion. Training, Advising, and Counseling Officers (TACs) and academic instructors concentrate primarily on training and secondly on assessing candidates' performance. This becomes apparent in the time and effort TACs and instructors devote to serving as role models, mentors, and coaches.

Throughout all the changes, rigor is maintained—even increased—and the goal continues to be to provide candidates the foundation they need to succeed as Warrant Officers in a changing Army, and to be adaptable to the ever increasing challenges of the Operating Environment.

Get in Shape:

PREPARE PHYSICALLY! You will participate in daily physical training to include weekly road marches up to 10K. Condition yourself in advance and bring comfortable marching boots. FM 21-18 discusses conditioning road marches, during the summer months you can expect high temperatures with extremely high humidity. At WOCS you will have to pass 3 Army Physical Fitness Tests (APFT). The APFT consists of three events: Push Ups, Sit Ups and a 2 Mile Run.

A 22-26 year old male is required to do 40 Push-Ups, 50 Sit-Ups and a 16:36 2 Mile Run.

A 22-26 year old female is required to do 17 Push-Ups, 50 Sit-Ups and a 19:36 2 Mile Run.

Remember: These are the *minimum scores.* I recommend you try to get 80%-90% in each event.

Complete score cards for all age groups are available at:

http://usarmybasic.com/army-physical-fitness/apft-standards

Wear of the Army Service Uniform (ASU)—It is required that candidates wear the ASU for WOCS graduation. Additionally, if you are attending flight school after WOCS, you will be required to wear the ASU for flight school graduation.

For questions regarding Phase 1 or 2 resident school, please contact HHC personnel section, (334) 255-1287/1967 or DSN 558-xxxx.

For questions regarding Phase 1 distance learning (DL), please contact the WOCS DL manager, (334) 255-1326 or DSN 558-xxxx.

Send email requests to usarmy.rucker.cac.mbx.wocc-web@mail.mil

WOCS General Information as of 09 Nov 2011:

1. The Institutional Training Directed Lodging and Meals (ITDLM) policy (previously known as Military Training Service Support, or MTSS) is in effect at Fort Rucker and is applicable to all Army military temporary duty (TDY) and active duty for training (ADT) resident service school students at WOCC. WOCS students will reside in Army barracks and be provided meals for their entire course.

   a. Initial lodging is provided through the Fort Rucker IHG Army Hotel (phone 334-598-5216, fax 334-598-1242), http://www.ihgarmyhotels.com/pal/en/us/home. A list of students is provided to the hotel in advance of arrival, but individual students must verify their reservation. During peak periods students may be referred to off post lodging, and transportation to on post facilities is limited. Units may wish to consider authorizing POV or rental vehicle. The WOCC neither approves nor funds reimbursement for student transportation.

   b. Students will be authorized under the ITDLM program to eat in the dining facility at no charge (building 5914). There will be a memorandum provided to the dining facility with the class roster after class begins the first day. Students may still eat without charge in the dining facility on the first morning by telling the dining facility personnel which WOCC course they are attending.

2. The WOCC website is the most current source of information. Unit Training Officers/NCOs and prospective students should check the WOCC website at http://usawocc.army.mil prior to the start of any course.

3. Dothan Municipal Airport, Dothan, Alabama, is located 22 miles from Fort Rucker. Taxi/bus service is available from Dothan Airport to Fort Rucker (approx $60).

4. Students should check orders upon receipt and verify authorization for dependent travel, POVs, or shipment of property. Failure to do so may result in inconvenience and hardship.

5. Students must meet height/weight standards as specified in AR 600-9.

6. Students must have their unit S2 or security manager ensure their security clearance is appropriately reflected in JPAS. They must then have the S2 send a visit request via JPAS to SMO code W0H0AA6S.

7. Students must have an AKO account that is not linked to another email account and can be accessed by both AKO user name and password, and CAC card. All correspondence will be conducted via official AKO email. AKO account may be initiated by contacting http://www.us.army.mil

Mail Services:

1. USPS will not deliver mail or packages to individuals residing in the IHG Army Hotel. Individuals will need to in-process Consolidated Mail Room #3 upon their arrival to Fort Rucker. More specific information is provided during the in-processing portion of each class. Mail should not be forwarded to the Ft Rucker IHG Army Hotel address, as it will be marked "Return to Sender."

2. UPS and FEDEX deliveries are accepted by the IHG Army Hotel

Uniform Issue to Navy, Marine Corps, Air Force, and Coast Guard selected for the Army WOC program.

The initial Army uniforms issue will be at the MEPS or HHC, Warrant Officer Career College, but, regardless of who does it, it is furnished by the Army before training.

What is a Normal Day at WOCS?

Wake up is at exactly 0530 hrs. No getting up early and you must sleep in the bed, not on top of the covers. Your class has 7-10 minutes to get outside for PT formation. Sundays you can sleep until 0600.

Expect to be late for most everything the first week. It takes a bit of co-ordination to get 65 or more people to formation in 10 minutes or less.

PT is from 0550 to 0700. Some days are hard, some are easy. Some classes are run into the ground and others do more grass/guerrilla drills. A lot depends on your fitness level, your TAC Officer and how well your class works as a team. Expect to do some PT while wearing Body Armor.

25 minutes or less to shower. You also must change clothes, do common area clean-up and get your room ready for daily inspection. Try to shower and change in 5-8 minute and dedicate the rest of the time to common area clean-up and getting your room ready for inspections. Be a team player, get out of your room and help your squad during common area clean-up.

Breakfast is highly disciplined. Your class will march over to the Dining Facility and file in by squad. No Coffee rights until they're earned. No talking, looking around or checking out the TV.

After breakfast your class marches off to Swartworth Hall for classes. The instructors are pretty cool so you can relax somewhat. Listen up, since almost everything is testable at the end of the week. Tests are given on Fridays so take notes and study when you can.

Lunch is much like Breakfast. Try to sneak in haircuts when you can. Our standards were 1/8th of hair on the sides and 1/4 on the top.

After lunch, go back to class. Afterwards return to WOCS in time for the afternoon/evening formation and then off to dinner. Occasionally you will be smoked by your TAC Officer for (Insert anything that comes to mind _____) on the PT field.

After dinner you can go to your room, pick up laundry or get smoked again; or sit outside in the quad and study. It really depends on your TAC Officer.

TIP: Time spent in the Quad is a good opportunity to practice Drill and Ceremony (D&C). Each Candidate in our class had to successfully lead the squad through 20 memorized D&C commands, to include several marching commands such as "Right Flank, Column Left" etc. Most of the Commands are given while the Squad is stationary, such as "Parade Rest, Attention, Present Arms, Order Arms, Left Face" etc., without leaving a 20 X 20 square. This one was quite the challenge for those without "Troop Time."

1900-2000hrs is the Mandatory Study Time. Study hour is one hour of dedicated study each evening. Your place of duty is sitting at your desk studying. Not writing letters home, not writing memos, not clipping your fingernails. Make sure you study! Do it to get ready for the Friday testing and do it to stay off of your TAC's radar. If you aren't sitting at your desk with your face in a book they will harass you and make you do a variety of things like write additional memo's or papers on obscure subjects, smoke you or worse; put you on Commander's Probation.

Lights out is 2245. Be in bed! No bathroom, studying, writing, or straighten up for inspections.

First 3 Minutes:

I checked my watch, mentally cataloging the time as 1442. It was sweltering hot outside and the air conditioning was `straining to keep the car interior below 95 degrees. I rifled through my dog eared processing papers for what must have been the 100th time, mentally checking off the pages against the WOCS checklist propped up on the glove box door. My Class A's itched, and I felt the sweat beads roll down my back. I recently changed out of my jeans and t-shirt 4 miles up the road at the Enterprise gas station and I could sense the humid October heat was causing the uniform's creases to sag. The Sun sparkled off the highly polished brass in the WOCS courtyard, causing my eyes to squint. Across the quad a more eager candidate, similarly dressed, casually cut across the grass to the 1st WOCS HHC orderly room door. I noticed his Class A's sagged a few degrees more south than mine, no doubt due to the harsh Alabama sun's direct exposure. I noticed his 82nd Airborne combat patch, polished combat boots, airborne wings and maroon beret. I saw we had the same Staff Sergeant rank on our sleeves and that he had a few more awards than I. This guy would be competition for Distinguished Honor Grad.

A TAC Officer rounded the corner and immediately took up an intersecting course with SSG Airborne. I watched intently, having only heard rumors of TAC Officers, to see how this meeting went. The TAC Officer wore a black baseball style cap, black t-shirt, starched BDUs, and possessed a skull piecing stare that totally fixated on SSG Airborne. Before SSG Airborne could say "Good Afternoon, Chief" the TAC Officer pounced on him, disregarding the in-processing paperwork in his right hand. You never, ever, carried anything in your right hand, I learned later on. "What do we have here?" shouted the TAC Officer, his clear, mocking, sing-song voice cutting the afternoon haze like a knife blade. "Someone wants to be an NCO!" Like the howling of a wolf call to the pack, 8 TAC Officers appeared from nowhere and encircled the confused candidate. In a flash he was on his back, on his stomach, doing flutter kicks, pushups, mountain climbers, dying cockroaches, the commands shouted at him like the retort of a 50 Cal machine gun on full auto. Within moments his Class A's, moments before proudly displaying his military achievements, were soaking up the red Alabama clay like an old sponge. SSG Airborne, to his credit, gamely counted off the repetitions, his voice barely audible over the staccato retort of barked commands.

As quick as I could I ripped the now offending Staff Sergeant stripes off my sleeves, picking the green threads off and trying to smooth down the vacant incriminating needle holes. The sweltering heat in the car, now benefiting me as an impromptu dry cleaner, steamed the wool fabric flat. The proud day I earned the rocker on those chevrons was now just a vague memory. I gathered my paperwork, killed the car's ignition and as quietly as possible pocketed my keys so as not to draw undue attention my way. I picked a route to the orderly room door that could only be described as nap-of-earth navigation, staying downwind and keeping to the low laying areas and shadows. I avoided all eye contact with the TAC Officers who were momentary distracted with their prey. As I triumphantly crossed the HHC door's threshold I couldn't resist the urge of one more glance at SSG Airborne. The sweat was pouring down his now red face as he gathered his scattered papers and beret from the ground and attempted to straighten his disheveled uniform. As suddenly as they appeared the TAC Officers disbanded, their need for utter dominance temporally sated. One TAC Officer caught my eye and his grin said it all, "Don't worry, you're next!" A glance at my watch reveled it was now 1445. My first 3 minutes of induction to the Warrant Officer Candidate School was complete.

NOTE: Currently Candidates report to WOCS wearing ACUs and Patrol Cap. I recommend you remove rank for the Patrol Hat and ACU jacket before signing in.

Black Monday:

Black Monday is the first day you're a member of one of the official classes, such as Red Class, Blue Class, Gold Class, etc. My Black Monday started after 5 days as a member of Grey Class, but it varies depending on your arrival date at WOCS. Grey Class was also sometimes called Snowbird Class. Snowbirds are candidates on physical hold pending medical clearance placing them back on full duty. The majority of Grey Class are candidates who will fill the next official WOCS class, the rest are the medical hold Snowbirds hoping to get medically cleared.

Black Monday starts at 0300. Every TAC Officer available arrives on your floor and shouts at the top of their voice for you to get up. Once you get past the shell shock from the rude awakening you realize they're telling you the PT dress is uniform pants and jacket, t-shirt, tennis shoes, CAC (ID) Card in the left cargo pocket, dog tags in the upper left pocket and full canteen in the right cargo pocket. The uniform may include gloves and PT cap based on the weather. A high stress inspection immediately occurs in the hall, with more shouting and pushups for anyone failing to follow directions to the letter.

I was one of the few to get it right and the TAC Officer told me to "Get Out!" I went down the stairs and out in the pitch black night to the street. No one was in front so I went behind the building and no one was there either. I felt weird. This was not good. A TAC Officer spied me from a second story window and yelled out "We got a deserter!" Also not good. I ran back into the building and snuck up the stairs, waiting just outside the doors. The yelling and shouting went on for a good 10 minutes and everyone was on the floor doing pushups and leg lifts. I didn't feel the least bit guilty and I sure as heck was not going to walk in.

Eventually everyone was chased out to the Grey Class formation area and issued rubber training M16's. It was raining cats and dogs and the TAC Officers didn't deviate one bit from the Op Order, so don't expect any mercy.

A quick formation followed and we started jogging at about a 6 minute a mile pace. We carried the M16's at a modified port arms. Five TAC Officers ran with us and the rest took off up the road in several cars. We met up with them down the road about a mile away. We broke into groups and went to stations and TAC Officers had us doing grass drills with the M16s. Other TAC Officers would roam and look for "slackers". You did not want to be labeled a slacker. Slackers got extra attention. Every few minutes you rotated to another station.

After 20 minutes we formed up again and ran about a mile, also at a 6 minute pace. A fresh group of TAC Officers ambushed us and we were directed to field number 2 where more abuse awaited us. This time it was 20 minutes of guerilla drills. More slackers were identified for extra attention, and every few minutes we rotated to a new angry TAC Officer.

Maybe the TAC Officers wouldn't be so angry if this was done later in the morning? Hey, I'm just thinking out loud.

Good Tip. Any time a TAC Officer asks if you need water, the answer is always yes. You get to take a break for a few minutes, catch your breath and get away from the madness while you fill up your canteen. Always get water, even if you dump your canteen on the way over to a water jug.

Finally it was time to run again. By now I was beyond exhaustion and actually looked forward to running. After a few hundred yards I realized we had run a large loop, and we were about a mile from WOCS. Most of the TAC Officers ran with us this time and the pace was a slower, leisurely 7 minute mile. We got back to the WOCS around 6am and for the first time had formation in the Red Class formation area. Every Red Class formation thereafter was in the same place. We were finally Red Class!

To this day I have no idea how many of us fell out, mostly because we didn't know each other well enough and because I never saw them again. If you quit on Black Monday you were drummed out of the course. After Black Monday, 61 males and 5 females started Red Class. Six weeks later 42 graduated, including 4 of the females.

Swartworth Hall:

The Warrant Officer Career College (WOCC) is a world class training facility located a short walk from WOCS. Air conditioned class rooms with individual student internet ready computers, coupled with some of the best Warrant Officer instructors in the Army provide an ideal learning environment. During your Warrant Officer career you will have many opportunities to attend WOCC. As a WOC you will receive many hours of instruction here and the opportunity to present and share with your fellow candidates on individual and group projects. Be prepared to defend your position on subjects such as human rights, ethical conduct, code of conduct, etc. Frank interaction with the instructors is expected during most class lectures.

Expect to spend about 40 hours a week in various classrooms. Each evening a block of time is dedicated to study. No other activity is authorized during study hour so use this time to prepare for your next day's class or exam. All course tests must be successfully passed prior to graduation, however not all course have exams.

In addition to providing training to WOCS, Swartworth Hall is used for training the US Army's Senior Warrant Officers when they return for their Warrant Officer Staff Course and Warrant Officer Senior Staff Course. All of these courses are elements of the Warrant Officer Education System goal to continually re-engage with the Warrant Officer community throughout their career and ensure they get the skills and education required to stay relevant in the US Army. Some course material is derived from or mirrors similar training plans from the Captain Career Course, Intermediate Level Education, and Command and General Staff Course.

If you happen to see any of these Senior Warrants in the halls, most likely swarming around the two huge coffee urns or discussing the merits of synthetic motor oils over fossil oil and the validity of the flux capacitor, avoid approaching them for anything. Best to hold your questions until you return to your unit to avoid any conflicts with your TAC Officers.

Coffee Drinkers, Soda Drinkers and Snack Food Junkies beware!

Swartworth Hall is lined with all the vices mentioned above. It behooves you to get your TAC Officer's approval before indulging, no matter how inviting and readily available these items appear. Many a Candidate has been caught in these hallowed halls consuming an ice cold Coke or Snickers bar by their TAC Officer, and believe me have paid dearly for it.

Army Service Uniforms Conversion—Enlisted to Officer:

Obviously you won't be wearing Enlisted uniforms on WOCS graduation day, but how, exactly, do you get the Officer version?

After 2-3 weeks into the WOCS course, the TAC Officers will direct you to send your uniforms to the Tailor Shop. The jacket will get the epaulets removed, the shoulder board clips sewn on, the NCO rank removed and the branch color sewn around each sleeve. Have the cleaners steam roll the sleeves to minimize the needle holes. The cost was about $65 in 1994 but I bet it's gone up a bit since then. Luckily, the ASU pants are good to go and interchangeable between Enlisted and Officer.

Many will feel converting a uniform is a waste of money, as almost everyone will only wear their converted uniforms once and end up buying a new one after graduation. They just don't look quite right. Resist the urge to buy a new one too soon. All the weight you lost during WOCS will most likely come back once you return to the land of beer and pizza. If you have to buy new ASUs, leave a little wiggle room in them.

Alternative 2: Buy a new ASU at Military Clothing Sales (MCS) before graduation. After graduation finance will give you a one-time clothing allowance of $400. This is the last time you will get a clothing allowance (it's an annual Enlisted benefit you lose once you transition to Warrant Officer) so spend it wisely.

Alternative 3: Before you arrive at WOCS, shop your Military Thrift Shop or EBay and find a used Officers ASU, get the cuffs converted to your future Officer Branch color, and bring them to WOCS. Many of the uniforms at the Thrift Shop or online are like new, and if you find one that fits you can save big bucks. Remember to tell your TAC Officer on the first day so there won't be any issues.

TIP: You also need shoulder boards in your branch color, shoulder tabs for your dress shirts, and rank for your beret and patrol cap. Fort Rucker's MCS never has enough of this stuff, so bring it with you to save a great deal of hassle. Ask a newly promoted CW2 for their rank and boards. It's a common practice to hand it down upon promotion. The boards cost over $25.00! By the way, networking is what Warrant Officers are all about!

Take a moment to ponder the future when you see your entire class' Uniforms racked and stacked at alterations just prior to getting converted. Makes you wonder about all the potential the future wearers will have to shape the Army.

Bottom Line Up Front (BLUF): Don't sweat it too much. If the class is getting uniforms converted, go with the program. After you leave WOCS in your rear view mirror and you start your new career as an Army Warrant Officer, you can decide if you want a new uniform. Either way you go, those WO1 shoulder boards sure look cool and I'll bet you'll be just as proud.

Guido Ball

Some of your gear will be marked with white medical tape and stenciled with your name. After a week the name tapes become unusable for display purposes and are replaced with new, freshly stenciled name tapes. What do you do with the old name tapes? You create a Guido Ball of course! Guido Balls are a WOCS tradition that goes back many years. The unusable name tapes are wrapped one on top of another and quickly form a ball. This is a class project, so with 60-90 candidates providing 8-12 name tapes weekly for 6 weeks, you can imagine how large the Guido Ball can grow.

Here's the rub. The TAC Officers will claim the Guido Ball is a static item. Static items, or items that can be used in lieu of your display items, are forbidden in the WOC SOP. The theory is that you the candidate, needing a replacement name tape for an upcoming inspection, will take the Guido Ball and start peeling names tapes off until you get to one with your name on it and use that name tape for the inspection, thus making it a static item.

So, the Guido Ball must be hidden and protected from the TAC Officers at all costs. The TAC Officers, true to their nature will hunt and poke and probe your area of responsibility incessantly looking for it. The difficulty is in the hiding, since as each week goes by it grows and grows until on Graduation day it's the size of a large butterball turkey and weighs over 10 lbs. It's considered a matter of class pride to present the elusive Guido Ball to your TAC Officers at the Graduation ceremony, and a bit embarrassing for them. The Guido Ball, if it survives, is normally displayed proudly with your class guidion long after you depart.

However, if you are misfortunate enough to ALLOW the TAC Officers to find your Guido Ball, the entire class is punished physically for honors violation, culminating in a full-fledged funeral for the Guido Ball held in the Quad, possibly including 21 gun salute, pall bears and other appropriate honors as spelled out in AR 600-25.

Your ENTIRE class should choose in the first few days whether to attempt to create a Guido Ball or not. Only the brave will survive!

Moving Day

Like everything else at WOCS, moving from the Snowbirds barracks to your class barracks is as stressful as possible. You are expected to quickly move all of your belongings, while the TAC Officers are barking commands and watching for candidates who aren't giving them the greeting of the day. Expect to spend most of the time dedicated for moving engaged in physical training due to displeasing one or several TAC Officers. To avoid some of the pit falls of moving day, here are a few tips to make the move less unpleasant.

Use you laundry bag and duffel bags to pack up your items. Take your rolled items and roll them tightly in your towel and pack them tightly in your bag. Replace all your uniforms in your garment bag to minimize wrinkling. Make sure your bags are securely locked or tied in case you have to toss them on the ground or pile them up during an impromptu PT session. If you must pile bags, think of it as a preparing for a formation. Every bag must be dress-right-dress, and sorted by type.

Never, ever, carry so many bags that your right hand is holding anything! Keep your right hand free at all times to ensure you can render a quick salute to a passing TAC Officer or grip the hand rail as you go up and down the fire escapes. Believe me when I tell you the TAC Officers don't care that your hands are full and you're moving. This is an ultra-high stress event designed to see who breaks.

This is not a time to be an individual. Move as squads, march in step, look like you are in a parade. No one benefits if you look like a soup sandwich. Help each other out and help carry each others moving bags over to the new barracks. Show the TAC Officers you are undertaking this activity as a class.

Expect several moves during the WOCS course. A second move is usually several weeks into the course to "Shake up "the class and change out your room mates. Each move is designed to make sure you don't get to comfortable and to see if you can come up with a "Plan". Expect to have a full blown inspection the following day after a move.

TAC Alley Procedures

Source: WO1 Jack Du Teil
http://www.il.ngb.army.mil/Recruiting/WOC/Survival.aspx

Every time you need to report to a TAC Officer in his office, you will have to negotiate TAC Alley. TAC Alley is the hallway on the first floor of the main building at 1st WOCS. This is where ALL the TAC Officers keep their offices. TAC Alley is entered only from the outside entrance at the end of the hall, as follows:

First you will ground your books outside of the entry door and complete three pull-ups on the bars located beside the walkway leading to TAC Alley. As you complete each pull-up you will loudly call out the count (i.e. ONE! TWO! THREE!)

Now enter TAC Alley and immediately locate a clear segment of the wall (one that does not contain pictures, thermostats, etc.) and brace against it, with your hat properly held in you left hand. **NOTE:** Bracing is standing at attention, with your heels, backside, head and shoulders making contact with the wall.

You will give the greeting of the day. This is to alert the TAC Officers, who may or may not be in the building that you are in their area. Think of a bleating lamb in the lion's den.

Next move at a brisk walk to the appropriate office and brace the wall immediately outside (**NOTE:** one side of the door jamb will have a black wooden cutout of a hand on the wall. Brace the wall on the other side of the door). Some TAC Officers have the wooden hands painted in their class color.

Warning! If you encounter a TAC Officer on your way down the hall, immediately find a clear piece of wall, brace, administer the greeting of the day and wait until the TAC Officer passes. Be wary of TAC Officers coming up behind you. After the TAC Officer passes you may continue. If the TAC

Officer remains between you and your destination, request permission to pass "Sir, Candidate Smith requests permission to pass, Sir! ".

Once you are properly positioned outside of your TAC Officer's office, extend your foot and peer into the office. If the TAC Officer is not present, you can either wait until he returns or leave. If they are in, this lets them know you are there. If you see they are on the phone or have someone in their office, wait until your TAC Officer is available.

The TAC Officer will acknowledge your presence. Usually this will be a gruff "Candidate, what do you want?" At this point, move and stand at attention precisely in the center of the doorway, with the imaginary center line cutting under the center of your boots.

Purposefully look at the left door jam, the top jam and the right jam to demonstrate that you ensured you are properly centered. Make minor adjustments if you are not centered.

Lean back into the hallway, look at the hand, look directly to your front and slap the wooden hand three times. Wait for the TAC Officer to acknowledge your presence again.

Give the greeting of the day to the TAC Officer and wait for him to return it.

Request permission to enter the office "Sir, Candidate Smith requests permission to enter, Sir!".

When you are given permission to enter, march smartly in and assume the position of attention, 30 inches from the front of the TAC Officer's desk. Execute a salute and report "Sir, Candidate Smith reports!"

When the TAC Officer returns your salute, stay at the position of attention until he gives you permission to stand at ease. **NOTE:** If at any time the TAC Officer asks you something, answer them. Don't get so caught up in TAC

Alley procedures that you don't assess the situation. The TAC Officer may not want you in their office or wants you to get to the point. Be Frosty!

When the TAC Officer is finished with you, you exit TAC Alley as follows: Return to the position of attention and give the greeting of the day. Quickly move out of the office and down to the end of the hall, observing the same traveling procedures you did on the way in (if you encounter more TAC Officers). Exit TAC Alley and secure any books you left on the ground.

Negotiating TAC Alley is nerve racking. If you make mistakes, you will be required to do ten four count push-ups to atone for each mistake. When performing push-ups in TAC Alley (or anywhere where you are required to carry your headgear), place your headgear in the small of your back, with the bill stuck in your waistband. Try not to become too flustered.

Dining Rights:

Source: WO1 Jack Du Teil
http://www.il.ngb.army.mil/Recruiting/WOC/Survival.aspx

It's a good idea to be familiar with the WOCS dining procedures before actually having to perform them. When you first arrive at WOCS go to the Dining Facility during the time the WOCS classes are dining and CLOSELY OBSERVE the highly structured dining practiced. There are several exceptions:

Pig Rights: If Pig Rights are awarded to a class they may eat in a normal, relaxed manner, without having to observe all of the rules and procedures required with Disciplined Dining.

Talking Pig Rights: These are Pig Rights, with permission to talk to fellow candidates during the meal. You almost never get these.

Desert Rights: This is the right to eat desert with your meal. Jell-O is considered desert, so do not get caught eating it without desert rights. This is usually awarded as an addition to either Pig Rights or Talking Pig Rights.

Caffeine Rights: This is the right to drink caffeinated beverages. This right is usually awarded during the second or third week and extends to the schoolhouse as well. Hot chocolate is considered a caffeinated beverage. Unlike the other rights, which are generally awarded a few meals at a time, caffeine rights are permanent, unless withdrawn by a TAC Officer.

Discipline Dining

Whether you have rights or not, you are expected to stand at parade rest in the chow line. Make sure you get two full glasses of water with each meal (you sign a contract saying you will, upon arrival at WOCS). After leaving the serving line and entering the dining room, a dining hall monitor will point to where you will sit. You will eat at rows of four place tables. When you get to your table, you will place your hat and pistol belt under the chair you will be sitting in.

When observing Discipline Dining procedures, immediately begin to set up your tray. The plate will be centered and "grounded" to the front edge of the tray. The Spoon will be balanced on the left side, with the rounded side resting on the edge of the plate and the handle on the edge of the tray. If, at any time, the spoon slips off the plate (and it will), stop what you are doing and say, "Excuse me, candidates," and replace it. The fork will be balanced on the right side, with the concave side resting on the plate and the handle on the edge of the tray. The knife will be laid across the top edge on the plate, with the blade pointing to the right. Misplacement of the knife is considered a safety violation.

All beverage containers will be grounded to the back of the tray, centered and approximately three finger widths apart. Auxiliary dishes (e.g. salad bowls) will be grounded to the top right hand corner of the tray. Any trash (e.g. empty sugar packets) will be placed in the top left-hand corner of the tray. After setting up your tray, stand at attention until the last candidate at your four-place table is ready to sit. They will give the command: "Takes seats!"

Make sure you slide into your chair from the side you entered the row from. First, take two napkins. Napkins are difficult to remove from the dispenser, so one candidate should hold the dispenser firmly on the table with the palm of their hand so the other candidates can quickly remove 2 napkins each. Place one napkin, fully opened, on your right thigh. The other will be placed around your left index finger and used to dab your mouth with. Immediately begin to cut up any food that needs to be cut, you are only allowed to use your knife once during the meal. Replace your knife and observe silent Pig Rights until you are instructed to stop eating.

The last two people in each row of tables are responsible for issuing dining instructions. They will execute facing movements and position themselves at the head of the table, side by side, facing their fellow candidates. **The candidate on the left will give the following commands:**

Candidates, stop eating.

Candidates, at this time, you will take all commands from the candidate on my right.

The candidate on the right will continue with the following:

Candidates, at this time, ensure that your headgear is properly positioned under your chair. (All candidates simultaneously and quickly glance to the right).

Candidates, at this time, ensure that your chair is properly positioned under the table (All candidates quickly move their chair a bit).

Candidates, at this time, ensure that you have two napkins in your lap. (All candidates quickly glance down).

Candidates, at this time, ensure that your tray is properly aligned with the edge of the table. (All candidates quickly touch the bottom edge of their plates).

Candidates, at this time, ensure that your plate is properly positioned. (All candidates quickly touch the bottom edge of their plates).

Candidates, at this time, ensure that your silverware is properly positioned. (All candidates quickly touch each piece of silverware).

Candidates, at this time, ensure that all of your auxiliary dishes and beverage containers are properly positioned and grounded to your tray. (All candidates quickly touch all containers).

Candidates, enjoy your meal. (Candidates begin eating at a modified position of attention).

After they have finished, the two candidates at the head of the table will execute facing movements and move back to their chairs. The candidate who issued the commands will receive the entire litany of Dining Rights from the candidate who had stood to his left. They will then eat. Every time you take a bite, you will lock the food with your teeth, dab your mouth with the napkin in your left hand, and then continue chewing. When you finish eating, you will exit from the opposite side of the chair you entered from. Anytime you come to an area in the dining facility where there might be cross traffic; you will stop and look both ways.

After you've turn in your tray and go outside to your class assembly area and stand at ease while waiting for the entire class to complete eating. Be wary of TAC Officers lurking about. After a quick formation your class will march off and continue training.

Pig Rights and Talking Pig Rights

When you first arrive at WOCS you do not have dessert, soda, or talking privileges at the Dining Facility (DFAC). These are rights that must be earned, usually by singing songs for the TAC Officers. Think I'm kidding?

The first song your class will sing is for the right to hang your hat, a WOCS tradition. The hanging of the class hat is usually right after your class receives its hats, shirts and guidion from the vendor.

Later, your class will also request to sing for Pig Rights and possibly Talking Pig Rights. Below is a great video link to Blue Class 10-6, the Trailblazers, as they sing several songs towards earning their rights: http://www.youtube.com/watch?v=dpVvBbap8Ds

NOTE: Usually the more songs you sing the more days of Pig Rights your class will be awarded, as a general rule. Of course the quality and enthusiasm displayed also plays a part. By the way, the songs are original material your class develops, sung to a well known tune.

Pig Rights and Talking Pig Rights can also be awarded for winning the WOCS Olympics or if your class scores well academically or on the APFT.

My class attended WOCS just before Christmas, so many of our songs were Christmas related. The hard part was selecting songs that people knew the words to, so we could change them up for our DFAC Class songs, Here is one we prepared for our TAC Officer, Mr. Clark. He was a rather quiet guy, but he, like the rest of them, had a sadistic streak in him that was a mile wide.

Our song is sung to the tune of "You're a Mean One, Mr. Grinch":

You're a mean one..., Mr. Clark;
You're a Dirty- Rotten-TAC!
You sneak upon us silently and give us a heart attack,
Mr. Clark!

You're so crafty, Mr. Clark.
You slither through the grass and Catch us taking a nap
Like a silent Egyptian Asp,
Mr. Clark.

You're a mean TAC, Mr. Clark.
You enjoy punishing our class, with the Leg Lifts, Push Ups, Pull Ups,
When you catch us on our ass,
Mr. Clark.

However, given the choice between you and being a Vietnam POW...
I'd take the Hanoi Hilton, EVERYTIME!

Rehearse your songs before the big show during class breaks or on Sundays. The guys up front cannot have cheat cards; however the rest can hide them in their hats. Everyone needs to sound off!

Seven Minute Drill

It behooves you to know what the seven minute drill is in the event it's discussed during casual conversation. During my time as a student at the WOCS I was assigned to Red Class, or the raging Red Bulls, as we called ourselves. Our class motto was "If you mess with the bull, you get the horns!"

Every morning, just prior to 0445, the Candidate Duty Officer of the Day (CDO) would call and get the weather forecast. At 0445, the CDO would walk each floor of the billets and announce the ambient temperature and likelihood of rain.

It's prohibited by the WOC SOP to get out of your rack prior to the CDO's daily announcement. It's considered cheating just getting up at 0430 to use the bathroom. Once the CDO passes through, we would get up, having slept in our PT shorts and t-shirts, and put on socks and shoes, rush to the bathroom and take care of business. Because it was difficult to deodorize the urinals properly, we would not use them and instead the 61 male candidates would jostle to use the 4 toilets. The five females assigned to our class used the second restroom on our floor. Also we would shave and brush our teeth. Another requirement was to take a full canteen of water to PT, so our canteens were topped off at this time. After returning to our rooms our racks had to be made to standard, all drawers closed, wall lockers locked (this was the only time we locked the wall lockers, since they were open for inspection the rest of the time) and slide our boots over to fill the vacancy left from removing our PT shoes, and turn off all lights except the fire lights.

Next, the entire Red Class of 66 candidates (61 Males and 5 Females) would gather in the hall in 2 columns facing the door and hold a canteen in their left hand. The Class 1st SGT would exit the Fire Escape door, walk down 2 flights of stairs while maintaining their right hand on the rail, walk on the sidewalk, double-time approximately 65 meters to the Red Class assembly, come to the position of Attention, and call out "Fall-In!" That was our cue to follow in a similar manner by exiting the Fire Escape door, walk down 2 flights of stairs while maintaining one hand on the rail, walk on the sidewalk, double-time to the Red Class assembly and fall-in to a platoon formation. The Security Officer was responsible to lock the door after the last candidate exited. Once the last candidate fell in the Class 1st SGT would order "Report" and each Squad Leader would render a salute and report either "1st Squad, Present or Accounted for." Or "1st Squad, Johnson reported to Sick Call, all others present." Once all Squad Leaders had reported the Class 1st SGT would give the command "Right Face" and "Column Left" to march us onto the parade field. Next would follow the commands "Class Halt", "Left Face", and "PT Instructor Post".

At this point the designated PT instructor for the day would look left and right, determine the shortest route to the Class 1st SGT, step backward 2 steps , fall out of formation, and double-time to the front and report to the Class 1st SGT by standing at attention and saluting. The Class 1st SGT would return the salute and fall into the formation and the PT instructor would assume his position, do an About Face and issue the following commands "At Double Arm Interval-Extend to the Left, March""Arms Downward, Move" "Left Face" "At Double Arm Interval, Extend to the Left, Move""Arms Downward, Move""Right Face""From front to rear, Count Off""Even numbers to the Left, Uncover", At this point everyone is still holding their canteen in their left hand. At the command "Ground your gear" the class would place their canteens on the ground, perfectly aligned. Imagine a single laser beam used for accuracy, with the name tape up and all caps facing forward. "Attention" would get everyone up again and PT would begin.

If it was after 0452, or seven minutes had expired, and you hadn't started exercising, your Class TAC Officers would come out and conduct PT, much to the dismay of the entire class. Trust me; you're so much better off if you conduct your own PT sessions, as the TAC Officers got brutally creative. One Inch Pushups, Tee-Pee Pushups, Leg-Lifts, Get Ups-Get Downs all come to mind.

WOC 500

The WOC 500 is a variation of the Indi 500 and is held every Sunday. Sundays are something of a No Training day and was the only day us candidates could go to our cars, start them up, and drive a few laps around the parking lot. So what's the big deal? Well for starters, your car has wonderful refreshing A/C. You can listen to the radio and catch up on news, the game or music. You can drive a few laps around the parking lot to charge up the batteries (yours and the car) and feel like a human being. The hard part for me was resisting the urge to drive right off the parking lot, out the Enterprise gate and get the heck out of Dodge.

If you were lucky, you could catch one of the WOCS carwashes that seem to happen every weekend. On the outside you appear to be supporting the charity carwash, but actually you are just extending the enjoyable driving experience. You can relax for awhile while someone else washes your car. Take in the water splashing, rhythmic sponging and Turtle Wax soap smells and towel drying. Treat yourself to the Armor All tire dressing. Many a candidate had to be woke up and told to put a donation in the can and drive off. A carwash can extend the WOC 500 for an hour.

Do not call home on your cell phone or use this time to wolf down pogie bait you hid in your car. The TAC Officers are on the lookout for this kind of stuff and you will be caught.

Afterwards, do a few last laps in your clean car, re-park in the student parking lot, lock the doors, take a breath, and rejoice that another week of WOCS is behind.

Fund Raisers and Charity Projects

Expect to spend a couple of Saturdays organizing and participating in fund raisers, usually consisting of car washes.

A successful car wash is dependent on good timing. A Payday weekend will do better than a non-Payday weekend. Also check the short- term weather forecast prior to selecting a date, as rain will definitely dampen your cash flow. Assign some duties out to your class. You will need someone to make flyers and post them throughout the area, especially at the Commissary, Shoppette / Gas Station / Barber Shop and PX areas. Assign someone to be responsible for supplying the necessary equipment. Preferable scavenge up car wash soap and Armor All from a previous Classes' car wash, but also get sponges, hoses, drying towels and trash cans. A coffee can makes for a good cash donation container.

We also spent a Saturday cleaning up a playground. You'll need to scrounge up trash bags, rakes, clippers, and maybe paint and brushes.

In any case, after the event, prepare a memorandum for record to present to your TAC Officer describing your classes' contribution to the community. Any event must be approved by your TAC Officer.

Class Colors

It took our class about 10 days to earn our "Colors." During these 10 days we spent a great deal of time learning to stop being individuals and become a class. I like to think we were the biggest bunch of knuckleheads that ever went through WOCS, but in retrospect we were no different than every other class since the inception of Warrant Officers. After a few weeks the TAC Officers had beat into our heads that we sink or swim as a class, and after we grew accustomed to the general concept, things started to go more smoothly.

We had to design an emblem, a t-shirt, a hat and come up with a motto, and have everything blessed off by the Senior TAC Officer.

After several return trips to the drawing board we finally had some approved designs. BTW, your design must be original!

We were given a phone number for a local vendor who had everything produced within a few days. Don't forget to include your TAC Officer's order in with your classes'. You also need a spare hat for the "Hang a Hat" ceremony at the DFAC. You can also order extras for your family.

15 Minute Drill

Ok, you survived another PT session and ended with a 3-4 mile run and at least 5 pull-ups. What now?

Its 0600 and your TAC Officer released your class from PT. You file back up the trusty fire escape stairs, taking your shoes off as you near the door. After you get on the floor, head for the Mop closet or nearest toilet bowl and thoroughly clean the bottom of your tennis shoes, removing even the smallest grain of sand or blade of grass. Tie the laces, position the tongue just right and place them under your rack, carefully lining the toes up with your shower shoes, low quarters and boots.

Next hang your PT uniform on the outside door of your wall locker with a hanger and while standing on your towel, dump your canteen over your head, and rub a little water on your soap so it appears slightly damp. Apply deodorant liberally and get dressed. Hang up your towel on your locker towel bar. Put your socks in the laundry bag and tie the bag to the foot of your rack IAW the WOC SOP. Remember if it's an odd day to wear your "I" boots and hat and if it's an even day you wear your "II" boots and hat. Make sure you use the next items in your display without disturbing your display. Straighten everything up, stagger your drawers 1 inch, 2 inches, and 3 inches respectively from top to bottom. Fill out you laundry slip and Display Items Missing and Display Items Serviceable (DIM & DISI) cards to reflect today's date. Check your rack, prepare your Discrepancy Card for the day's inspection and check that the hangers in your wall locker are evenly spaced down to 1/32th of an inch. Remove the class books for the day, based on the posted training schedule, from the stack on your shelf and carefully square up the stack, with thickest, largest book on the bottom and thinnest smallest Field Manual (FM) on top. Be sure to ground everything.

NOTE: Grounding is lining items up with the nearest vertical furniture plane, such as the edge of the rack or edge of the shelf. Nearly everything in your room is grounded in some fashion. The easiest way to get it right the first time is to press one end of a ruler against an edge, and line everything up along the ruler's length.

In addition to getting yourself dressed and your area straight for the day's inspection, your squad is also assigned 1 of 4 main common areas to maintain. Those areas are:

1. **Latrine No. 1** (toilets, urinals, sinks, mirrors, showers and floors)

2. **Latrine No. 2** (toilets, urinals, sinks, mirrors, showers and floors)

3. **Halls** (sweeping, mopping, base boards, mop closets, buffing)

4. **Brass** (shining everything from brass, door knobs, fire door glass, the 2 water fountains, and any outside brass plaques assigned).

Next, the entire Class will line the hall in 2 columns facing the door and holding their books and laundry bags in their left hand. You also have your WOC Wallet and full canteen or Camelback with you. The Class 1st SGT would exit the Fire Escape door, walk down 2 flights of stairs while maintaining their right hand on the rail, walk on the sidewalk, double-time approximately 65 meters to the Class assembly, come to the position of Attention, and call out "Fall-In!" That is your cue to follow in a similar manner by exiting the Fire Escape door, walk down 2 flights of stairs while maintaining one hand on the rail, walk on the sidewalk, double-time to the Class assembly and fall-in to a platoon formation. The Security Officer is responsible to lock the door and make sure all lights are out after the last candidate exited. Once the last candidate fell into formation the Class 1st SGT would order "Report" and each Squad Leader would render a salute and report "1st Squad, Present or Accounted for" and so forth through 4th squad. Once all Squad Leaders had reported the Class 1st SGT would give the command "Right Face", "Forward March" and "Rear March" to march us to the DFAC.

During our first 2 weeks we were given until 0625 to start marching to the DFAC. Weeks 3 and 4 we had to be marching at 0620. During weeks 5 and 6, as the Senior Class preparing for graduation, we had to be marching at 0615.

Remember, you can't do everything, so prioritize and decide what you can afford to take a hit on during the inspections.

Field Week

In keeping with how the Army currently operates, WOCS has added a week long Field Training Exercise (FTX). After the initial planning and training, OP Orders and FRAGOs are generated. The FTX includes Flight School Instructors, TAC Officers, Chinook Student Pilots (recent WOCS Graduates) as well as current WOC students. The FTX is usually held during your class' 3rd or 5th week of training.

The FTX Week kicks off with a CH-47 Chinook Helicopters transporting your class to Tactical Training Base (TTB) Freedom, deep in the country of "WOC-anistan". Upon arrival you'll be assigned a CHU (Containerized Housing Unit) where you'll bed down for the week. The FTX consists of classes, Military Operations on Urban Terrian (MOUT) and a Patrol Day where your class will experience encountering a hostile force. You'll be evaluated on First Aid, Evacuation Procedures, Security and Communications. Included at no extra cost is a trip to the Leader's Reactionary Corse (LRC). Your Squad will have to safely navigate the entire team across several puzzling stations while safely transporting Ammo Cans or Injured Personnel, using provided tools such as two boards, a rope and a lot of imagination. Expect to encounter a hostile enemy force anytime day or night.

MOUT operations are designed to provide the experience of identifying and defeating dismounted enemy combatants embedded into a civilian population. Beware of snipers, pyrotechnics, trip wires, booby traps, suicide bombers and so forth as your team clears houses and rooms. The normal Rules of Engagement (ROE) are simple, don't kill the civilians, friendly Foreign Military, or hostages and don't get killed in the process.

Also recently added is a HMMWV rollover trainer. The HMMWV Egress Assistance Trainer (HEAT) is an Up-Armored HMMWV chassis with a hydraulic motor that rolls the vehicle over in a 360-degree rollover simulation. The trainer provides soldiers confidence in the vehicle's seat-belt and familiarizes them to what a roll-over condition will feel like. Also taught is the importance of pulling the Gunner down from the turret to prevent them from getting crushed, and lastly how to properly and safely exit the vehicle, especially if under enemy fire.

No matter what WOCS throws at you, remember there is a light at the end of the tunnel named GRADUATION!

WOCS graduations are held in the Aviation Museum and will be the next to final activity before you leave Fort Rucker. You still have to clear the installation, which only takes about 2 hours.

All the effort you applied and lessons learned, all you went through to get those bars pinned on your shoulders, will stay with you for the rest of your career. Expect to get orders reassigning you to your new duty station shortly after returning to your unit, as well as a few stares from folks who remember you as an NCO and now see you as an Officer.

TIP: Remember now you have to salute virtually everyone you meet. As a newly promoted Warrant Officer you DROP your return salute FIRST when saluting Enlisted Soldiers. You smile, but it will happen. You will be holding your salute and an enlisted soldier will be saluting you back and you both will be thinking "Isn't that bum ever going to drop their salute?"

Chapter 14

How to be a Good Warrant Officer

Eight Rules to Live By:

Adapted from a paper written by:
Adam W. Burritt
Captain, Logistics
Education Services Officer
Commander, A Co, 3643rd BSB

1. A Warrant Officer is a leader who understands and adapts to the dynamics of the people he/she leads.

    Get to know your Soldiers, their skills, how best to apply their talents and be receptive to their problems.

2. A Warrant Officer can accept comments/critique from his/her NCO's and then make a decision and stick to it. Leading by committee works for some when you have time, but eventually someone has to make the call when the chips are down.

    Listen to your Soldiers, but be decisive; always do the hard right over the easy wrong.

3. A Warrant Officer is technically and tactically proficient, and understands how to implement the assets provided to them in an effective and safe way to obtain results.

    > Know your job better than anyone else in your unit; use what you have to get the task done without excuses.

4. A Warrant Officer understands that leadership in command is only part of the job, and that leadership on staff is just as important, but requires a different skill set.

    > You'll have to work twice as hard on a staff as the RLOs {Real Live Officers} since they went to the Captain's Career Course, Intermediate-Level Education (ILE) and possibly Command and General Staff College (CGSC) before assuming a staff job. But remember, they have never been down your path, so learn from them, be just as detail oriented, and in the end you will earn their respect.

5. A Warrant Officer seeks to constantly refine his/her knowledge, understands rules and regulations and employs those rules and regulations to the letter when required.

    > Be able to back up your decisions with the regulations and sound judgment. After awhile, people will stop questioning you.

6. A Warrant Officer praises in public. Corrections are always made behind closed doors. However, a Warrant Officer knows when it is time to show his Soldiers they will be required to toe the line, and that those who refuse to do so will be reprimanded.

    > Be discrete when possible, but be prepared to discipline in public if required.

7. A Warrant Officer has a plan. Hopefully it's a good plan. Maybe it's a written plan, but a plan for everything. Every new job requires a new plan, and if you go into an assignment thinking you can just wing it because you know your stuff, you are dead wrong.

    Look at your SOP, keep it up-to-date and always strive to improve it. Synch maintenance with your supported units. Use the WOPA and learn from the Senior Warrants in your branch.

8. You are as good as your integrity, don't lie, cheat, or abuse your soldiers. Don't tolerate those that do.

This is not an all inclusive list, just a list of lessons learned. A Warrant Officer is no longer an NCO, and the bottom line is the buck stops with you now. As your career progress, you can add and subtract from the 8 rules above. But for now, these tips are provided to get you started on the right path.

Chapter 15

Your First Year as a Warrant Officer

Arriving at Your Unit

Prior to arriving to your first duty station, call and make an appointment to report to your Commanding Officer, Rater, and Senior Rater. Call the S1 section and tell them when you expect to arrive so they can prepare the in-processing paperwork. Get phone numbers and email addresses for the Warrant Officers in your new unit. They can give you the lay of the land, the unit's mission and provide some Intel on any upcoming deployments and exercises. Also, if luck is with you, the Warrant Officer you are replacing is still assigned and can give you some insight on your new job requirements and your duty description. At any rate request their latest support form, which will provide you with your rating chain information.

I can only hope your first year as a Warrant Officer is not as confusing as mine was. My hardest lesson was to learn I was no longer a NCO.

My first assignment was as the Missile Maintenance Technician to the 3rd Armored Cavalry Regiment at Fort Bliss Texas. I was assigned as the Officer in Charge (OIC) for the Missile Shop and the Integrated Family of Test Equipment (IFTE) Shop as well as the Platoon Leader. The previous Warrant had left several months prior and I was the only MOS 912 series Warrant on Fort Bliss. I had no one to glean prior experience from, but I did have an awesome group of Warrant Officers who helped me to become a Warrant. CW3 Charlie Mills , CW3 Dan McLeish, and CW2 Bill Bono were terrific at getting me settled in. Charlie could lay 8 M2 Machine Guns out on a table and fix 5 of them within a few minutes by swapping out a few parts. Charlie always had a pot of coffee brewing, whether we were in the shop or in a raging thunder storm at Arrowhead at the National Training Center (NTC) and Dan would always be nearby with a joke and the latest Smokin' Hot bottle of hot sauce that you just had to try, just so you could brag about putting red hot lava on your tongue. Remember, we didn't have AKO accounts, Warrant forums, or even individual computers in 1994.

Meetings, Formations, Staff Calls and Parades

The Bottom Line Up Front (BLUF) is if it's important to your Rater and Senior Rater, then it should be important for you to attend. The section, maintenance shop or motor pool will function without you. It means a lot to your Rater and Senior Rater when you make the effort to attend Change of Command, after hour socials and Promotion ceremonies. Beside, who can say "No" to cake and punch?

After awhile you will figure out what to avoid. Use some common sense; if you're a Maintenance Warrant, then it behooves you to attend a weekly or monthly maintenance meeting.

Team Building
Forming

In the first stages of team building, the FORMING of the team takes place. As the new Warrant Officer, you may be assigned immediately as the section OIC. My best bit of advice is to not make any major changes for at least 30 days. Take this time to OBSERVE and IDENTIFY the key performers, as well as whom the slackers are. When you first join a new group your initial behavior is driven by a desire to be accepted by the section and other Officers in your unit, and avoid controversy or conflict. Serious issues and feelings are avoided, and your focus will be to LEARN the Unit's Battle Rhythm, getting into routines regarding reports and maintenance, understanding the unit's organization, who does what, where and when meetings occur, etc. This is a great time to learn what is required from you at these meetings and what level of information your Senior Officers want from you.

Just remember others are gathering information and impressions about you- such as how you act under stress, so take this time to comprehend the scope of the mission and the tasks assigned and how to approach it. This is a comfortable stage to be in, but the avoidance of conflict and threat means that not much actually gets done.

When you meet the Soldiers and Non-Commissioned Officers (NCOs) in your section, Unit and other fellow Officers, you'll learn about the mission and challenges your section faces, and also be told of the goals and start to lead the section in tackling the tasks required to achieve those goals. Your section members will tend to behave quite independently for most tasks. They may be motivated and show some initiative but are usually relatively uninformed of the unit's issues and objectives. Section members are usually on their best behavior at first but their true personalities will eventually appear. Be wary of anyone wanting to INFORM you of the slackers in your section. What may have been an issue with the previous Warrant could now be resolved since you took over. Come to your own opinions based on your own observations. Usually your best NCOs and Soldiers will model appropriate behavior even at this early phase and be supportive of your new assignment.

As the section OIC you need to be decisive during this phase as well as somewhat of an enigma. There is a reason the Army puts as much effort in training and grooming NCOs as they do, and you need to use them as a buffer between you and the Soldiers assigned to your section. The United States Military has the world's finest NCO corps. Remember, you are no longer an NCO and don't continue to be one. Tell your NCOs what you expect and what the standard is and check that it's done.

The forming stage of any section is important because, in this stage, the section members get to know one another, exchange some personal information and make new friends. This is also a good opportunity to see how each member of the team works as an individual and as a group, who your small group leaders are, what personality conflicts exist and how the section responds to pressure. Lucky for you individuals leave and join Army sections routinely, but even so expect some speed bumps along the way.

Transforming

The transformation phase is a period after forming where the performance of the section gradually improves. It is usually entered after the section breaks out of its norms after a series of successful creative problem-solving or intense section level activities are completed. The interference of the Warrant, who is content with the section's level of performance, can prevent a team from progressing through the storming stage to achieve its true performance potential. This puts the emphasis back on the team and leader as the storming stage must be actively engaged in order to succeed—too many 'diplomats' or 'peacemakers' especially in a leadership role may prevent the team from reaching their full potential.

Storming

Every group will next enter the storming stage in which different ideas compete for consideration. You and the NCOs addresses issues such as what problems they are really supposed to solve, how they will function independently and together and what leadership model they will accept. Your section NCOs and Soldiers will began to open up to you and each other and openly confront your orders and the section's goals and the how to tackle the tasks associated those goals. In some cases storming can be resolved quickly. In others, the section never leaves this stage, and takes an extraordinary amount of time to get even the most routine tasks accomplished. The maturity of some Section members and especially the professionalism of your NCOs will determine whether the section will ever move out of this stage. Some section members will focus on minutiae to evade the real issues and try to derail your authority. As the OIC, you must show the ability to chart a course thru all the chaos and background static with results that meet or exceed the unit's goals, not your personal agenda or the section's. Avoid direct conflicts with your soldiers by working with your NCO and giving guidance thru them.

250

The storming stage is necessary to the growth of the section. It can be contentious, unpleasant and even painful to some section members who are averse to conflict. Tolerance of each section member and their differences should be emphasized. Without tolerance and patience the section and its mission will fail. This phase can become destructive to the section and will lower motivation if allowed to get out of control. Some teams will never develop past this stage.

You, the OIC, and the section NCOs, will need to be more accessible and really listen to your soldiers, but also provide firm guidance and decision-making and above reproach professional behavior. The section members will therefore resolve their differences and members will be able to participate with one another more comfortably. The ideal is that they will not feel that they are being judged, and will therefore share their opinions and views. Some rearrangement of team members and NCOs may come out of this phase, but the section will be stronger for it.

Norming

Congratulations, the section has finally become a cohesive unit and all agree to the goals and have come to accept your leadership as well as understand your standards. You have successfully communicated the mutual plan for the section at this stage. Certain section members may have compromised on their own ideas, but all agree to work together to make the section function as a coherent unit. In this stage, all section members take the initiative and have the ambition to work for the success of the section's goals.

Performing

Hopefully, your section will evolve to the performing stage. These high-performing sections are able to function as a unit as they find ways to get the job done smoothly and effectively without inappropriate conflict or the need for external supervision. Eventually they become motivated and knowledgeable. The section members are now competent, autonomous and able to handle the day to day decision-making process without excess supervision. A small amount of dissent is expected and even becomes customary as long as it is channeled through means acceptable to the section.

Leadership over your section during this phase is almost always to make course corrections and to assign priorities. The NCOs will make most of the necessary decisions. With time however, be aware that even the most high-performing teams will revert to earlier stages under certain circumstances. Many long-standing sections go through these cycles routinely as they react to changing circumstances, such as absorbing new NCOs and Soldiers or when members are reassigned. For example, a change in the NCO leadership may cause the team to revert to storming as the new NCO challenges the existing norms and dynamics of the section. The original section members have already gone thru this process and the transition from forming, transforming, storming, to norming, and hopefully back to performing, should be swift. These minor fluctuations are to be expected and with your leadership can be controlled.

Chapter 16

Army Officer Evaluation Report (OER's)

On 31 March, 2014, the Army Officer Evaluation Report Form (DA Form 67-10-1 & 67-10-2) policy changed to better align with current Army leadership doctrine, to more accurately evaluate performance and potential of Army Officers, to increase accountability, and to better inform a transparent, talent management process.

The OER enhancements, and changes, apply to all OERs. The changes include reinstating senior rater box check for company-grade Officers, senior rater successive assignment recommendations, incorporating a statement on the OER, if the rated Officer has completed or initiated a Multi-Source Assessment and Feedback/360 (MSAF), within the last three years, and a reduction in short-term evaluations. The requirement to conduct initial discussion with the rated Officer, regarding missions, goals, duties and objectives remains; the method of documenting that discussion is at the discretion of the rating Officer.

Specific modifications for each of these enhancements and changes:

Senior rater box check: The Senior rater box check (Part VI a.) is reinstated for company-grade Officers, Warrant Officer, Chief Warrant Officer 2, second lieutenant, first lieutenant , and captain, and Senior Raters will provide comments on the Rated Officer's potential in Part VI c. indicating the rated Officer's potential. Senior raters will also complete the check box (Part VI a.) and provide comments on potential (Part VI c.) on DA Form 67-10-2 for rated Officers in grades Chief Warrant Officer 3-5, Majors and Lieutenant Colonels.

Senior rater successive assignments: — senior raters will be required to indicate three successive assignments, instead of three future assignments for the rated Officer. The senior rater should look three-to-five years in the future, and list the next three, succeeding positions, appropriate to the rated Officer's grade and career path.

Multi-Source Assessment and Feedback/360 (MSAF)

The rater will include a comment stating that the rated Officer has completed, or initiated, a "360"/Multi-Source Assessment Feedback, within the last three years. The new OER form will eventually have a, "Yes or no" box to check for "360" completions. The MSAF provides input from peers, superiors, and subordinates which will help the rated Officer develop as a self-aware and adaptable leader. Officers can access the 360 Assessment at https://msaf.army.mil. Results of the feedback will still remain confidential, and only be available to the rated Officer; the results are to be used for self-development, not evaluative purposes. The purpose of the rater's check on 360 assessments is to help ensure that leaders are encouraging subordinate development and that rated Officers are benefitting from available leader development programs.

The new policy, regarding short-term evaluation reduction, reduces multiple, short-term evaluations, particularly in deployed situations, by permitting Officers who change raters but continue to perform the same duties under the same senior rater, to receive a memorandum of input from their departing rater, rather than a "Change of rater" evaluation. The memorandum of input is intended to be used by the rater of record when they complete the final OER; this is at the senior rater's discretion.

The Army anticipates more changes as they continue to develop the current evaluation forms to make certain that they reflect current doctrine, increase rater accountability, further stratify the senior rater profile technique for Officer evaluation reports, and include an interactive leader development tool.

Army Officers, except for those recalled from retired status, are required to receive periodic evaluation reports. The most important periodic report is the official rating provided by the Officer Evaluation Report (OER). The OER is used to determine potential for promotion, assignments, and selection for military training.

In an Officer's rating chain, he or she is first evaluated by a rater. Your rater is determined by the rating chain of your senior rater, and is usually your immediate supervisor. Your rater is responsible for evaluating all Officers assigned to them by the senior rater, and is free to use input, from a variety of sources, to develop your OER. It is your rater who will describe, in the OER, the rated Officer's overall performance and potential. In some cases, an intermediate rater is also assigned; still, the final person in the rating chain is the senior rater. It is the senior rater's job to review the rater's comments, provide important career-influencing input to the evaluation, and check a "rating block."

A recent update to the OER process that significantly affects the rated Officer, directly, is rater and senior rater accountability. To decrease the tendency for rating inflation, the rater and senior rater can only award top blocks to a limited number of Officers in their rater/senior rater population pool. Only 49%, less than half, of the rated Officer groups in the rater or senior rater's profile can receive an "excels" or "most qualified" rating. Getting consistent, top-block ratings is no longer necessary for promotion, and in fact, the majority of rated Officers will have some mid-range ratings, and still compete, successfully, against their peers for promotion, assignments, schools, and in some cases, even command.

About thirty days before your OER is due, the S1, G1, or even your rater, should remind you to submit a digitally-signed OER support form, and forward it to your rater. It is the rated Officer's responsibility to submit an OER support form to their rater by the due date. This allows your rater, and senior rater, sufficient time, ninety days, to complete and sign their portions, get your signature, get the OER reviewed, make any necessary rewrites, and send it to HQDA in time to avoid penalization for a late OER.

The three sections of the OER

1. Duties and Responsibilities (Part IV a.): This is the section of the OER support form that defines your position. If this is the first time you are completing the OER support from, or if this is a new duty position, ask for a copy of the previous Officer's duty description to help fill out this section. Caution: Some equipment quantities, dollar values, and personnel numbers may be out of date. Use the most up-to-date information available. This section should mimic the duty section from your support form. Be sure to capture any unique, additional duties assigned to you by your rater. Space is limited, so use it wisely.

2. Major Performance Objectives (Part IV b.): Ideally, this portion is to be filled out by both the rater and the rated Officer within thirty days of the start of the rating period, and then adjusted throughout the rating period as opportunities arise. State, in this section, what you expect to accomplish, or were expected to accomplish if you are filling this out retrospectively, during that rating period. The more specific you can be, the better!

3. Significant Contribution (Part IV c.): This section of the support form is similar to a "brag sheet" that states specifically what you, the rated Officer have accomplished over the rating period. This section provides the rater, and senior rater, elements to pick and choose from when they write the rated Officer's evaluation. The more detailed and well-defined these accomplishments are written, the easier it is for your raters to transmit the information to the actual OER. Use bullet statements, or exact sentences, that can be cut and pasted to the OER. The rater and senior rater may then embellish these descriptions as they see fit and/or appropriate. These statements should contain an action verb and a clear result. Example: Candidate completed Lean Six Sigma Green Belt project with $235K in cost avoidance benefits to the Army.

A continuation sheet can be attached if you exceed the character limits for any field.

Remember to view the OER support form as your projected image to your rater and senior rater, and after the OER is created from it and the OER is submitted to HQDA, it's part of your permanent record. Below is an example that can guide you through creating a worthy OER support form.

Selling yourself on your OER Support Form

The OER (Officer Evaluation Report) Support Form, DA Form 67-10-1A, is a wonderful tool, used to establish priorities, focus, and goals for you, as a Warrant Officer. Unfortunately, we are not formally trained on how to complete one effectively, and we must, usually, rely on others to give us advice; therefore, I pass hints on how to successfully sell yourself on your support form and build the foundation for your own OER.

Each position in a unit has similar positions throughout the Army. The way that a Warrant Officer fills that particular position, and decides what is important and relevant, is what makes the position so unique. Also, the significant achievements that a Warrant Officer writes down, and the way that they convey their achievements to their rater and senior rater, are also unique.

Every position in the Army is vital, and it's up to you to get the importance of the job, and the achievements of your soldiers and yourself, across to your rating chain. You must do this by communicating clearly the position requirement goals, and how you succeeded in completing them.

Duties and Responsibilities (Part IV c.)

The "duty and responsibilities" portion of the support form defines your position. The individual Officer can redefine the duties and responsibilities, but keep in mind that the previous Officer to hold your position has already submitted a support form, and you can use their entries as an example. It's OK to improve the duties, or to refine them in order to capture changes as discussed with your rater and senior rater. Remember, the duties are based on the mission of that position, but you should also cover additional duties assigned that will be unique to you. The rater, or S1, should have a duty description for each position in the unit. After you fill it in and make minor changes to reflect your understanding of your duties and responsibilities, schedule a meeting with your rater to see if they agree that you have captured the essence of the position. Face-to-face meetings are the essence of the rating system, and provide a mutual understanding of the requirements for a successful rating period. Try to successfully complete this section within the first thirty days.

Notice on the DA Form 67-10-1A provided, how the mission is defined in terms of 5Ws, number of Soldiers supervised, equipment, and dollar value.

No goals or additional duties are described in this description, unless they are a recurring event that goes along with this position.

The rest of the support form hinges off this duty description.

Support Form DA Form 67-10-1A
Indicate your Major Performance Objectives (Part V a.)

The next portion of the support form should be completed by the rater and rated Warrant Officer, together, within thirty days of the rating period, and adjusted throughout the rating period. The rater should give the Warrant Officer definite goals, and/or projects that are required to be completed during the rating period. The rated Warrant Officer can then incorporate those goals into their performance objectives. Example of this section:

b. INDICATE YOUR MAJOR PERFORMANCE OBJECTIVES:

1. Make safety a number-one priority, with zero preventable accidents.

2. Ensure 100% accountability of all assigned property.

3. Confirm that assigned soldiers and NCOs are counseled and evaluated on-time, and receive appropriate recognition for their contributions to the unit's success.

4. Complete annual 100% training requirements, and verify that the resources are available to my assigned soldiers, so they may do the same.

5. Guarantee that mission support exceeds our customers' expectation.

6. Improve readiness of assigned vehicles from 72% to 90%.

7. Achieve a 270 on my next APFT, a twenty-point improvement, and encourage my soldiers to do the same.

8. Continue working towards a Master's Degree.

The duties in this portion of the support form should be specific, and measurable objectives should be discussed. For instance, how does the Rated Officer show that the performance objective of exceeding customer expectations, No. 5, is achieved? Periodic phone calls, surveys, and reduction of complaints received may all contribute to measuring this goal. If the objective is not measurable, attainment will be difficult; for example, don't write "aim to improve APFT score," instead write "achieve a 270 on my next APFT, a twenty-point improvement."

Always define specific goals on your support form. Always keep in mind that if the goal is not achieved due to unforeseen circumstances, they can be rewritten as the rating period goes by to show what you did obtain. A support form is a working document until your OER is due and the significant contributions portion is completed.

Performance Objectives and Accomplishments Continued (Part V)

In this section you will have to list your major performance objectives (2-3) and list your significant contributions and accomplishments (2-3) for each of the six performance focus areas.

1. Character	4. Leads
2. Presence	5. Develops
3. Intellect	6. Achieves

Significant contributions: (Part V b.)

This section of the support form provides the rater and senior rater the ammo to fill out the rated Warrant Officer's OER. I recommend that you write your sentences so that they mimic what you would like to see on your OER, enabling your chain of command to "cut and paste" the "significant contributions" over into your OER. A rated Officer that cannot define their achievements will have a difficult time convincing others. Below are some poorly written contributions that will offer no help to your rater and senior rater when writing your OER. Read the contributions below.

1. Instilled safety awareness daily.

2. Conducted hand receipt inventories.

3. Prepared awards and conducted counseling.

4. Monitored training.

5. Made customer satisfaction a priority.

6. Supervised PMCS.

7. Passed APFT and worked on Master's Degree.

Now read the contributions below. These are well-defined, and can be easily transferred from this form to be used on your OER.

1. (Your Name) revitalized safety boards to raise safety awareness, discussed safety at weekly staff meetings, conducted monthly safety inspections, and directed the replacement of missing safety devices in the motor pool which resulted in no safety incidents in the last twelve months.

2. (Your Name) conducted monthly ten percent hand receipt inventories resulting in one-hundred percent accountability of all assigned property and zero loss of equipment, valued at over $3 million dollars.

3. (Your Name) recommended two NCOs and six soldiers to receive awards, completed evaluations for assigned NCO, and confirmed they were received by HQDA on time. All soldiers were counseled one time.

4. (Your Name) made sure that MOS and DA required training occurred on time. One-hundred percent of section completed annual training requirements. His driver, SGT Alpha, received NCO of the quarter. (Your Name) has successfully completed training at National Training Center (NTC).

5. (Your Name) created interactive customer survey to capture supported unit satisfaction and performed spot checks of equipment at the unit's location, resulting in a readiness improvement of fifteen percent.

6. (Your Name) conducted weekly ten-percent PMCS spot-checks of assigned vehicles. He worked with NCOs to verify that faults found were noted on 2404, and operators were available to assist motor pool in repairs. (Your Name)'s vehicles average, monthly, readiness rate is now ninety-six percent, a twenty-four percent improvement.

7. (Your Name) scored 278 on my last APFT, a twenty-eight point improvement. (Your Name)'s platoon was awarded the PT Streamer for the months of June and September.

8. (Your Name) completed four night classes for an additional twelve semester credits, with a 3.8 GPA.

Below is a collection of action verbs useful for filling out contributions:

Management skills	Communication skills	Clerical/Detailed skills
administered	addressed	approved
analyzed	arbitrated arranged	arranged
assigned	authored	catalogued
attained	corresponded	classified
chaired	developed	collected
contracted	directed	compiled
consolidated	drafted	dispatched
coordinated	edited	executed
delegated	enlisted	generated
developed	formulated	implemented
directed	influenced	inspected
evaluated	interpreted	monitored
executed	lectured	operated
improved	mediated	organized
increased	moderated	prepared
organized	motivated	organized
oversaw	negotiated	prepared
planned	persuaded	processed
prioritized	promoted	purchased
produced	publicized	recorded
recommended	reconciled	retrieved
reviewed	recruited	screened
scheduled	spoke	specified
strengthened	translated	systematized
supervised		tabulated

Research skills	Technical skills	Teaching skills
clarified	assembled	adapted
collected	built	advised
critiqued	calculated	clarified
diagnosed	computed	coached
evaluated	designed	communicated
examined	devised	coordinated
extracted	engineered	developed
identified	fabricated	enabled
inspected	maintained	encouraged
interpreted	operated	evaluated
interviewed	overhauled	explained
investigated	programmed	facilitated
organized	remodeled	guided
reviewed	repair	informed
summarized	solved	initiated
surveyed	trained	instructed
systematized	upgraded	persuaded
validated		set goals
		stimulated
		wrote

Financial skills	Creative skills	Helping skills
administered	acted	assessed
allocated	conceptualized	assisted
analyzed	created	clarified
appraised	designed	coached
audited	developed	counseled
balanced	directed	demonstrated
budgeted	established	diagnosed
calculated	fashioned	educated
computed	founded	expedited
developed	illustrated	facilitated
forecasted	instituted	familiarized
managed	integrated	guided
marketed	introduced	referred
planned	invented	rehabilitated
projected	originated	represented
researched	performed	
	planned	
	revitalized	
	shaped	

In all cases, write your sentences and significant achievements with bullets, beginning with strong action verbs, and include how this achievement has contributed to the organization, or to you. Remember to use numbers, dollar amounts, and percentages as much as possible. The rater and senior rater may then embellish each bullet in a more laudatory and professional tone to convey your achievements to HQDA.

It's been several years since HRC began using the new automated evaluation reports processing system. From my point of view, we have made great strides in achieving the OER processing goals established when the new system was implemented. Today, we have a fully automated processing system. OERs are received at HRC; scanned into a computer system; examined section by section on-line; Senior Rater profiles are calculated automatically and applied electronically; OERs receive a final quality control check; and then, they are forwarded to PERMS (Personnel Evaluation Reports Management System) via computer. Anytime during this processing cycle, we have the capability to amend OERs with minor errors without returning the OERs to the field. Rating officials can be contacted using e-mail, or by telephone using the senior rater's e-mail address or phone number on the OER. In return, e-mails from the rating chain are received by HRC, which authorize the necessary corrections to be made. This greatly reduces the time involved in processing OERs; however, certain types of errors cannot be corrected at HRC, and those reports are still returned to the field for correction.

The latest OER guidance, posted in DA PAM 623-3, 31 March 2014, mandates the use of valid Common Access Card (CAC) enabled digital signatures in electronic form templates and forms producing applications. DA PAM 623-3 emphasizes the Army-wide use of the Interactive Web Response System as a virtual tool to monitor the acceptance and processing of evaluation reports at Headquarters, Department of the Army (HQDA).The OER branch is always available to answer your questions.

The Officer Evaluation Report DA-67-10-1: (Front)

Your admin should fill out the top portion and the duty description is a cut and paste from your Support Form.

HQDA#

COMPANY GRADE PLATE (O1 - O3; WO1 - CW2) OFFICER EVALUATION REPORT		See Privacy Act
For use of this form, see AR 623-3; the proponent agency is DCS, G-1.		Statement in AR 623-3.

PART I - ADMINISTRATIVE (Rated Officer)

a. NAME (Last, First, Middle Initial)	b. SSN	c. RANK	d. DATE OF RANK (YYYYMMDD)	e. BRANCH	f. COMPONENT (Status Code)
DOE, JOHN	000-00-0000	1LT	20130901	EN	

g. UNIT, ORG., STATION, ZIP CODE OR APO, MAJOR COMMAND	h. UIC	i. REASON FOR SUBMISSION
50th MRBC, 5th EN BN, Ft. Leonard Wood, MO 65473 FORSCOM	WBAOAA	02	Annual

j. PERIOD COVERED		k. RATED MONTHS	l. NON RATED CODES	m. NO. OF ENCLOSURES	n. RATED OFFICER'S EMAIL ADDRESS (.gov or .mil)
FROM (YYYYMMDD)	THRU (YYYYMMDD)	12			john.doe18671@mail.mil
20140401	20150331				

PART II - AUTHENTICATION (Rated officer's signature verifies officer has seen completed OER Parts I-VI and the administrative data is correct)

a1. NAME OF RATER (Last, First, Middle Initial)	a2. SSN	a3. RANK	a4. POSITION
SMITH, JOHN	111-11-1111	CPT	Company Commander

a5. EMAIL ADDRESS (.gov or .mil)	a6. SIGNATURE	a7. DATE (YYYYMMDD)
john.smith18981@mail.mil	DIGITAL SIGNATURE	20120315

b1. NAME OF INTERMEDIATE RATER (Last, First, Middle Initial)	b2. SSN (Optional)	b3. RANK	b4. POSITION

b5. EMAIL ADDRESS (.gov or .mil)	b6. SIGNATURE	b7. DATE (YYYYMMDD)

c1. NAME OF SENIOR RATER (Last, First, Middle Initial)	c2. SSN	c3. RANK	c4. POSITION
GRANT, JOE	222-22-2222	LTC	Battalion Commander

c5. SENIOR RATER'S ORGANIZATION	c6. BRANCH	c7. COMPONENT	c9. EMAIL ADDRESS (.gov or .mil)	
5th Engineer Battalion Fort Leonard Wood, Missouri, 65473	EN	RA	joe.doe183906@mail.mil	
	c8. SENIOR RATER PHONE NUMBER 777-888-9999		c10. SIGNATURE	c11. DATE (YYYYMMDD)

d. This is a referred report, do you wish to make comments?			
☐ Referred	☐ Yes, comments are attached	☐ No	

f1. Supplementary Review Required?		f2. NAME OF REVIEWER (Last, First, Middle Initial)
☐ Yes ☒ No		

f3. RANK	f4. POSITION	f5. Comments Enclosed	
		☐ Yes	☐ No

f6. SIGNATURE	f7. DATE (YYYYMMDD)	g. MSAF Date (YYYYMMDD)
		20140601

PART III - DUTY DESCRIPTION

a. PRINCIPAL DUTY TITLE	b. POSITION AOC/BRANCH
Executive Officer	12A00

c. SIGNIFICANT DUTIES AND RESPONSIBILITIES

(See DA Pam 623-3, para 2-5)

PART IV - PERFORMANCE EVALUATION - PROFESSIONALISM, COMPETENCIES, AND ATTRIBUTES (Rater)

a. APFT Pass/Fail/Profile: _____ Date: _____ Height: _____ Weight: _____ Within Standard? _____

Comments required for "Failed" APFT, or "Profile" when it precludes performance of duty, and "No" for Army Weight Standards?

(See DA Pam 623-3, para 2-6)

b. This Officer's overall Performance is Rated as: (Select one box representing Rated Officer's overall performance compared to others of the same grade whom you have rated in your career. Managed at less than 50% in EXCELS.)

I currently rate _____ Army Officers in this grade.

A completed DA Form 67-10-1A was received with this report and considered in my evaluation and review: ☐ Yes ☐ No (explain in comments below)

EXCELS (49%)	PROFICIENT	CAPABLE	UNSATISFACTORY
☐	☐	☐	☐

Comments:

(See DA Pam 623-3, para 2-6)

DA FORM 67-10-1, MAR 2014

Page 1 of 2
APD LC v1.00ES

The Officer Evaluation Report DA-67-10-1: (Back)

HQDA#

NAME: DOE, JOHN	SSN 000-00-0000	PERIOD COVERED:	FROM (YYYYMMDD) 20140401	THRU (YYYYMMDD) 20150331

c. 1) Character:	
(Adherence to Army Values, Empathy; and Warrior Ethos/ Service Ethos and Discipline. Fully supports SHARP, EO, and EEO.)	(See DA Pam 623-3, para 2-6)
c. 2) Presence:	
(Military and Professional Bearing, Fitness, Confident, Resilient)	(See DA Pam 623-3, para 2-6)
c. 3) Intellect:	
(Mental Agility, Sound Judgment, Innovation, Interpersonal Tact, Expertise)	(See DA Pam 623-3, para 2-6)
c. 4) Leads:	
(Leads Others, Builds Trust, Extends Influence beyond the Chain of Command, Leads by Example, Communicates)	(See DA Pam 623-3, para 2-6)
c. 5) Develops:	
(Creates a positive command/ workplace environment/Fosters Esprit de Corps, Prepares Self, Develops Others, Stewards the Profession)	(See DA Pam 623-3, para 2-6)
c. 6) Achieves:	
(Gets Results)	(See DA Pam 623-3, para 2-6)

PART V – INTERMEDIATE RATER

(See DA Pam 623-3, para 2-7)

PART VI - SENIOR RATER

a. POTENTIAL COMPARED WITH OFFICERS SENIOR RATED IN SAME GRADE (OVERPRINTED BY DA)	b. I currently senior rate _____ Army Officers in this grade.
	c. COMMENTS ON POTENTIAL:
☐ MOST QUALIFIED (limited to 49%)	(See DA Pam 623-3, para 2-8)
☐ HIGHLY QUALIFIED	
☐ QUALIFIED	
☐ NOT QUALIFIED	
	d. List 3 future SUCCESSIVE assignments for which this Officer is best suited:
	(See DA Pam 623-3, para 2-8)

DA FORM 67-10-1, MAR 2014

Page 2 of 2
APD LC v1.00ES

1. Part VI c. Rater Comments

Most errors occur because the rater goes beyond what is requested, and recommends projected assignments tied to unique skill or adds comments on the Officer's future potential. All recommendations for future assignment, schooling, and/or command for Company Grade Officers is made by the Senior Rater in Part VI c. The Rater provides "Broadening Assignment" recommendations for Field Grade Officers on the DA 67-10-2 and Senior Raters will provide "Successive Assignments" recommendations. The rater's comments demonstrate the Officer's performance. The raters comments could include comments on: excellent use of limited resources, proactive in developing others, uses critical thinking skills, effective communicator, innovation, influential, and so forth.

OER completion requires rating officials to make a conscientious assessment of a rated officer's performance in his or her assigned position and his or her potential for increased responsibility and service in positions of higher ranks.

OER part VI: block d—Three Future (Successive) Assignments: In this block the Senior Rater will list at least two but no more than three different successive duty positions that the Rated Officer is "best suited to".

These assignments should serve to broaden and enrich the Rated Officer's future potential to the Army over the next 3 to 5 years.

2. Rater Commenting on Potential (Part IV e.)

Another major error occurring in Part IV e, in the rater's narrative, are comments on the rated Officer's potential (promotion, command, future assignment and schooling recommendations). Such comments are mandatory but only for the Senior Rater. Rater's comments will focus on the Rated Officer's performance. Overall, OER process time can be reduced significantly, if all raters focus their comments on performance and Senior Raters focus their comments on potential.

3. Lack of three successive assignments (Part VI d.)

The second most frequent error is the failure, by the senior rater, to make recommendations for 2-3 successive assignments for the rated Officer. The senior rater enters narrative comments in this block (Part IV c.). Bullet comments are prohibited. Potential comments should primarily focus on the rated officer's potential for promotion, command, schooling (military and civilian), broadening assignments, successive duty assignments and level of assignments, and/or retention, when applicable. Even in cases of adverse OERs, these recommendations are required, and are valuable to determine a suitable assignment for the rated Officer, while awaiting any administrative action that may be pending.

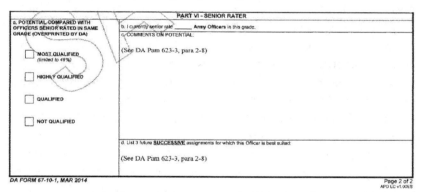

4. Senior rater not senior enough

OER branch still receives a significant number of OERs with invalid senior raters. The most common problem is that the designated senior rater is not always "senior enough" to evaluate the Officer. Often, this occurs because the rated Officer has been promoted or selected for promotion during the rating period. When an Officer is promoted, the rating chain should be reviewed to determine if a new senior rater is required. For example:

CPT Smith is rated by MAJ Jones and senior rated by LTC Johnson. Four months into the rating period, CPT Smith is promoted to MAJ. LTC Johnson is no longer eligible to Senior rate CPT Smith because the minimum grade for a senior rater of a MAJ is a COL/GS15. A new senior rater must be identified. LTC Johnson, if he chooses, and if all requirements are met, can render a senior rater option OER, prior to CPT Smith's promotion to Major.

A second example:

CPT Smith is rated by MAJ Jones and senior rated by LTC Johnson. Four months into the rating period, CPT Smith is selected for promotion to MAJ. CPT Smith is working in an authorized O-4 billet. LTC Johnson is not eligible to senior rate a CPT(P), who is serving in a Major's position; therefore, a new senior rater must be designated.

Rater and Senior Rater qualifications are discussed in DA PAM 623-3 para. 3-8 d. Use this reference as your guide in determining senior rater qualifications. Officers who have had an OER returned, due to "senior rater grade not met," know that there is no easy fix for these reports. You cannot designate another Officer as the senior rater and evaluate the rated Officer. Usually, the invalid senior rater narrative is moved to the intermediate rater portion of the OER, and a new senior rater is appointed to perform the review function only. The bottom line is that the rated Officer gets an OER without senior rater comments, or a block check. I urge you to discuss senior rater qualifications at your S1/PSNCO conferences, and ask them to send you a copy of their rating schemes so that your clerks can pick up on the invalid senior raters before reports are generated.

5. Use of narrative gimmicks

The use of BOLD type or exaggerated margins, or"picture-framing," has never been permitted when preparing an OER. Raters, or senior rater, who use BOLD type, or "picture-framing," to emphasize, highlight, or bring attention to a rated Officer's performance, often do the Officer a disservice. OERs with BOLD type, or "picture-framing," will not be accepted and will be returned to the submitting organization for correction, thus delaying the processing of the rated Officer's OER.

6. Completion of Part IV b, (Raters) & Part VI b.(Senior Raters)

Many OERs have reached HRC with this block only partially completed. In addition to the block check, evaluating the Officer's potential, the Raters and Senior Raters are required to identify the number of Officers of the same grade and component that the senior rater rates. When that space is blank, the OER cannot be finalized; again, this small omission results in unnecessary processing delay, since the examiner must contact the senior rater and request the necessary information before the OER can be processed. By reviewing OERs more carefully, prior to submission, to HRC, this can be an easily eliminated error.

7. "Relief for Cause" OERS

A great deal of time is lost attempting to process incomplete Relief for Cause (RFC) OERs. To ensure that these OERs are processed in a timely manner, several things must be completed. Below is a short questionnaire that should serve as a checklist, identifying actions required to ensure prompt processing of RFC OERs:

Does the OER identify who directed the actual relief?

- Rater?
- Senior rater?
- Other? (If outside the rating chain, a memo, by the relieving official, must be submitted with the OER).

Does the OER require a supplemental review?

- Yes or no
- If it does, is the supplemental review documentation included with the OER when submitted to HQDA?

Who conducts the supplemental review?

- If the rater did the relief, the review should be done by the senior rater. The senior rater should state he or she has reviewed the action, and it is correct. No additional paperwork is required.
- If the senior rater directs the relief, the review must be done by the first Officer in the chain of command, above the senior rater. A memorandum is required.
- If the relief is directed by someone other than the immediate rating chain, rater or senior rater, the review should be conducted by the first Officer in the chain of command, above the individual who directed the relief. A memorandum is required.

Must the senior rater complete Part VI. d.?

- Yes. Even if the senior rater has recommended that the rated Officer not be retained on active duty, the Officer will not be released from the Army immediately. In most cases, recommending positions and assignments, where the rated Officer can be utilized, will assist those responsible for the Officer, pending further action.

Are the following documents included in the RFC OER packet?

- Acknowledgement of the referral, by the rated Officer, unless the rated Officer checked "no" in Part II. d., and signed.
- Comments from the rated Officer, if he chooses to make comments.
- A statement by the senior rater, if the rated Officer refused to sign the OER.
- A statement by the relieving official, if different than rating officials, with reasons for relief (AR 623-3, paragraph 3-36).
- Supplementary Review, unless rater directed the relief.

If any of the required documentation is not included with the OER, processing the OER will be delayed and the OER may even be returned; therefore, it is imperative that you review the OER carefully before sending it to HRC.

Helpful hints
OER profiling

Once the OER is received at HRC, it is date-stamped with the received date. All reports, from the same senior rater, for Officers in the same grade, received at HRC on the same day, will be added to the senior rater's profile, as of the same date (batch processing). For example: A senior rater's profile currently reflects two Most Qualified (MC) reports, and four Highly Qualified (HQ) reports. The senior rater forwards two more MQ reports to HRC; if both reports arrive on the same day, the profile will reflect four MQ and four HQ. Since the MQ category is not less than fifty-percent, both incoming reports should receive a HQ label. If the same two reports arrive on separate days, the profile on the first day should reflect three MQ reports and four HQ; thus, the incoming report would get an MQ label because the profile has less than fifty-percent in the MQ category. The profile, on the day that the second OER arrives, would reflect four MQ and four HQ, and since the MQ category is not less than fifty-percent, the incoming OER should receive a HQ label.

HRC contact information can be found at: www.hrc.army.mil

Some other reminders about profile management:

- Plan ahead, and know when OERs are due and when selection boards meet.
- Start off with, and maintain, a credible profile; establish a goal of one-third for the top block.
- MQ Ratings. Your ability to give "MQ" ratings depends on effective profile management, and proper sequencing of reports to HRC.
- Control the mailing and sequencing of OERs, and ensure that the first batch of OERs has arrived at HRC, before you send a second batch.
- Know your profile at all times. If unsure, call the Evaluation System Office at HRC.
- Remember, 2LTs through CPT, WO1, CW2 use the 67-10-1 and MAJ, LTC and CW3-CW5 use the 67-10-2.

Sequencing and processing delays

Sequencing is still not routine for most senior raters. In an effort to manage their profiles successfully, senior raters have a tendency to hold "top block" OERs for excessive periods of time. This can become an issue if the OER, when it finally arrives at HRC, has major errors. While the OER will be profiled, based on the date it arrives in OER Branch, an OER with errors is often put in a "Hold" status while we wait to get the information needed to resolve the errors. By the time that OER branch receives the information, corrects the OER, and sends it to Officer Records, the OER may be six or eight months old. Just remember that when OERs are sent in at or after the ninety-day mark, they will not be processed until all errors have been corrected.

OERs delayed because of errors also have a major impact on OERs submitted for selection boards. While board OERs have processing priority, OERs can only be profiled once all OERs, submitted through the profile date, are completed. It becomes a critical issue when a non-board OER is not corrected or completed, and it holds up the processing of board reports.

OER myths revisited

1. Rating officials and the rated Officer should always leave the signature dates blank for the administration personnel to fill in.

    ABSOLUTELY WRONG: Rating officials and the rated Officer have to digitally sign the report.

2. Signature dates determine whether or not an OER is considered late.

    WRONG: Rating officials have ninety days, from the "Thru" date of the report, to have a report reach OER Branch, HRC. On the ninety-first day after the "Thru" date of the report, the OER is considered late. Signature Dates have nothing to do with the calculation.

3. LTC may senior rate CPT (P), serving in an authorized MAJ position.

    WRONG: An LTC may not senior rate a CPT (P) serving in an authorized MAJ position. If a CPT is in an S3 slot, authorized for a MAJ, and is selected for promotion to MAJ, then you must change the rating scheme immediately, with a COL (or GS-15) or higher, as the senior rater.

4. Officers going before a promotion board, below-the-zone, may receive Complete-the-Record (CTR) reports.

    ABSOLUTELY NOT: DA PAM 623-3 is very specific in that only Officers in or above the primary zone qualify for a CTR OER. If I submit a CTR report on an Officer going before a promotion board, below-the-zone, HRC may not catch it, and it may go before the board.

    NOT TRUE: There are many "gates" at HRC that an OER must pass through prior to being seen by the board. First, the computer that processes OERs identifies individuals eligible for selection boards that are below-the-zone, and not authorized CTR OERs. Second, an OER examiner reviews every OER. Based on his or her review, and the list of computer generated errors, the invalid OER will be identified and withdrawn. Third, the person responsible for profiling OERs and distributing them to the DA Secretariat also checks to ensure that the OER is valid. Fourth, branch managers who conduct board scrubs also check. (**NOTE:** Below-the-zone files are physically segregated from primary zone files.) Fifth, board recorders, for each board, check hard copy files. Finally, board members themselves are certainly not timid in identifying possible irregularities in a file to the board recorders. Don't do it! You will simply be wasting your time, as well as the time of many other people, and the report will not go before the board.

Appeals and corrections branch notes
Reserve and National Guard OERs

The Appeals and Corrections Branch receives numerous inquiries from Officers who have Reserve and National Guard reports on the performance data of the OMPF, which they received while assigned to the Army Reserve or National Guard. In accordance with AR 600-8-104, table 2-2, all U.S. Army OERs will be filed on the performance data. Once started, the Officer Official Military Personnel File (OMPF) will be continued in use even if the Soldier changes Army components. There are no provisions to remove these reports, or transfer them to the restricted data, except through the process of appeals. If the Officer decides to appeal these reports, then the appeal must be submitted to the Appeals Branch at the respective component headquarters, Reserve or National Guard. The HRC Appeals and Correction Branch processes appeals, only on active duty OERs. Addresses and information on appealing Army Reserve and National Guard reports are contained in AR 623-3, Chapters 4 and 5.

Timely submission of OER appeals

The Appeals and Corrections Branch continues to receive a number of appeals requesting a waiver of the five-year limit on submission of substantive appeals. Approval of the waiver is given by the DCSPER Officer Special Review Board (OSRB), and waivers are only approved when "exceptional" justification is provided by the rated Officer. The OSRB policy, and the intent of AR 623-3, is that the appeals process is, and was at the time that the report was rendered, designed to encourage timely efforts to seek relief when a report is believed to be inaccurate. That belief presumably arises at the time the report is rendered. Rated Officers are responsible for initiating an appeal as soon as possible, as part of their share of the responsibility for their own career development and management. This is what the appeals process is designed to support, and failure to submit the appeal in a timely manner may result in loss of eligibility to appeal. Officers are reminded that all appeals on reports prepared on the DA Form 67-9 must be submitted within three years of the completion date. The five-year rule applies to all other reports.

General information

The OER information page. You can access the information page on the internet through the U.S. Army Human Resources Command website at http://www.hrc.army.mil.

Complete-the-record reports. These reports are authorized only for Officers in or above the zone for consideration by a selection board. To qualify for this type of OER, you must have a minimum of ninety rated days, excluding non-rated time, in the same position under the same rater. This must meet the "Thru" date, established for Complete-the-record reports for that board.

Clarification of AR 623-3, paragraph 3-60

All signatures on the OER should be dated on or after the "Thru" date of the report. The intent of AR 623-3 is that the rated Officer will sign the OER last; for example, the dates should be in sequential order (rater, intermediate rater, senior rater, rated Officer), or all on the same date. As an exception, to facilitate the rated Officer signing the OER after its completion and signature by the rating officials, the OER may be signed and dated by each rating official, up to fourteen days prior to the "Thru" date of the report. This is specifically for cases where the rated Officer, and/ or rating official(s), departs, immediately following the "Thru"date of the OER. Restrictions to this procedure are detailed in AR 623-3;, regardless of the signature dates, OERs will not be accepted for processing at HRC any earlier than the "Thru" date of the report.

OER Support Form (DSF) DA 67-10-1A

Raters of WO1-CW5 and 2LT-COL will use the Support Form DA 67-10-1A to encourage performance counseling and regular 2-way communication. The most important periodic report is the official rating provided by the Officer Evaluation Report (OER). The OER is used to determine potential for promotion, assignments, and selection for military training.

An Officer is first evaluated by a Rater. Your Rater is determined by your Senior Rater's rating chain and is usually your immediate supervisor. Your Rater is responsible for evaluating all Officers assigned them by the Senior Rater, and is free to use input from a variety of sources to develop your OER. It is your Rater who will describe in the OER the Rated Officer's overall performance. In some cases, an intermediate Rater is also assigned, and the final person in the rating chain is the Senior Rater. It is the Senior Rater's job to review the Rater's comments and to provide important career influencing remarks in your evaluation regarding your potential.

Most OERs are submitted annually, however many different situations such as PCS, change of responsibilities, Change of Rater, School, can trigger an out-of-cycle OER requirement. More information on the Officer Rating System can be found in AR 623-3

A successful Warrant Officer understands how to use the OER process. A good OER accurately reflects your duties, strengths, accomplishments, and portrays your future potential to the Army. Your accomplishments during the rating period should be clearly related to your duties and quantifiable and included on your DA Form 67-10-1A OER Support Form.

Raters of Officers will also conduct quarterly follow up counseling sessions to discuss performance, update and revise developmental tasks, and check on developmental progress. Summary and key comments will be recorded on the Support Form, which is considered a "working document." Senior Raters initial on the form. Senior Raters will also ensure compliance with Support Form requirements. The bottom line is a properly conducted counseling session and open command climate fosters honest, two-way communication between Raters and Rated Officers.

The Support Form is designed to support developmental actions and integrate the developmental action plans with performance objectives. The Rater directs the process, with active participation from the Rated Officer. The Support Form is used to build a developmental plan based on tasks targeting major performance objectives listed on DA Form 67-10-1A.

The Rater conducts quarterly counseling sessions to discuss performance, highlight observed progress and strengths as well as developmental shortcomings that need addressing, as they relate to adherence to the 6 leadership attributes and demonstration of competencies, and notes key points discussed in block Part V of the Support Form. The Rated Officer puts their initials in block III. The date the counseling(s) occurred is also recorded before the initials.

Part V - Six Performance Objectives and Accomplishments:

Character:	Army Values, Empathy, Warrior Ethos/ Service Ethos, Discipline
Presence:	Military and Professional Bearing, Fitness, Confidence, Resilience
Intellect:	Mental Agility, Sound Judgment, Innovation, Interpersonal Tact, Expertise
Leads:	Leads Others, Builds Trust, Extends Influence Beyond the Chain of Command, Leads by Example, Communicates
Develops:	Creates a Positive Environment/Fosters Esprit de Corps, Prepares Self, Develops Others, Stewards the Profession
Achieves:	Gets Results

OER Support Form DA 67-10-1A (Front)

HQDA#

COMPANY GRADE PLATE (O1 - O3; WO1 - CW2) OFFICER EVALUATION REPORT	See Privacy Act
For use of this form, see AR 623-3; the proponent agency is DCS, G-1.	Statement in AR 623-3.

PART I - ADMINISTRATIVE (Rated Officer)

a. NAME (Last, First, Middle Initial)	b. SSN	c. RANK	d. DATE OF RANK (YYYYMMDD)	e. BRANCH	f. COMPONENT (Status Code)
DOE, JOHN	000-00-0000	1LT	20130901	EN	

g. UNIT, ORG., STATION, ZIP CODE OR APO, MAJOR COMMAND	h. UIC	i. REASON FOR SUBMISSION
50th MRBC, 5th EN BN, Ft. Leonard Wood, MO 65473 FORSCOM	WBAOAA	02	Annual

j. PERIOD COVERED		k. RATED MONTHS	l. NON RATED CODES	m. NO. OF ENCLOSURES	n. RATED OFFICER'S EMAIL ADDRESS (.gov or .mil)
FROM (YYYYMMDD) 20140401	THRU (YYYYMMDD) 20150331	12			john.doe18671@mail.mil

PART II - AUTHENTICATION (Rated officer's signature verifies officer has seen completed OER Parts I-VI and the administrative data is correct)

a1. NAME OF RATER (Last, First, Middle Initial)	a2. SSN	a3. RANK	a4. POSITION
SMITH, JOHN	111-11-1111	CPT	Company Commander

a5. EMAIL ADDRESS (.gov or .mil)	a6. SIGNATURE	a7. DATE (YYYYMMDD)
john.smith18981@mail.mil	DIGITAL SIGNATURE 123456789	20120315

b1. NAME OF INTERMEDIATE RATER (Last, First, Middle Initial)	b2. SSN (Optional)	b3. RANK	b4. POSITION

b5. EMAIL ADDRESS (.gov or .mil)	b6. SIGNATURE	b7. DATE (YYYYMMDD)

c1. NAME OF SENIOR RATER (Last, First, Middle Initial)	c2. SSN	c3. RANK	c4. POSITION
GRANT, JOE	222-22-2222	LTC	Battalion Commander

c5. SENIOR RATER'S ORGANIZATION	c6. BRANCH	c7. COMPONENT	c9. EMAIL ADDRESS (.gov or .mil)
5th Engineer Battalion Fort Leonard Wood, Missouri, 65473	EN	RA	joe.doe188906@mail.mil
	c8. SENIOR RATER PHONE NUMBER 777-888-9999		c10. SIGNATURE c11. DATE (YYYYMMDD)

d. This is a referred report, do you wish to make comments?	e1. SIGNATURE	e2. DATE (YYYYMMDD)
☐ Referred ☐ Yes, comments are attached ☐ No		

f1. Supplementary Review Required? ☐ Yes ☒ No	f2. NAME OF REVIEWER (Last, First, Middle Initial)	
f3. RANK	f4. POSITION	f5. Comments Enclosed ☐ Yes ☐ No
f6. SIGNATURE	f7. DATE (YYYYMMDD)	g. MSAF Date (YYYYMMDD) 20140601

PART III - DUTY DESCRIPTION

a. PRINCIPAL DUTY TITLE	b. POSITION AOC/BRANCH
Executive Officer	12A00

c. SIGNIFICANT DUTIES AND RESPONSIBILITIES

(See DA Pam 623-3, para 2-5)

PART IV - PERFORMANCE EVALUATION - PROFESSIONALISM, COMPETENCIES, AND ATTRIBUTES (Rater)

a. APFT Pass/Fail/Profile: _____ Date: _____ Height: _____ Weight: _____ Within Standard? _____

Comments required for "Failed" APFT, or "Profile" when it precludes performance of duty, and "No" for Army Weight Standards?

(See DA Pam 623-3, para 2-6)

b. This Officer's overall Performance is Rated as: (Select one box representing Rated Officer's overall performance compared to others of the same grade whom you have rated in your career. Managed at less than 50% in EXCELS.)

I currently rate _____ Army Officers in this grade.

A completed DA Form 67-10-1A was received with this report and considered in my evaluation and review: ☐ Yes ☐ No (explain in comments below)

EXCELS (49%)	PROFICIENT	CAPABLE	UNSATISFACTORY
☐	☐	☐	☐

Comments:

(See DA Pam 623-3, para 2-6)

DA FORM 67-10-1, MAR 2014

Page 1 of 2

OER Support Form DA 67-10-1A (Back)

NAME:		SSN		PERIOD COVERED:	FROM (YYYYMMDD)	THRU (YYYYMMDD)
DOE, JOHN		000-00-0000			20140401	20150331

c. 1) Character: *(Adherence to Army Values, Empathy, and Warrior Ethos/ Service Ethos and Discipline. Fully supports SHARP, EO, and EEO.)*	(See DA Pam 623-3, para 2-6)
c. 2) Presence: *(Military and Professional Bearing, Fitness, Confident, Resilient)*	(See DA Pam 623-3, para 2-6)
c. 3) Intellect: *(Mental Agility, Sound Judgment, Innovation, Interpersonal Tact, Expertise)*	(See DA Pam 623-3, para 2-6)
c. 4) Leads: *(Leads Others, Builds Trust, Extends Influence beyond the Chain of Command, Leads by Example, Communicates)*	(See DA Pam 623-3, para 2-6)
c. 5) Develops: *(Creates a positive command/ workplace environment/Fosters Esprit de Corps, Prepares Self, Develops Others, Stewards the Profession)*	(See DA Pam 623-3, para 2-6)
c. 6) Achieves: *(Gets Results)*	(See DA Pam 623-3, para 2-6)

PART V – INTERMEDIATE RATER

(See DA Pam 623-3, para 2-7)

PART VI - SENIOR RATER

a. POTENTIAL COMPARED WITH OFFICERS SENIOR RATED IN SAME GRADE (OVERPRINTED BY DA)	**b.** I currently senior rate _____ Army Officers in this grade.
	c. COMMENTS ON POTENTIAL:
☐ MOST QUALIFIED *(limited to 49%)*	(See DA Pam 623-3, para 2-8)
☐ HIGHLY QUALIFIED	
☐ QUALIFIED	
☐ NOT QUALIFIED	
	d. List 3 future SUCCESSIVE assignments for which this Officer is best suited:
	(See DA Pam 623-3, para 2-8)

DA FORM 67-10-1, MAR 2014

Page 2 of 2
APD LC v1.00ES

282

The Senior Rater's role is to validate the initial developmental tasks and enforce developmental counseling.

The purpose of the Support Form is to:

(1) Promotes a top-down emphasis on leadership communication.

(2) Integrates the Rated Officer's participation in the objective setting, performance counseling, and the evaluation process.

(3) It enhances planning and relates performance to mission through Rater and Rated Officer joint discussion of the duty description and major performance objectives.

(4) During the rating period, encourages performance counseling and the best use of individual talent through continuous communication to update and revise the performance objectives.

(5) And, at the end of the rating period, enables the Rated Officer to provide input to the OER.

In-depth information of DA Form 67-9-10A is given in AR 623-3, chapter 2, section I.

The purpose of the Support Form is to define your rating chain (your Rater and Senior Rater), your job description, a section for goals, a section for accomplishments, and a section for you to identify your major performance objectives and another section to list your significant contributions and accomplishments. Simply put, the OER Support Form is a simple and effective two-page document to input your objectives and accomplishments. Supervisors (Raters) are required to get an OER Support Form from you before they write your OER. The Rated Officer benefits from the direct two-way communication with their Rater and is better able to:

(1) Direct and develop their subordinates.

(2) Plan for accomplishing the mission.

(3) Gain valuable information about the organization.

(4) Find better ways to accomplish the mission.

Performance objectives identified usually belong to one of five areas:

(1) **Routine objectives** deal with repetitive duties. These duties do not ordinarily produce visible results, but if they are not properly done, serious consequences could occur. (Example: Process administrative discharge within a 45-day period; carry out a program that ensures on time responses to suspense items.)

(2) **Problem solving** objectives deal with problem situations. These objectives will allow time for dealing with problems without disrupting other objectives. (Example: Prepare for logistical support to activate a battalion; improve vehicle maintenance readiness.)

(3) **Innovative** objectives create new/improved methods of operation. These may involve a degree of risk because they are untried ideas. (Example: Create and or carry out a new property accountability system; develop and test a new maintenance program.)

(4) **Personal development** objectives further the professional growth of the Rated Officer. These objectives will be oriented toward skills that will help the Officer in their careers or job performance. These may be in any assigned specialty. (Examples: Complete Warrant Officer Staff Course, get Lean Six Sigma Green Belt certified or earn Masters degree;)

(5) **Special items of Interest.** Army-wide areas of interest to include but not limited to: Safety, Property Accountability, Command Inspections, Soldier Annual Training, and so forth.

Your key to success is to submit a complete, accurate and well written OER Support Form to your Rater and Senior Rater that they can reference when writing your Officer Evaluation Report. Here's how it normally works.

At the beginning of any rating period and preferable within 30 days, you, the Rated Army Officer, meets with your Rater for an initial counseling. During the initial counseling, the Rater outlines performance expectations, identifies conduct expectations and shares unit goals via their own OER Support Form. In essence, their OER Support Form covers 6 areas: Character, Presence, Intellect, Leads, Develops, Achieves. Each one of these sections might have 3 to 5 specific goals.

Once the initial counseling is complete, the Rated Officer normally has 30 days to prepare his or her own OER Support Form. They take into consideration their Rater's goals, expectations and OER Support Form and then set their own goals for their duty position. Once their OER Support Form is complete, they initial it and return it to their Rater.

Next, the Rated Officer keeps a working copy of their OER Support Form and routinely inputs their key accomplishments. Accomplishments might include operational readiness rates, reenlistments, promotions, Soldiers graduating from school, etc. This allows the Officer to keep track of their accomplishments and also provides quantifiable achievements that will eventually be reflected on their OER.

Remember, a year is a long time. If you wait until the end of your rating period, you will likely forget many of your major accomplishments during the past 12-months. Don't let this happen to you. Be proactive and update your OER Support Form regularly.

As the quarter passes by, continue to update, edit and review your OER Support Form. Make it as organized and quantifiable as possible. When you sit down quarterly with your Rater for counseling, provide a copy of your OER Support Form. That way, you can show your Rater an organized list of your accomplishments during the previous three months.

Your Rater will transcribe the highlights of the counseling and your updated Support Form onto your Developmental Support Form (DSF). The DFS is required until you are promoted to CW2.

Every 90 days, the Rater should follow up with you, the Rated Officer, with additional follow-up counseling. They should repeat the process listed above throughout the rating period. When the rating period is complete, the Rated Officer should update, review and finalize their OER Support Form and give a copy to their Rater.

Many Raters will also request an OER "Shell". Get with the orderly room or the S1 section and use examples whenever possible Always fill in the OER using the online OER wizard and start by filling out the administrative section, get your Rater and Senior Rater's information and your APFT data. DO NOT GUESS! Call the training NCO to get your last height, weight, Army Physical Fitness Test (APFT) PASS/FAIL and date. Remember integrity is huge in the Officer corps. If you are due an APFT, go take one! Some Raters will also want you to fill in a draft of their proposed comments. Discuss this with them in advance. Write your Rater's comments regarding your achievements and performance in each of the 6 performance areas. Raters are just as busy as everyone else, and most prefer to make minor edits to a sentence rather than create one from scratch.

Officers who have questions about the OER Support Form changes can contact Army Human Resources Command directly at 1-888-276-9472, or via email at askhrc.army@us.army.mil

Officer Evaluation Report DA FORM 67-10-1

The new OER system is now in effect as of 1 Apr 2014 and is being used to evaluate all officers (WO1 – BG). The new OER clarifies the distinction between Raters, who should be discussing the Rated Officer's performance and Senior Raters, who should be providing insight on the Rater Officer's potential. The new OER is used by all Officers in all branches, including the Regular Army, Army Reserves, and Army National Guard.

A major update to the current OER is a clear distinction of the responsibilities of Raters and Senior Raters. Raters will focus on the Rated Officer's performance, while Senior Raters will focus on the Rated Officer's potential and capability to handle additional responsibility, something that is not always occurring at this time. Another update is that Raters now have a Profile, similar to the Senior Raters Profile. Raters, like Senior Raters, must limit the number of "excels" awarded to an Officer Grade to below 50% during the Rater's career. The OER online tool will prevent Raters from "Busting" their profiles.

Example: If the Rater has rated a total of 6 WO1's since establishing a profile, only 2 WO1's can be awarded "Excels" thus staying below 50%.

Raters will evaluate W1-W2 and Company Grade Officers by writing 2-3 sentences on "Performance" in each of the 6 areas:

1. **Character** *(Adherence to Army Values, Empathy, and Warrior Ethos/ Service Ethos and Discipline. Fully supports SHARP, EO, and EEO.)*
2. **Presence** *(Military and Professional Bearing, Fitness, Confident, Resilient)*
3. **Intellect** *(Mental Agility, Sound Judgment, Innovation, Interpersonal Tact, Expertise)*
4. **Leads** *(Leads Others, Builds Trust, Extends Influence beyond the Chain of Command, Leads by Example, Communicates)*
5. **Develops** *(Creates a positive command/workplace environment/Fosters Esprit de Corps, Prepares Self, Develops Others, Stewards the Profession)*
6. **Achieves** *(Gets Results)*

There are three grade based OER forms.

- WO1-CW2 and Company Grade Officers (O1-O3)

- CW3-CW5 and Field Grade Officers (O4-05)

- Strategic Leaders (06-07)

Three forms are developed, one for WO1-CW2 Warrant Officers and O1-O3 Company Grade Officers. Another will be used for CW3-CW5 Warrant Officers and O4-O5 Field Grade Officers, and finally a third form will be used to evaluate the "Strategic Leaders," namely Colonels and Brigadier Generals. Major Generals and above will not be rated.

Company Grade OER DA Form 67-10-2 (Front)
(CW3–CW5 / MAJ–LTC)

FIELD GRADE PLATE (O4 - O5; CW3 - CW5) OFFICER EVALUATION REPORT For use of this form, see AR 623-3; the proponent agency is DCS, G-1.			*See Privacy Act Statement in AR 623-3.*

PART I - ADMINISTRATIVE *(Rated Officer)*

a. NAME *(Last, First, Middle Initial)*	b. SSN	c. RANK	d. DATE OF RANK *(YYYYMMDD)*	e. BRANCH	f. COMPONENT *(Status Code)*
DOE, JOHN	000-00-0000	MAJ	20130701	AG	

g. UNIT, ORG., STATION, ZIP CODE OR APO, MAJOR COMMAND	h. UIC	i. REASON FOR SUBMISSION
HHC, 5th EN BN, Fort Leonard Wood, MO 65473 FORSCOM	WBAOAA	03 | Change of Rater

j. PERIOD COVERED		k. RATED MONTHS	l. NON RATED CODES	m. NO. OF ENCLOSURES	n. RATED OFFICER'S EMAIL ADDRESS *(.gov or .mil)*
FROM (YYYYMMDD)	THRU (YYYYMMDD)	4			john.doe18980.mil@mail.mil
20140401	20140801				

PART II - AUTHENTICATION *(Rated officer's signature verifies officer has seen completed OER Parts I-VI and the administrative data is correct)*

a1. NAME OF RATER *(Last, First, Middle Initial)*	a2. SSN	a3. RANK	a4. POSITION
SMITH, JOHN	111-11-1111	MAJ	Brigade Executive Officer

a5. EMAIL ADDRESS *(.gov or .mil)*	a6. SIGNATURE	a7. DATE (YYYYMMDD)
john.smith187890.mil@mail.mil	DIGITAL SIGNATURE 123456789	20120315

b1. NAME OF INTERMEDIATE RATER *(Last, First, Middle Initial)*	b2. SSN *(Optional)*	b3. RANK	b4. POSITION

b5. EMAIL ADDRESS *(.gov or .mil)*	b6. SIGNATURE	b7. DATE (YYYYMMDD)

c1. NAME OF SENIOR RATER *(Last, First, Middle Initial)*	c2. SSN	c3. RANK	c4. POSITION
GRANT, JOE	222-22-2222	COL	Brigade Commander

c5. SENIOR RATER'S ORGANIZATION	c6. BRANCH	c7. COMPONENT	c9. EMAIL ADDRESS *(.gov or .mil)*	
4th Maneuver Enhanced BDE, Fort Leonard Wood, Missouri, 65473	EN	RA	joe.grant7789.mil@mail.mil	
	c8. SENIOR RATER PHONE NUMBER		c10. SIGNATURE	c11. DATE (YYYYMMDD)
	777-888-9999		DIGITAL SIGNATURE 123456789	20120315

d. This is a referred report, do you wish to make comments?	e1. SIGNATURE	e2. DATE (YYYYMMDD)
☐ Referred ☐ Yes, comments are attached ☐ No		

f1. Supplementary Review Required? ☐ Yes ☒ No	f2. NAME OF REVIEWER *(Last, First, Middle Initial)*	

f3. RANK	f4. POSITION	f5. Comments Enclosed ☐ Yes ☐ No

f6. SIGNATURE	f7. DATE (YYYYMMDD)	g. MSAF Date (YYYYMMDD)
		20140601

PART III - DUTY DESCRIPTION

a. PRINCIPAL DUTY TITLE	b. POSITION AOC/BRANCH
Brigade S-1	42A00

c. SIGNIFICANT DUTIES AND RESPONSIBILITIES

(See DA Pam 623-3, para 2-11)

PART IV - PERFORMANCE EVALUATION - PROFESSIONALISM, COMPETENCIES, AND ATTRIBUTES *(Rater)*

a. APFT Pass/Fail/Profile: ___ Date: ___ Height: ___ Weight: ___ Within Standard? ___
Comments required for "Failed" APFT or "Profile" when it precludes performance of duty, and "No" for Army Weight Standards?

(See DA Pam 623-3, para 2-12)

b. THIS OFFICER POSSESSES SKILLS AND QUALITIES FOR THE FOLLOWING BROADENING ASSIGNMENTS

(See DA Pam 623-3, para 2-12)

c. THIS OFFICER POSSESSES SKILLS AND QUALITIES FOR THE FOLLOWING OPERATIONAL ASSIGNMENTS

(See DA Pam 623-3, para 2-12)

d1. Character. *(Adherence to Army Values, Empathy, and Warrior Ethos/Service Ethos and Discipline. Fully supports SHARP, EO, and EEO.)*	(See DA Pam 623-3, para 2-12)

DA FORM 67-10-2, MAR 2014

Page 1 of 2
APD LC v1.00ES

DA Form 67-10-2 (Back)
(CW3–CW5 / MAJ–LTC)

SAMPLE

HQDA#:					
NAME DOE, JOHN		SSN 000-00-0000	PERIOD COVERED: FROM (YYYYMMDD) 20140401		THRU (YYYYMMDD) 20140801

d2. Provide narrative comments which demonstrate performance regarding field grade competencies and attributes in the Rated Officer's current duty position. (I.e. demonstrates excellent presence, confidence and resilience in expected duties and unexpected situation, adjusts to external influence on the mission or taskings and organization, prioritizes limited resources to accomplish mission, proactive in developing others through individual coaching counseling and mentoring, active learner to master organizational level knowledge, critical thinking and visioning skills, anticipates and provides for subordinates on-the-job needs for training and development, effective communicator across echelons and outside the Army chain of command, effective at engaging others, presenting information and recommendations and persuasion, highly proficient at critical thinking, judgment and innovation, proficient in utilizing Army design method and other to solve complex problems, uses all influence techniques to empower others; proactive in gaining trust in negotiations, remains respectful, firm and fair. Fully supports SHARP and creates a positive command/workplace environment.)

COMMENTS:

(See DA Pam 623-3, para 2-12)

e. This Officer's overall Performance is Rated as: (Select one box representing Rated Officer's overall performance compared to others of the same grade whom you have rated in your career. Managed at less than 50% in EXCELS.)

I currently rate _____ Army Officers in this grade.

A completed DA Form 67-10-1A was received with this report and considered in my evaluation and review: ☐ Yes ☐ No (explain in comment below)

EXCELS (49%)	PROFICIENT	CAPABLE	UNSATISFACTORY
☐	☐	☐	☐

Comments:

(See DA Pam 623-3, para 2-12)

PART V - INTERMEDIATE RATER

(See DA Pam 623-3, para 2-13)

PART VI - SENIOR RATER

a. POTENTIAL COMPARED WITH OFFICERS SENIOR RATED IN SAME GRADE (OVERPRINTED BY DA)

☐ MOST QUALIFIED (limited to 49%)

☐ HIGHLY QUALIFIED

☐ QUALIFIED

☐ NOT QUALIFIED

b. I currently senior rate _____ Army Officers in this grade.

c. COMMENTS ON POTENTIAL

(See DA Pam 623-3, para 2-14)

d. List 3 future SUCCESSIVE assignments for which this Officer is best suited:

(See DA Pam 623-3, para 2-14)

DA FORM 67-10-2, MAR 2014

Raters will Comment on Performance

Raters will use one of four blocks to indicate the Rated Officer's performance level. The new blocks in Part IV b. are labeled:

☐   Excels (can only be awarded to less than 50%)

☐   Proficient

☐   Capable

☐   Unsatisfactory

Raters, as well as Senior Raters, are subject to the not more than 49% rule. Raters are restricted in the number of high performers they can indicate on the OER. The not more than 49% top block rule for exceptional Officers will apply and Raters, for the first time, will have a Rater profile that shadows them for the remainder of their career. No restarts of a Rater's profile will be authorized. A Rater's profile will have an initial three "Excels" block credit to enable them to award a top block in the initial rating sessions, which is especially important for Raters with small populations. Additionally board members will see the Rater's profile under the performance boxes, thus providing the board insight into the Rater's prior evaluations for that Grade/Population.

Raters will also provide input into future assignment recommendations for CW3-5 Warrant Officers and Field Grade Officers. Recommended assignments will be to operational units, not training units, and indicate position as well, such as G4 assigned to an Air Defense Artillery unit. Recommendations are intended to broaden an Officer's experience, provide for growth, and will be fully visible to the board. Also Career Managers will use the recommendation in the assignment decision process.

Promotion & Selection Board Recommendations

Promotion and selection boards have stated narrative statements are more important in determining an Officer's potential than check boxes.

Raters will evaluate Rated Officers by writing 2-3 sentences on "Performance" in each of the 6 areas. The Rater is required to write a few sentences on the Rated Officer's performance, aligned with each of the attributes / competencies. The six attributes / competencies are:

1. **Character** (*Adherence to Army Values, Empathy, and Warrior Ethos/ Service Ethos and Discipline. Fully supports SHARP, EO, and EEO.*)
2. **Presence** (*Military and Professional Bearing, Fitness, Confident, Resilient*)
3. **Intellect** (*Mental Agility, Sound Judgment, Innovation, Interpersonal Tact, Expertise*)
4. **Leads** (*Leads Others, Builds Trust, Extends Influence beyond the Chain of Command, Leads by Example, Communicates*)
5. **Develops** (*Creates a positive command/workplace environment/Fosters Esprit de Corps, Prepares Self, Develops Others, Stewards the Profession*)
6. **Achieves** (*Gets Results*)

The Rater's narrative will be a performance based assessment of the Rated Officer and assist in developing the Officer. The Rater will "Paint a Picture" of the Rated Officer's mental, physical, and emotional characteristics, as well as their conceptual, interpersonal, technical and tactical skills. The web based software will prevent the Rater from busting their profile and accidently exceeding 49% top block "Excels" in their Rating pool.

Senior Raters will Comment on Potential

Senior Raters will focus their comments and inputs on the Rated Officer's potential for promotion and/or command in the unit and for the Army.

There are four Senior Rater blocks in Part VIb.

- Most Qualified (potential for below-the-zone promotion/selection)

- Highly Qualified (strong potential for promotion/selection among peers)

- Qualified (can function at the next higher level and should be promoted/ selected if there are requirements)

- Not Qualified (Not recommended)

Senior Raters still must limit the percentage of "Most Qualified" ratings awarded to less than 50% of the Officers they Senior Rate. The rating of "Qualified" is equivalent to the previous rating of "Center of Mass" rating.

Senior Raters will also provide comments on "Potential" in Part VI block c. and list 3 future "Successive' assignments for the Rated Officer in block d. Part VI.

Today's Army has many opportunities that extend beyond the typical Army unit. Fellowship programs, Training with Industry, Instructor at one of the Military Academies, or Program Acquisition positions are all available for the right Officer. Any of these positions can be identified in block d. Of course standard assignments, such as Shop Officer, Platoon Leader and S4 can also be listed.

CW3-CW5 and Field Grade Officers will be rated using DA Form 67-10-2. The 6 "Performance" areas are replaced with Part IV Block d2 were Raters will provide narrative comments. The Rater's comments will demonstrate the Rated Officer's performance regarding Field Grade competencies and attributes in the Rated Officer's current duty position.

The Senior Rater portion of DA Form 67-10-2 is essentially the same as described for the WO1-CW2 Company Grade Officers.

Raters will adhere to awarding not more than 49% "Excels" to CW2-CW5 and O4-05 Officers.

Senior Raters will adhere to awarding not more than 49% to their "Most Qualified" CW2-CW5 and O4-05 Officers.

Masking of Warrant Officer (WO1) and Lieutenant (O1-O2) OER Senior Rater blocks will continue to occur-once they are promoted to CW3 or Captain (See AR 623-3, Para. 1-12, Access to evaluation reports). This prevents a poor OER, received during the developmental phase of an Officer's career, from haunting the Officer for the rest of their career.

OER Goals and Implementation

The main goal of the revised OER is determining an Officer's capabilities and how to best develop that Officer for the Army's future.

The current OER system went into effect on 1 April 2014.

It will take two to three years for the new system to mature.

The latest update to AR 623-3, the Army Evaluation Reporting System, was published on 31 March 2014. This is a major revision, but in summary it:

- Adds policy and procedures for designating a Uniformed Army Advisor to perform supplementary reviews on evaluation reports, when required.

- Includes a new rater's managed assessment for DA Form 67-10-1 (Company Grade Plate (O1-O3; WO1-CW2) Officer Evaluation Report) and DA Form 67-10-2 (Field Grade Plate (O4-O5; CW3-CW5) Officer Evaluation Report), reinvigorating the importance of the rater to the overall assessment process and reinforcing accountability .

- Redefines the senior rater four-box check system and label technique for all grade plate forms.

- Updates procedures for when three future successive assignments are required for entry on DA Form 67-10 series.

- Includes "operational" and "broadening" assignments recommendations for inclusion on DA Form 67-10-2 to assist in talent management.

- Includes "strategic" assignment recommendations for inclusion on DA Form 67- 10-3 (Strategic Grade Plate (O6) Officer Evaluation Report) to assist in talent management.

- Updates and clarifies procedures for "interim" DA Form 1059 (Service School Academic Evaluation Report)and DA Form 1059-1 (Civilian Institution Academic Evaluation Report) reports, when required (chapter 4).

- Incorporates new Evaluation Entry Processing System for completing and submitting evaluation reports to HQDA (throughout).

- Includes a new DA Form 67-10-1A (Officer Evaluation Report Support Form), mandated for use by officers in the grade of Warrant Officer one through colonel, and linking development with attributes and competencies outlined in ADRP 6-22 (throughout).

- Includes new DA Form 67-10-1, DA Form 67-10-2, DA Form 67-10-3, DA Form 67-10-4 (Strategic Grade Plate (O7) Officer Evaluation Report), based on grade plates, and linking performance to attributes and competencies outlined in ADRP 6-22 (throughout).

- Replaces DA Form 67-9-1 (Officer Evaluation Report Support Form) and DA Form 67-9-1A (Development Support Form)(throughout).

- Replaces DA Form 67-9 (Officer Evaluation Report) (throughout).

- Makes administrative changes (throughout).

The Army is also considering a redesign of the Service School Academic Evaluation Report—DA 1059.

The Warrant Officer Mantra

Deny Everything,

Admit Nothing,

Act Surprised,

Make Counter-Accusations,

Demand Proof,

Show Concern.

Provided by 1LT "Slay" Slaymaker, USMC

About the Author

Jim Boroch published his first book, "The Best of Military Cartoons", featuring his cartoon character PVT Hazard , in 2011 along with 5 other cartoonists. "Surviving WOCS, The Path to Warrant" is Boroch's first solo non-fiction book.

Boroch is a retired Army Warrant Officer with over 28 years Military experience, 17 of those years as an Army Warrant Officer. He deployed to Desert Storm, Bosnia and Korea and most recently to Iraq. He also led Soldiers successfully in military operations stretching from the National Training Center at Fort Irwin to the desert sands of Iraq. Boroch has carried his M16 rifle, writing pen and drawing pencils across the Atlantic and Pacific Oceans many times and throughout Germany, Bosnia, Korea, Saudi Arabia, Iraq, Qatar and Kuwait.

Boroch is credited with leading the first US Army Missile Shop to successfully integrate the Direct Support Electrical Test Set (DSETS) equipment for Bradley TOW 2 sustainment. He also successfully led fielding teams that brought the advanced TOW 2 Anti-Tank weapon, TOW Field Test Set (TFTS), and Dragon Anti-Tank AN/TAS 5 Night Sight and he was a team led for the fielding of the Bradley Fighting Vehicle (BFV) to the 24th Infantry Division. As a squad leader during Desert Storm he lead his squad to remote sites in Iraq to perform Bradley TOW Missile system repairs and AN/TAS 6 Thermal Sight repairs. During his assignment to Fort Bragg, Boroch applied successfully for Warrant Officer and after graduation was assigned as the Missile Shop Officer for the 3rd Armored Cavalry Regiment. He deployed to Bosnia with the 3rd ACR to Stabilization Forces (SFOR) 7 with the 108th Air Defense Artillery Brigade and supported the 49th Armored Division to SFOR 11. As a member of the 108th ADA BDE's advance party during Operation Iraqi Freedom, Boroch was responsible for safeguarding the 108th ADA's shipment of Patriot Missiles into Kuwait and leading resupply and sustainment missions transporting all classes of supply throughout Kuwait and Iraq, averaging 450 kilometers of driving daily with his good friend and section NCOIC SFC Will Grevel and good buddy and fellow Warrant Officer CW4(r) Dave Sookbirsingh. Together they provided resupply to the Combined Forces Land Component Command (CFLCC) and 32nd Army Air Missile Defense Command's Patriot PAC3 and PAC2 Brigades.

Boroch also completed several Ulchi Focus Lens training exercises in South Korea and successfully led his soldiers to complete four National Training Center exercises and three Hohenfels and Grafenwoehr live fire TOW gunnery exercises.

More recently, Boroch was the led for the Cruise Missile Defense Systems Project Office 2010 Level 1, and 2011 Level 2, State of Alabama Quality Award winning submissions. The Alabama Quality Award (modeled after the Malcolm Baldrige National Quality Award) recognizes and honors organizations whose past or recent innovations in areas of production, service or management have resulted in increased productivity and quality.

In addition to being a certified Green Belt Lean Six Sigma Process Efficiency professional, Boroch is a US Cavalry Spur Holder, a member of the Order of Saint Barbara, an Eagle Scout and member of the Order of the Arrow. Besides writing, Boroch is a cartoonist whose artwork has been published weekly in newspapers since 2003. His cartoon, PVT Hazard , has appeared regularly in the Fort Carson Mountaineer, the Fort Bliss Bugle, the Fort Gordon Globe, and the Redstone Rocket, and also appeared in the NCO Journal. Jim Boroch and his wife live in Alabama.

Admission to a U.S. military flight training program is highly competitive-to qualify, each candidate must earn top scores on a specific test for his or her chosen military branch. Peterson's Master the Military Flight Aptitude Tests offers exactly what a candidate needs to prepare for each of the military flight aptitude tests, including reviews of instrument comprehension, cyclic orientation, spatial apperception, and much more, with in-depth descriptions of each question type.

Peterson's guide also provides detailed data on career opportunities as a military pilot, flight officer, airplane navigator, helicopter pilot, and more PLUS information on flight training programs for the Air Force, Coast Guard, Marine Corps, Army, and Navy.

Find Master the Military Flight Aptitude Tests at:
www.MentorMilitary.com

MENTOR MILITARY

Why Shop from **MentorMilitary.com?**

- Our product selection is curated **specifically for servicemembers.**

- **Competitive pricing**, our prices are often lower than Amazon.

- Most orders ship within 1 business day.

- We ship to **APO/FPOs.**

- We offer a 30-Day Money Back guarantee on our books.

Visit MentorMilitary.com